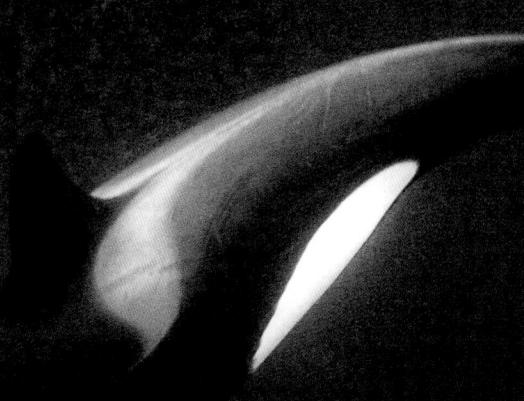

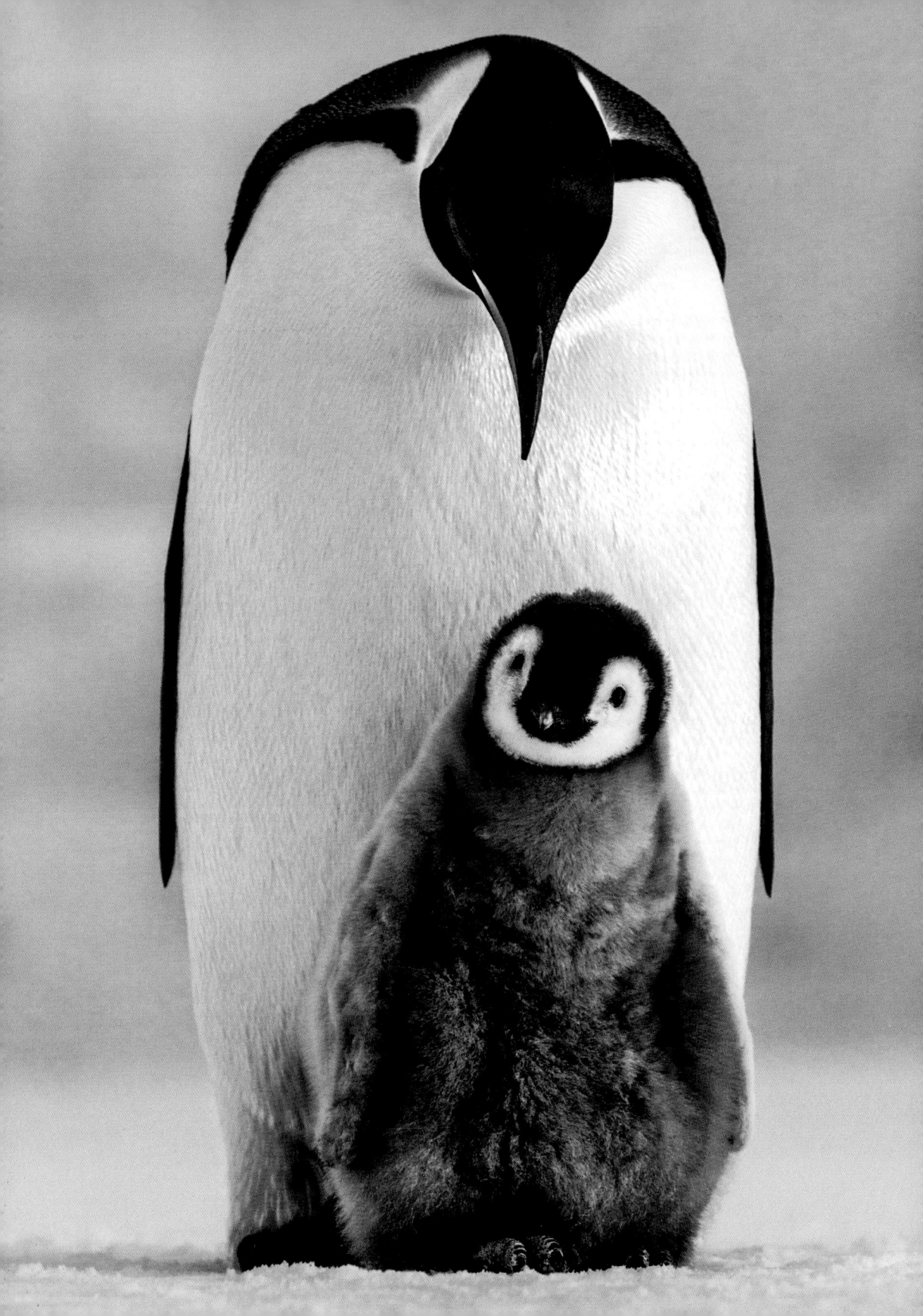

MASTERS
OF.PHOTOGRAPHY

Paul Nicklen

A Photography Masterclass

*Dedicated to nature, to the animals and
to this extraordinary planet – thank you
for being both subject and teacher.*

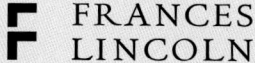

FRANCES
LINCOLN

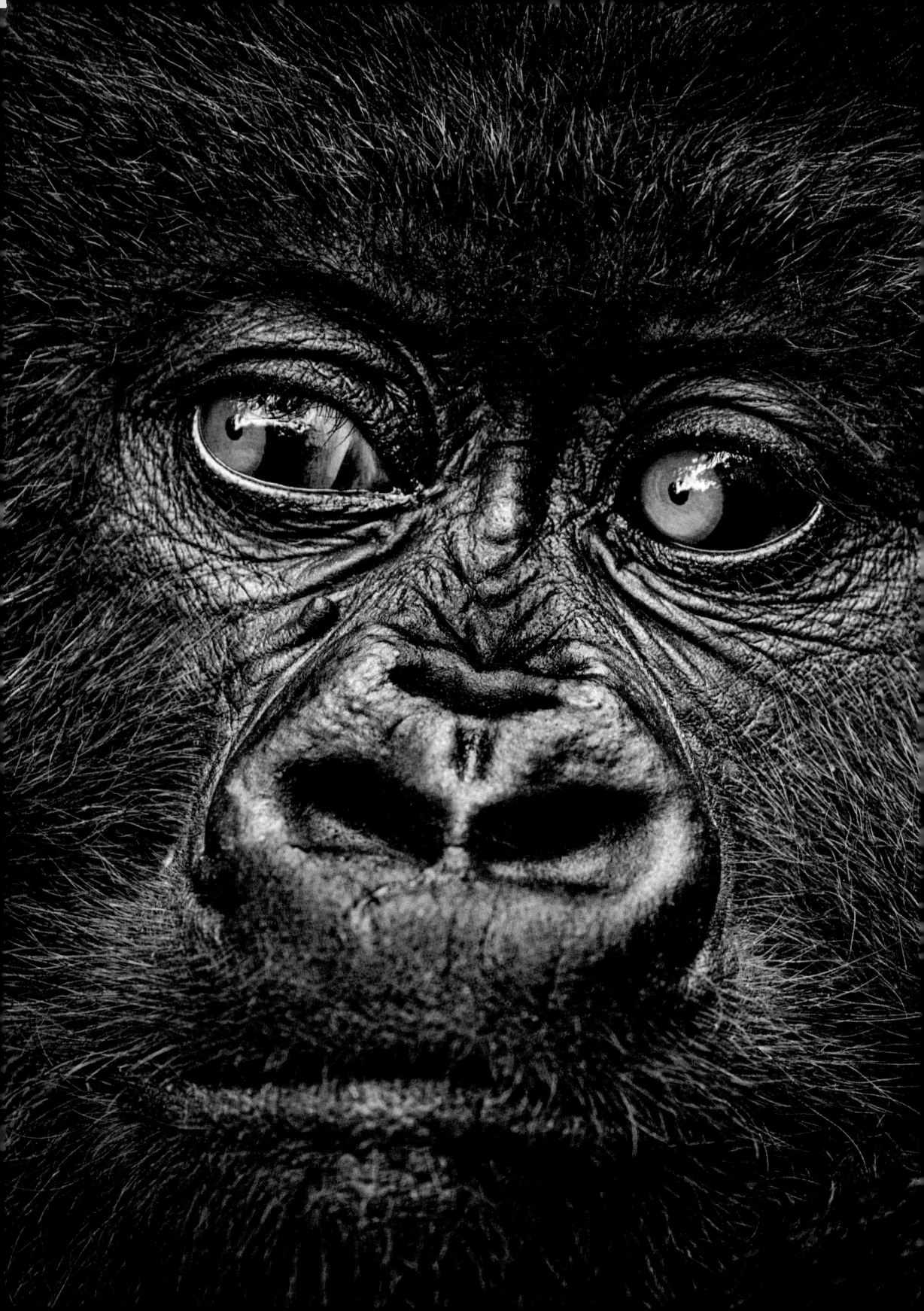

CONTENTS

Page 1: *Orca Ballet*,
Lofoten, Norway, 2014.
Page 2: *Commitment*,
Ross Sea, Antarctica, 2011.
Left: *The Beholder*, Rwanda, 2018.
Overleaf: *Face to Face*,
Svalbard, Norway, 2008.

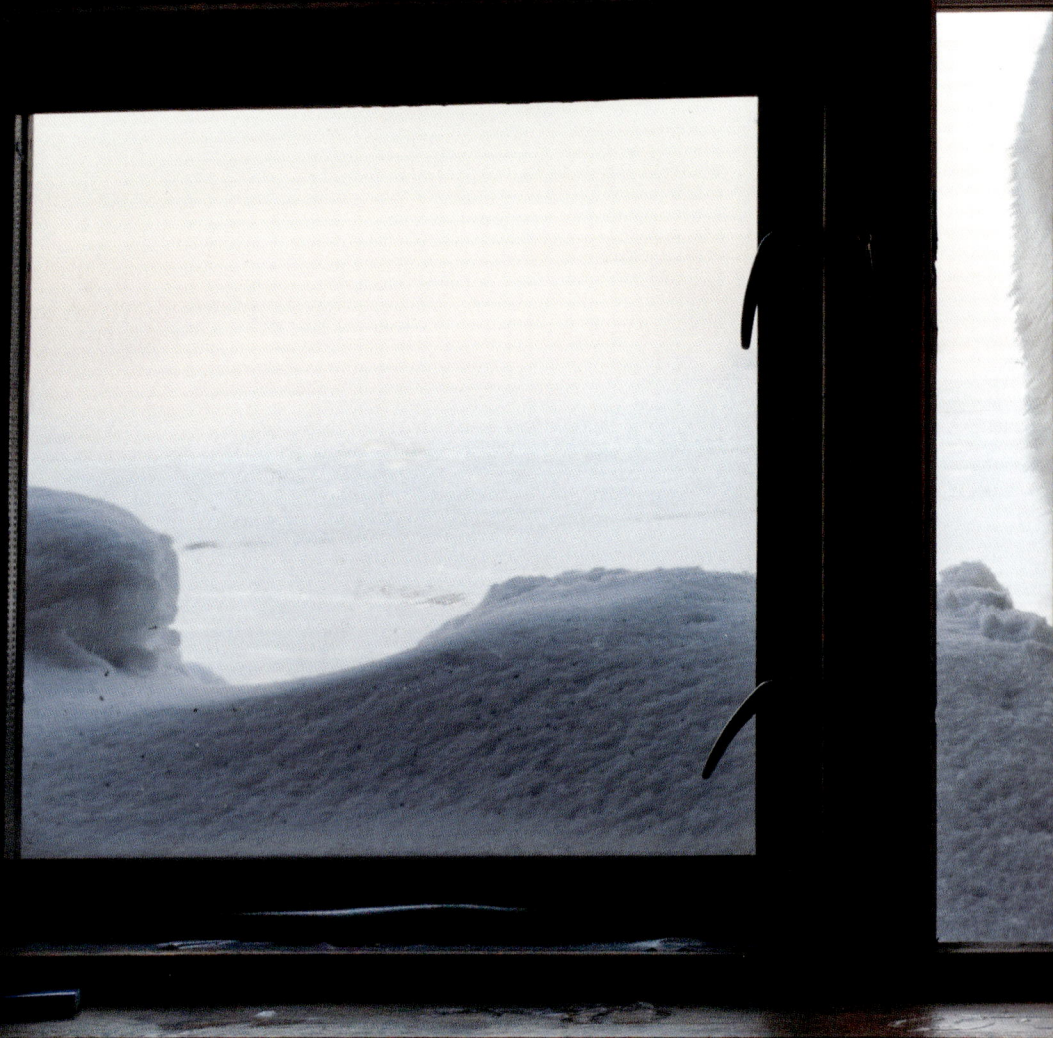

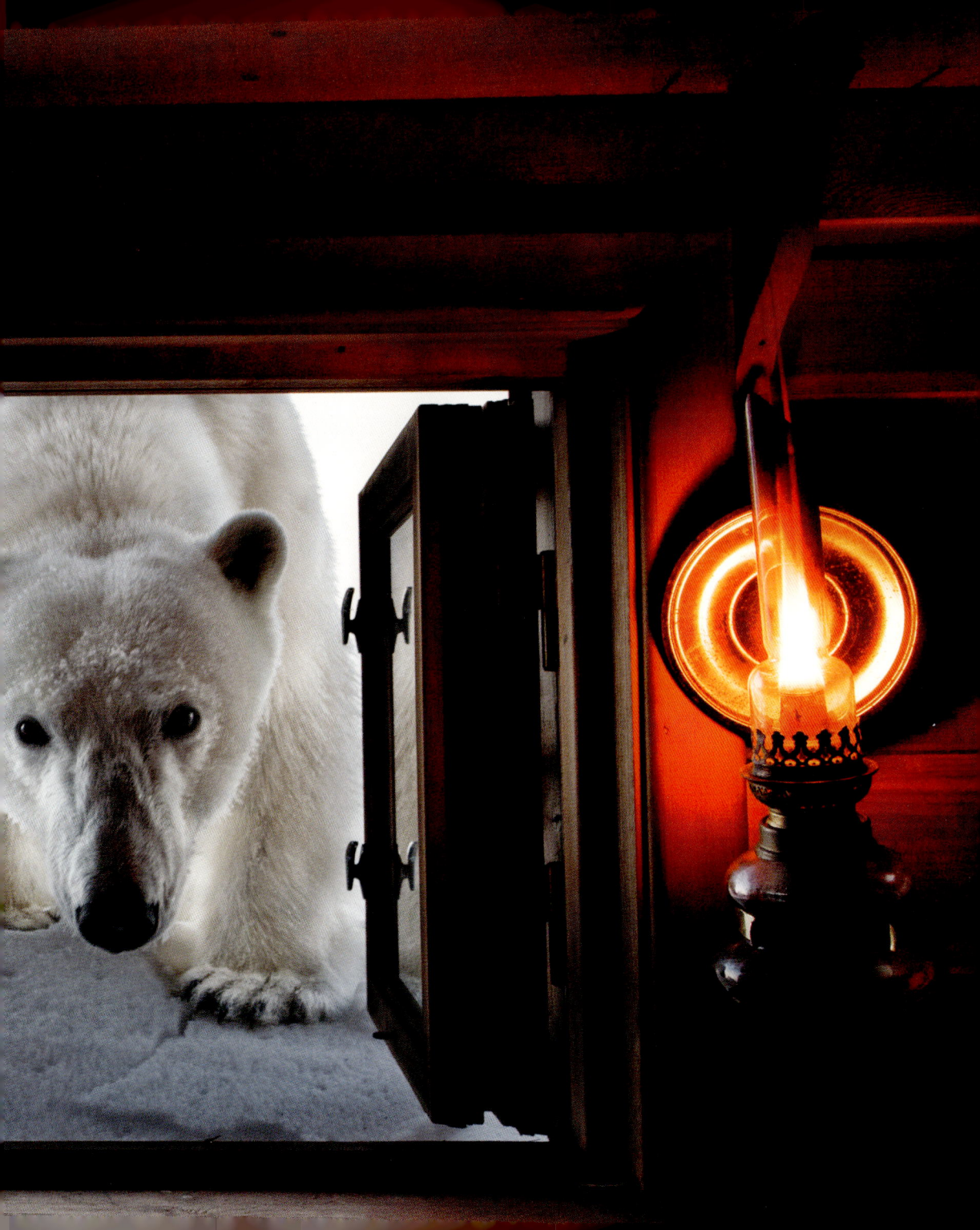

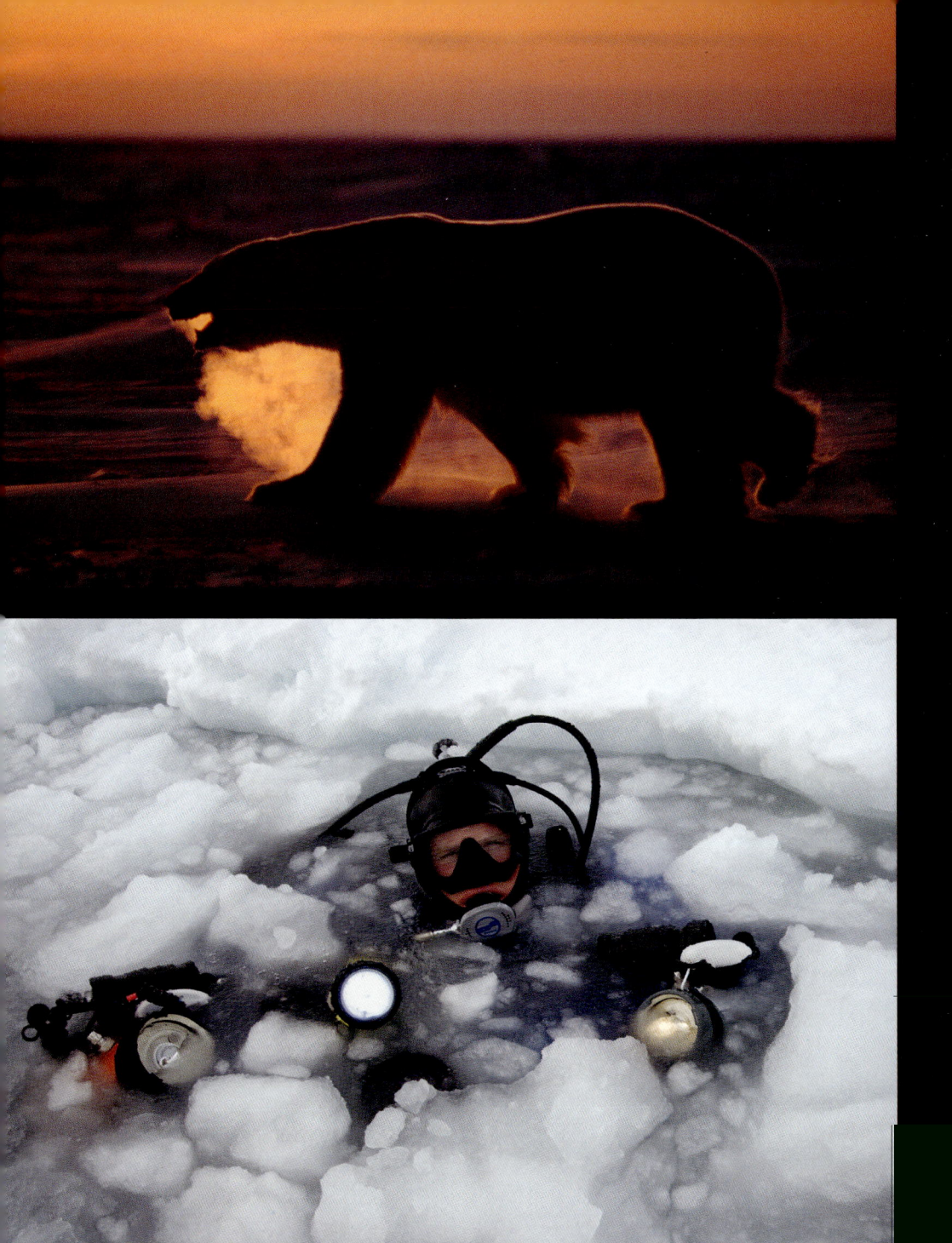

What kind of photographer are you?

Draw on early life experiences

I'm only going to teach photography once in my life, and this is it. This book is my 'tell-all'. I've been working as a full-time professional photographer for thirty years. Twenty of those were with *National Geographic*. I am going to tell you every secret of the trade, every background story behind a photograph, and every technique I use as a photographer. I'll explain how I photograph bears, coastal wolves, leopard seals, sea otters and salmon. I'll share the psychological exercises and drills I use to push myself to the furthest reaches of this profession.

Over the following pages, we will explore where art, science and conservation intersect. Most of all, we're going to learn how to shoot powerful images that tell stories and help effect change. I want you out there with me, changing this world for the better. Whether you want to be a *National Geographic* photographer or are picking up a camera for the first time, this book is for you.

My journey towards photography began when I was four years old and my family moved from Saskatchewan in Canada to Iqaluit (formerly Frobisher Bay), and then to the tiny Inuit community of Kimmirut (formerly Lake Harbour). Situated on Baffin Island, next to Greenland in the Canadian territory of Nunavut, it is a

Top: A polar bear crosses the frozen ground with backlit breath at 1 a.m., Ellesmere Island, Canada, 1995.
Bottom: Paul surfacing from diving under arctic sea ice (taken by Jed Weingarten), Nunavut, Canada, 2005.

cold, windswept, icy, frozen landscape. In winter, temperatures can plummet to minus 20 degrees Fahrenheit (–30°C). Winters are tough, and the summer months aren't much easier, but it's impossible not to feel uplifted by the seemingly never-ending sunlight of summer.

Despite the challenging conditions, this was home. Looking back, it is an environment that had a lasting impact on me and on the photographs I would go on to make.

All my time was spent out on the sea ice, in the snow, with the Inuit. The ice and snow were my sandpit. As a young boy, one of my favourite things to do after school was to hike up into the mountains and sit, sometimes for hours, taking in the entire scene. I noticed the distant snow-capped mountains and the sea ice. I watched the clouds moving over the landscape and the shadows dancing across the ice, which seemed to 'breathe' with the 30-foot (9-metre) tide as it went up and down. I took in this visual feast every day.

In winter, in the middle of the night, a little sliver of light that appears across the horizon can, within minutes, become a full-blown explosion of northern lights – the aurora borealis dancing across the horizon.

The Inuit children and I would play a game where you whistle to the aurora. You call the spirits closer to you. According to oral tradition, the spirits of the aurora borealis can 'chop off' your head if you call them in too close. That's what they're doing up in the sky – playing catch with your head. We would clap to make them go away. This 'dancing' of the aurora borealis, or 'breathing' – coming back and leaving – fed my creative brain and made me fall deeply in love with this place.

People who move to the Arctic either fall in love with it or can't wait to get out of there. My brother dreamed of a life back in the South, to be surrounded by trees, but I couldn't get enough of it. I couldn't get enough of the vast, wild, rugged landscape. It was like living inside a high-key painting with different shades of white and grey, where shadows moved and danced across the landscape.

You might see an Arctic hare appear from behind a snowbank, or a polar bear pad across the sea ice in the distance. As the sun gets lower in the sky, you can sometimes spy a polar bear's shadow

" The 'dancing' of the aurora borealis . . . fed my creative brain and made me fall deeply in love with this place."

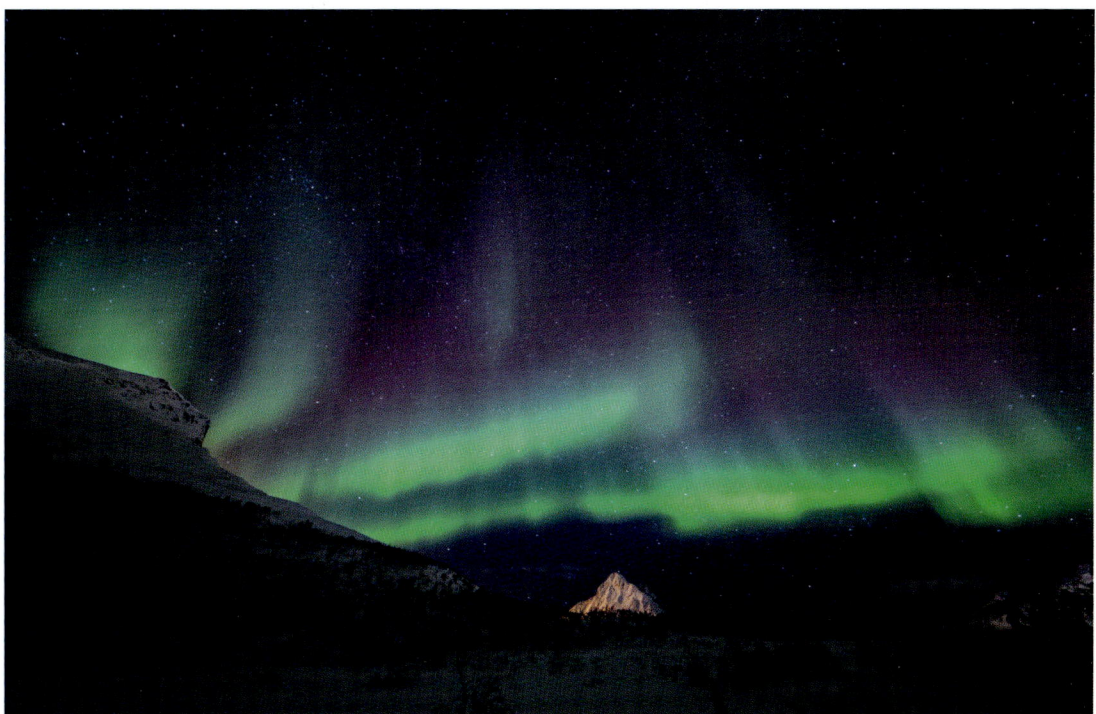

Above: The long, dark days of winter come alive under the aurora borealis, Norway, 2015. Overleaf: *Arctic Dance*, Norway, 2015.

stretching out over the ice. I vividly remember those images; images I would take with my mind and with my eyes. Those moments, those experiences fuel me today. They feed my soul.

For me, the creative process really began to unfold after watching and learning from my mother, who was a keen, talented photographer. She had the only darkroom in town. In fact, she had one of the only cameras – a Pentax K1000.

My mother would go out and photograph Inuit culture. Seeing her make photographs of the beauty of that landscape and seascape, and the people who were living a very beautiful, artistic and poetic life connected to the land and the sea, was a very special experience.

Watching her develop those images in her darkroom and then seeing those moments come to life as black-and-white prints was a magical process for me. I was in awe. I respected my mother for being a great photographer and admired the craft of photography, but I never thought I would become a photographer.

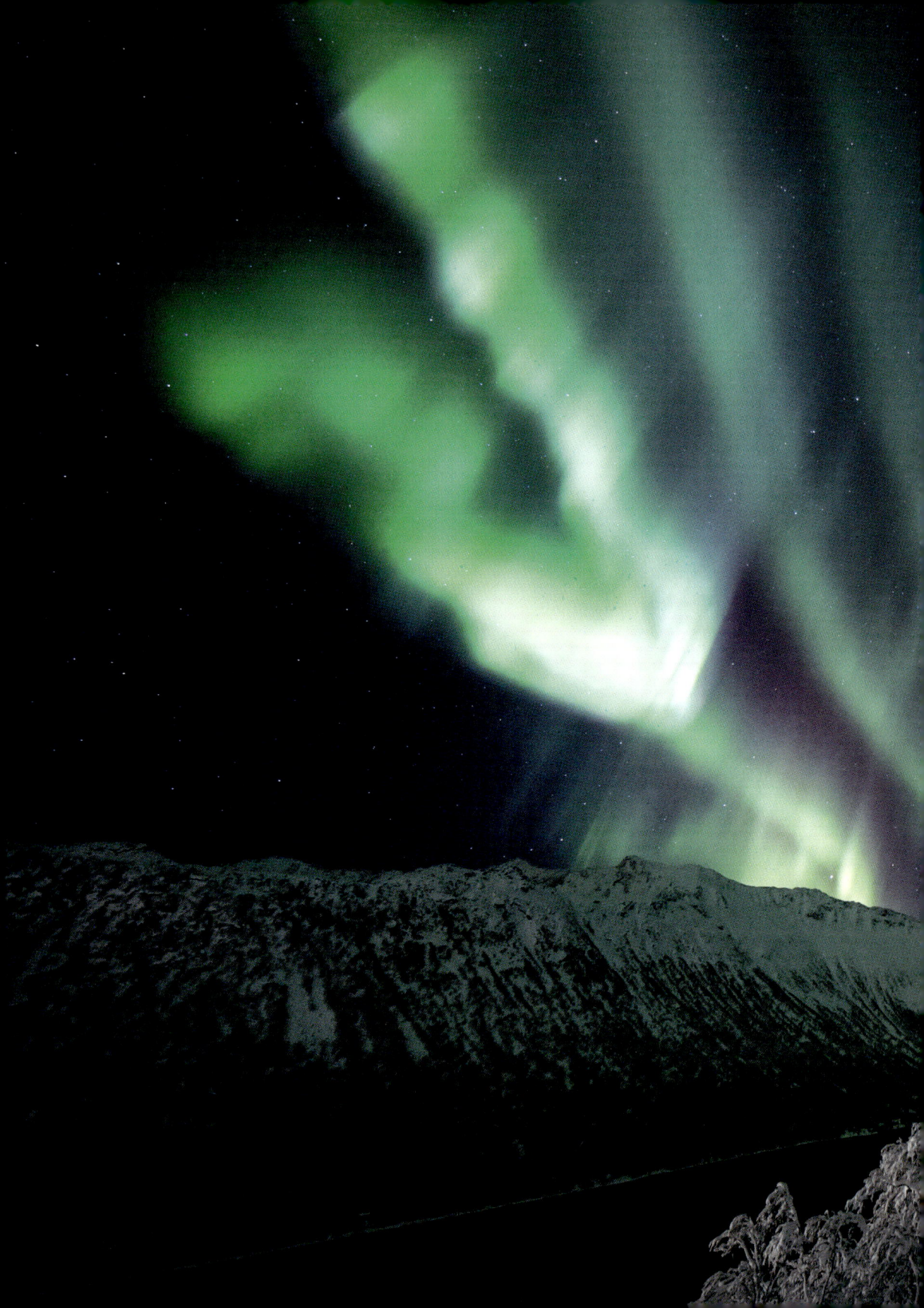

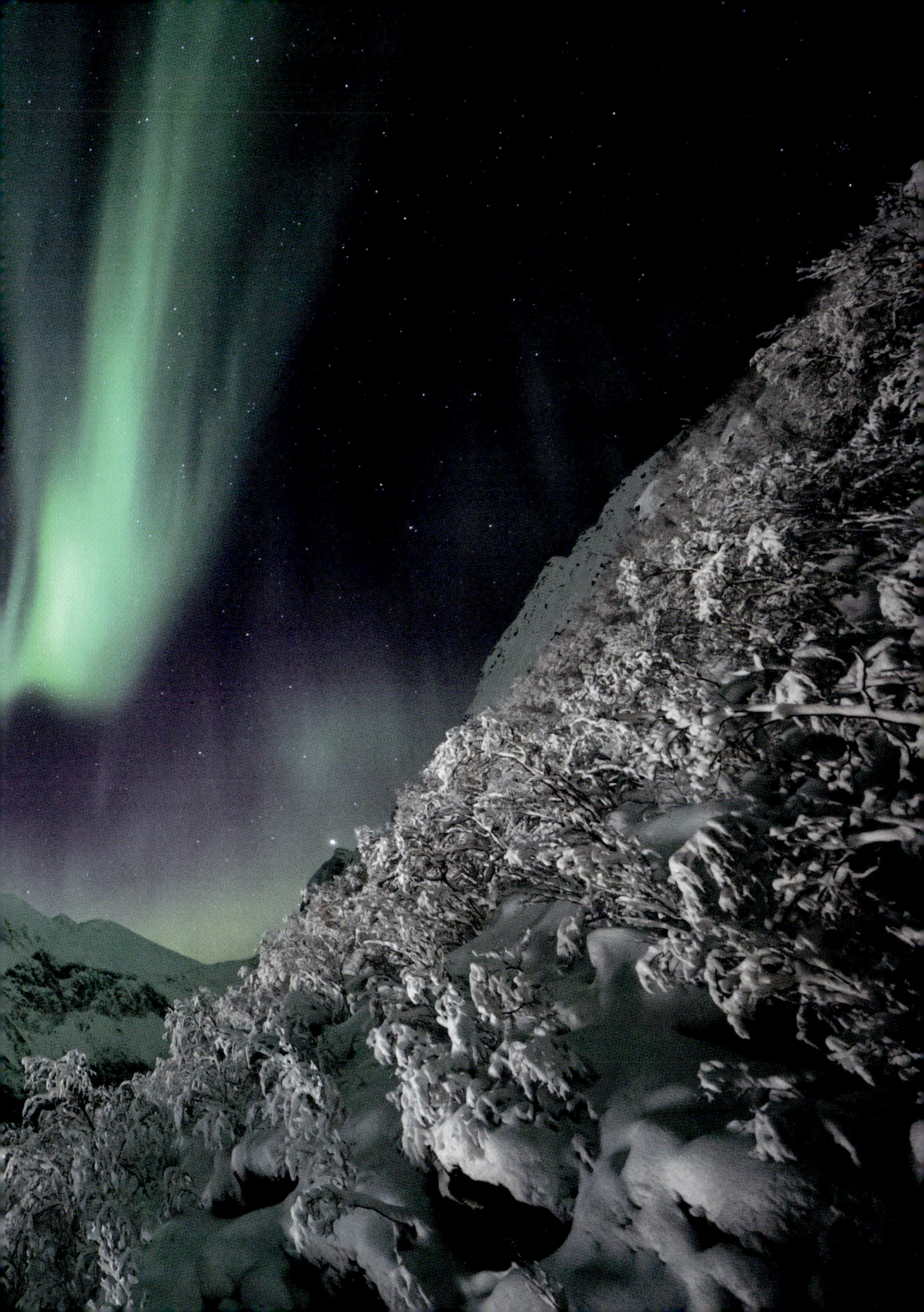

When you're out there as a child playing, sometimes through the night under the aurora borealis or on the sea ice with your friends, you're feeding your senses – and in many ways, your heart and spirit. It sets you off on a path.

When I left the Canadian North to study biology at the University of Victoria on Vancouver Island, British Columbia, where I now live, I would dream about being back on the sea ice with the polar bears, the wolves and the Arctic hares. I knew deep down I was going to do something, someday, to do with photographing and protecting this place. But at that young age, I did not yet know what that might be.

I didn't know it at the time, but I was learning survival skills from the Inuit: how to deal with extreme temperatures and navigation; how to be out on the sea ice and up in the mountains, navigating dangerous conditions. I'm good at being frozen and miserable, at coping in the cold – losing feeling in my fingers, hands and feet, and having frostbite on my ears, nose and face. I can deal with all of that. I'm indebted to the Inuit for teaching me how to survive on the land.

It's funny how life turns out. I did end up pursuing a life in photography, of course, via a career as a biologist, and there have been many twists and turns along the way. Reflecting on my journey through life and image-making, I recognize that the years I spent growing up in the Canadian North had a profound impact on me creatively and practically; my younger years indelibly shaped my work as a photographer – how I approach making photographs, my attitude, everything.

Your path into and through photography will be different to mine, of course, and it will be unique to you. Perhaps you are in awe of the grace of the wildlife that roams the Serengeti, or maybe you are fascinated by the birds that flock to your local park. Good photographs can be made anywhere. Tuning in to your early experiences, taking the time to reflect on the journey you have made so far and the direction you hope to take, will inform your photography immeasurably. It will enable you, I believe, to confidently and authentically forge a fulfilling life in this challenging yet endlessly rewarding profession.

" Watching [my mother] develop those images . . . seeing those moments come to life as black-and-white prints was a magical process for me."

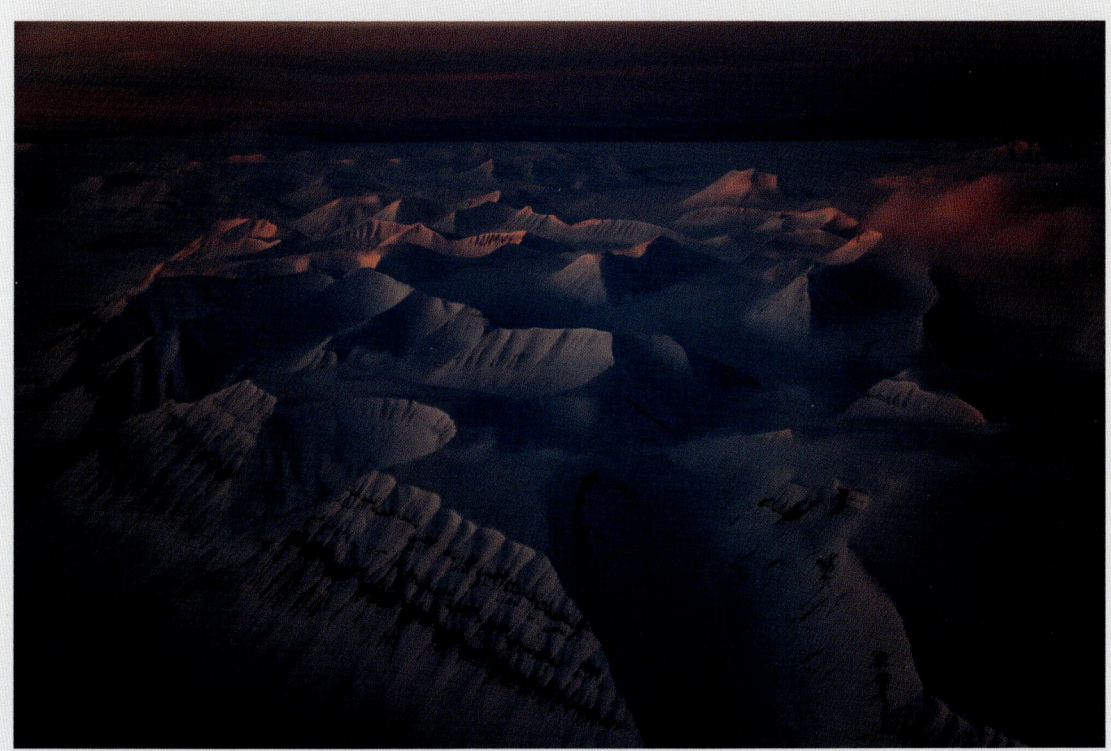

Above: *Winter Dawn*, Spitsbergen, Norway, 2007.
Overleaf: Paul in a camoflauge survival suit searching
for polar bears, East coast of Spitsbergen, Norway, 2007.

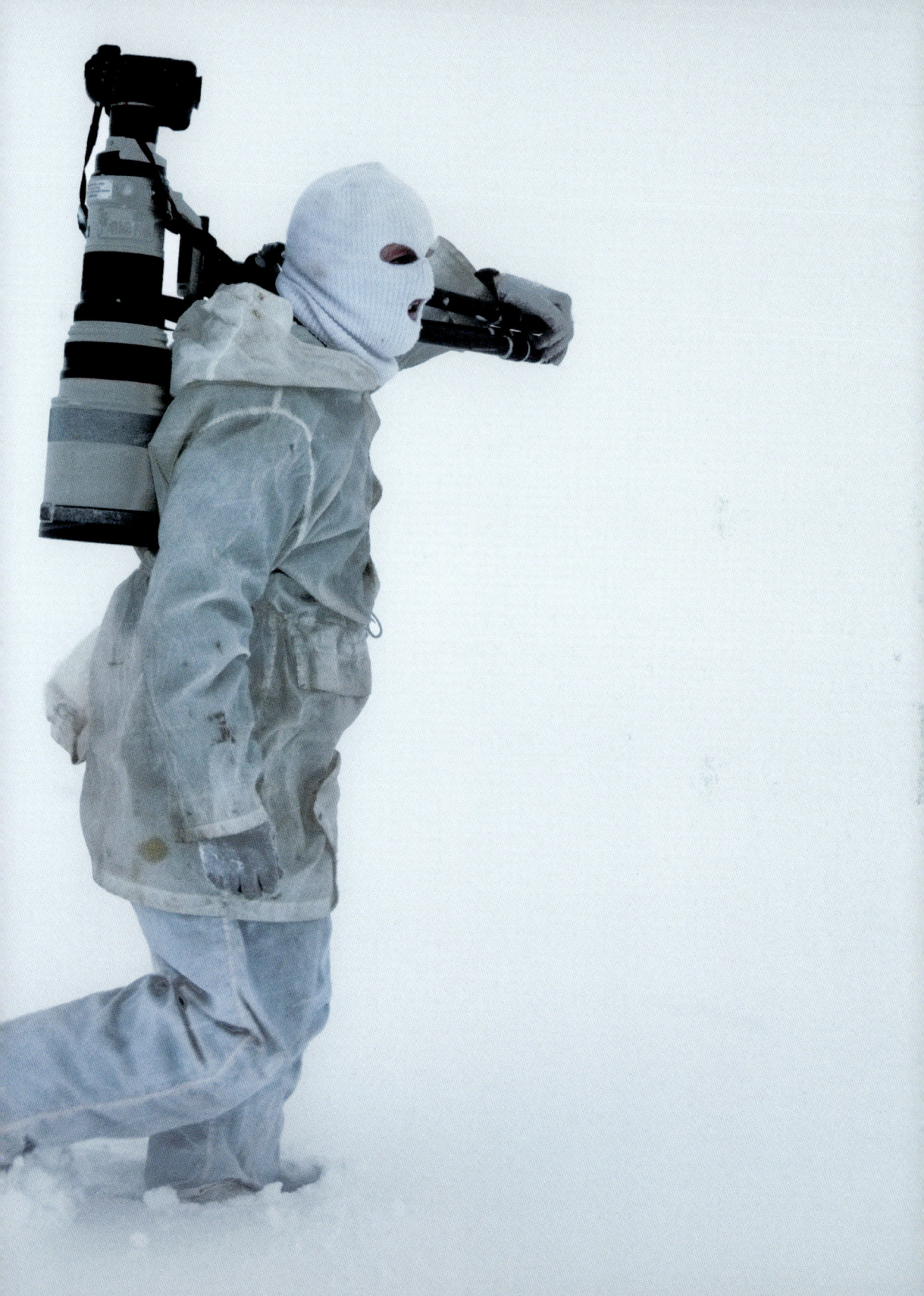

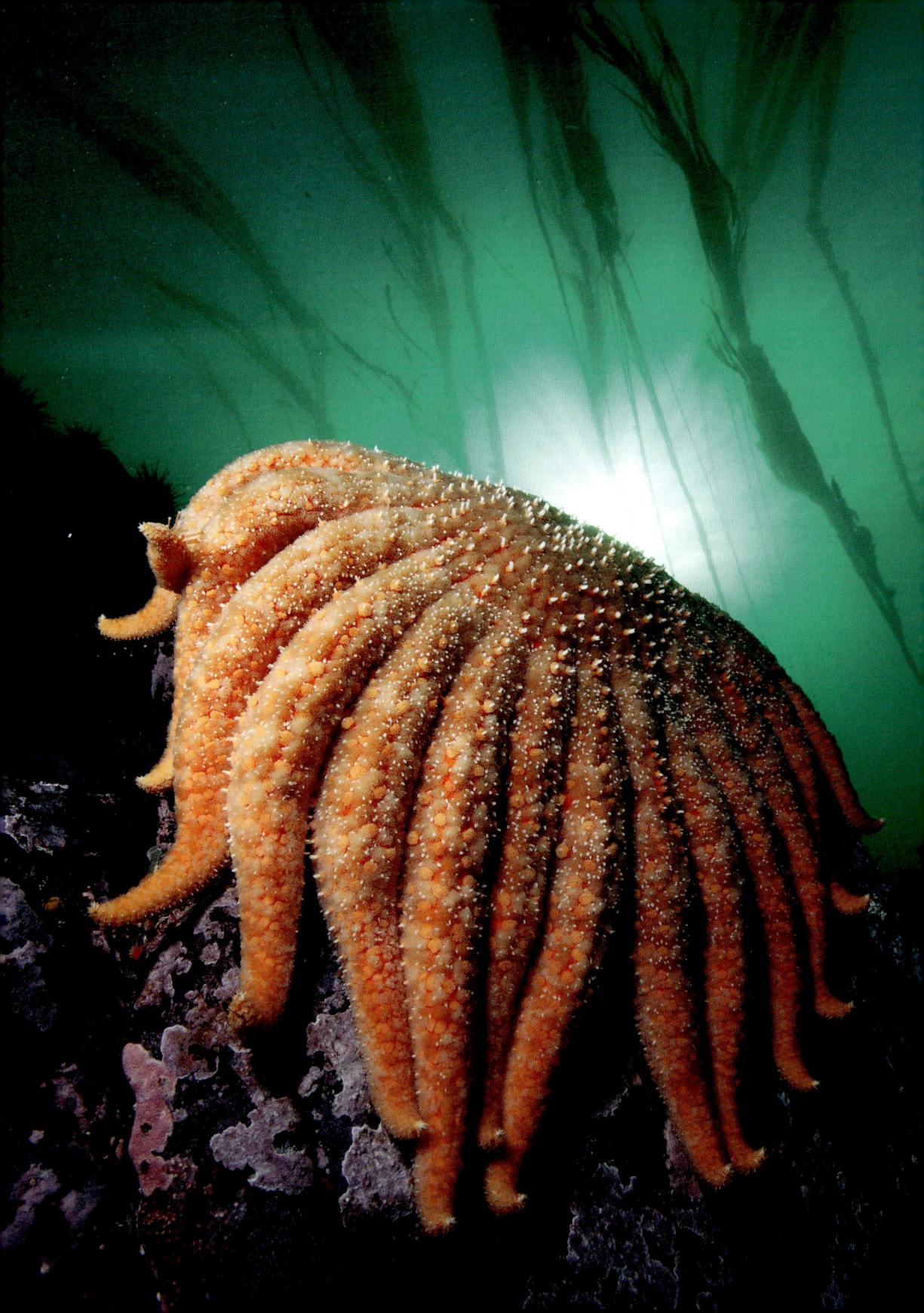

2 Grow as an artist

Hone your creative vision and find your style

Developing an individual approach to image-making or a personal style is an ongoing process. It's a lifelong endeavour. No one picks up a camera and is the finished article. In fact, I don't think it's possible to reach a definitive place with your photography; the way one makes pictures is always evolving. But that is something to embrace.

By embarking on a life in photography you are making a commitment to yourself to keep doing the work – developing your eye (Chapter 8) and knowledge (Chapters 7, 10 & 11), nurturing your self-belief (Chapter 5), regularly checking in with your reasons for doing what you're doing and remaining focused on your goals (Chapter 3).

One of the most useful things I learned at the beginning of my career was how *National Geographic* edits photography (Chapter 16). It's a model I use to this day. Let's say I had shot 10,000 images on an assignment. An editor would narrow down the images to around 1,000 'top' images. We'd then look at the images together and whittle them down to 500, 200, 100, a top 50, and then 25 to 35 standout images. Those images would make it into the final story 'tray'. (We called it a 'tray' because we used to use Kodak carousel slide projectors that were fed by a rotating tray of slides.)

Left: Sunflower sea star, Quadra Island, British Columbia, Canada, 2004.

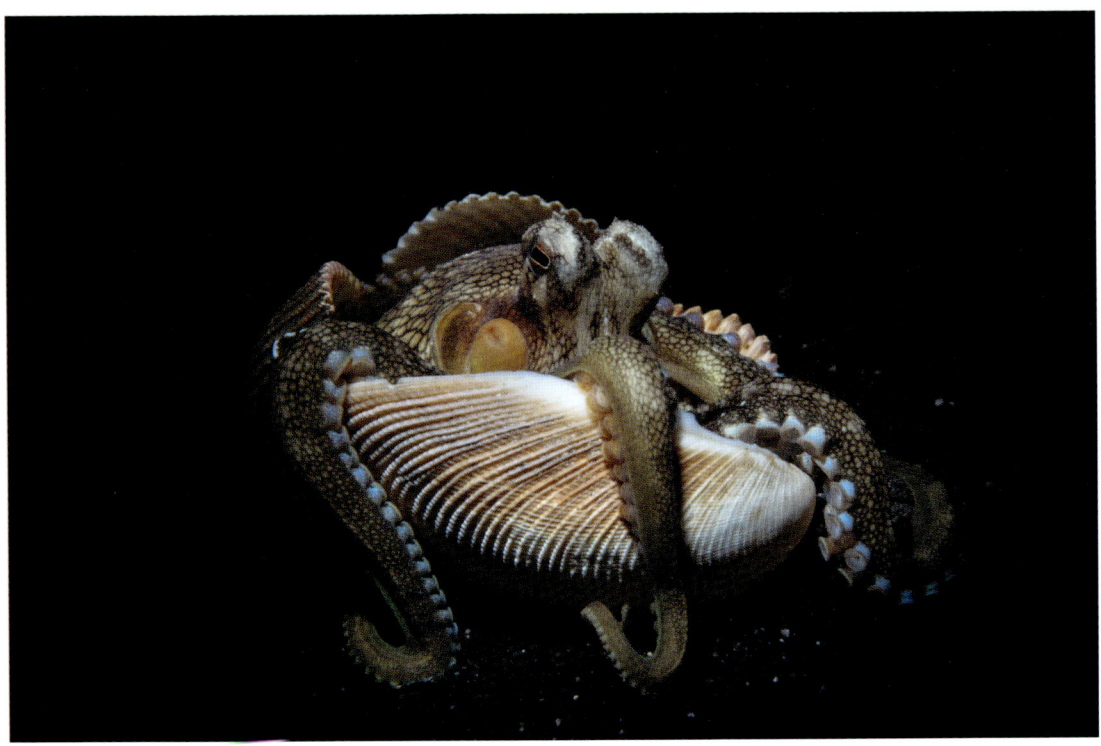

Above: A coconut octopus clings
to a shell, Indonesia, 2025.

I mention this because having insight into the editing process and style will help you learn about *your* style, your way of shooting, and identify those of your images that will hopefully live on forever. Aside from the 'home run' images, to use a baseball analogy, it's also a chance to identify 'second base' and 'third base' hits – the solid B and C-level images that serve as a supporting cast. These are the images that capture key journalistic storytelling moments, images that are perhaps not as powerful as those 'big hitters', but that help to tell the story. They're like legs on a table that give the whole story structure.

When it comes to refining your approach to photography, I implore you not to overthink things, not to force yourself into a box, especially when you're starting out. Go out there and let your style find you. Shoot from every angle, find subjects in your backyard or close by; go out and 'sketch'.

Sketching with a camera is one of the greatest things you can do. I like to draw my ideas for images on paper, but I also love to go into a situation, hold my camera to my eye and 'sketch' in a less literal sense. That's when I start to let myself go. I let myself be free and see the world through my camera without distractions from what is outside the frame.

Over time, you'll start to see images that repeat themselves or a style or a technique you've used, where you start to say, 'That is mine, it's my own'. By going out and exploring, sketching and not overthinking, you'll set yourself on a path of discovery, and you'll find your style. But you need to shoot tens of thousands, hundreds of thousands of images before you start to see your style unfold.

It's important you don't get disheartened if somebody doesn't 'get' your style straightaway. For my first few assignments at *National Geographic*, none of the editors understood my style. I am in love with wildlife and nature. I want my images to be either extremely full frame – where you're looking at the eye or into the mouth of an animal that is taking up the whole frame – or to convey a sense of place – where the animal is just a speck in the distance against a big, beautiful landscape. Those kinds of images really speak to me, but they are not necessarily what the editors at *National Geographic* are looking for. What will work as a large fine art print on the wall may not work in the pages of a magazine. A strong journalistic image tells a clear story with context and consequence – it's about truth revealed, not just beauty captured. Fine art, by contrast, invites interpretation and emotion, often leaving the narrative open.

So, don't get discouraged if your style doesn't immediately fit with what an editor wants. Right now, I'm really enjoying going back through the two million or so images I shot for *National Geographic* over the last 20 years and mining those images for beautiful moments that work as fine art prints. Most didn't work for the magazine, but that doesn't mean they are without merit.

> " A strong journalistic image tells a clear story with context and consequence – it's about truth revealed."

I shoot in a very creative, artistic way – images that convey a sense of place; beautiful, moody imagery that might work in a fine art situation, but not in a journalistic context. I always made sure I shot

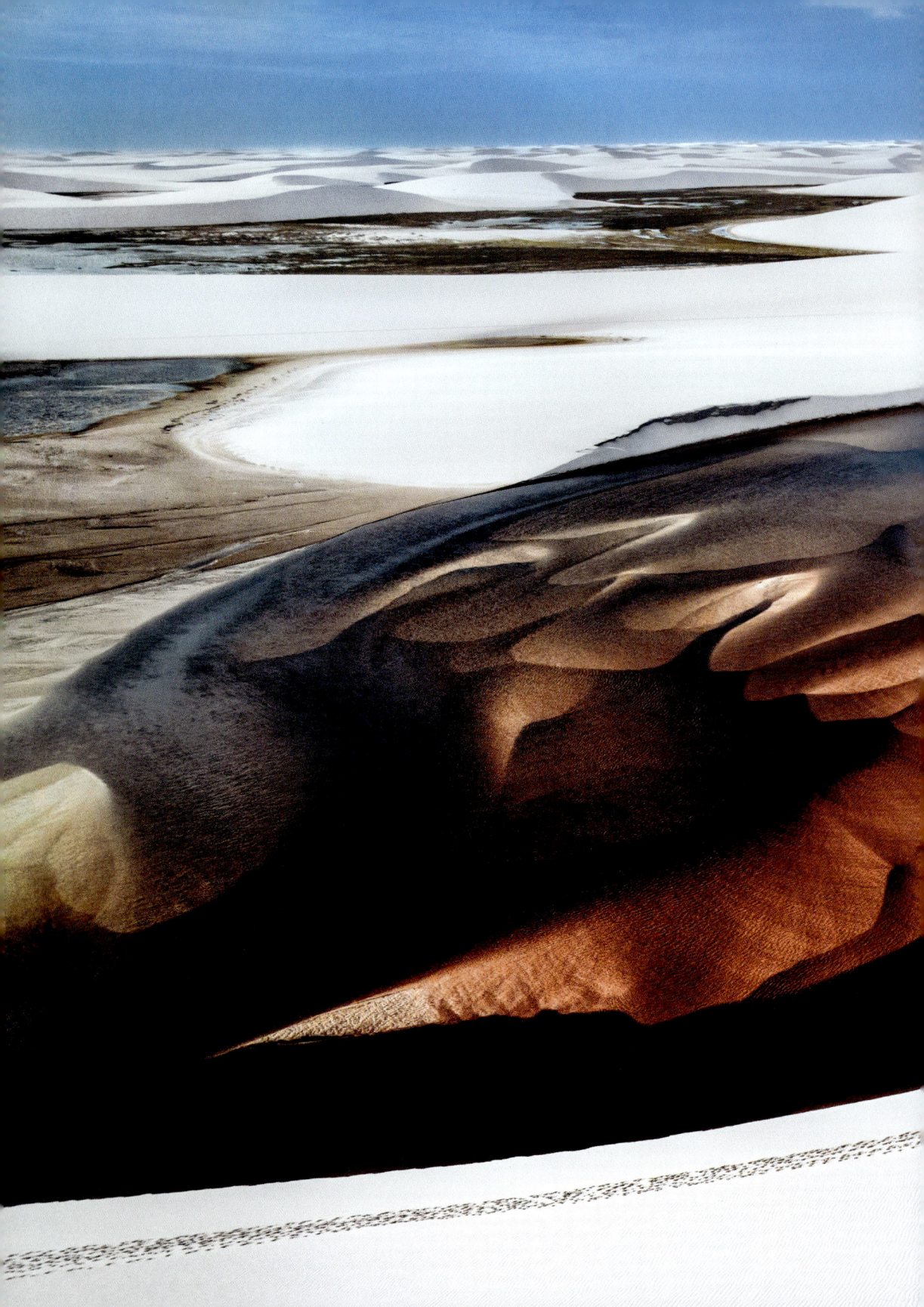

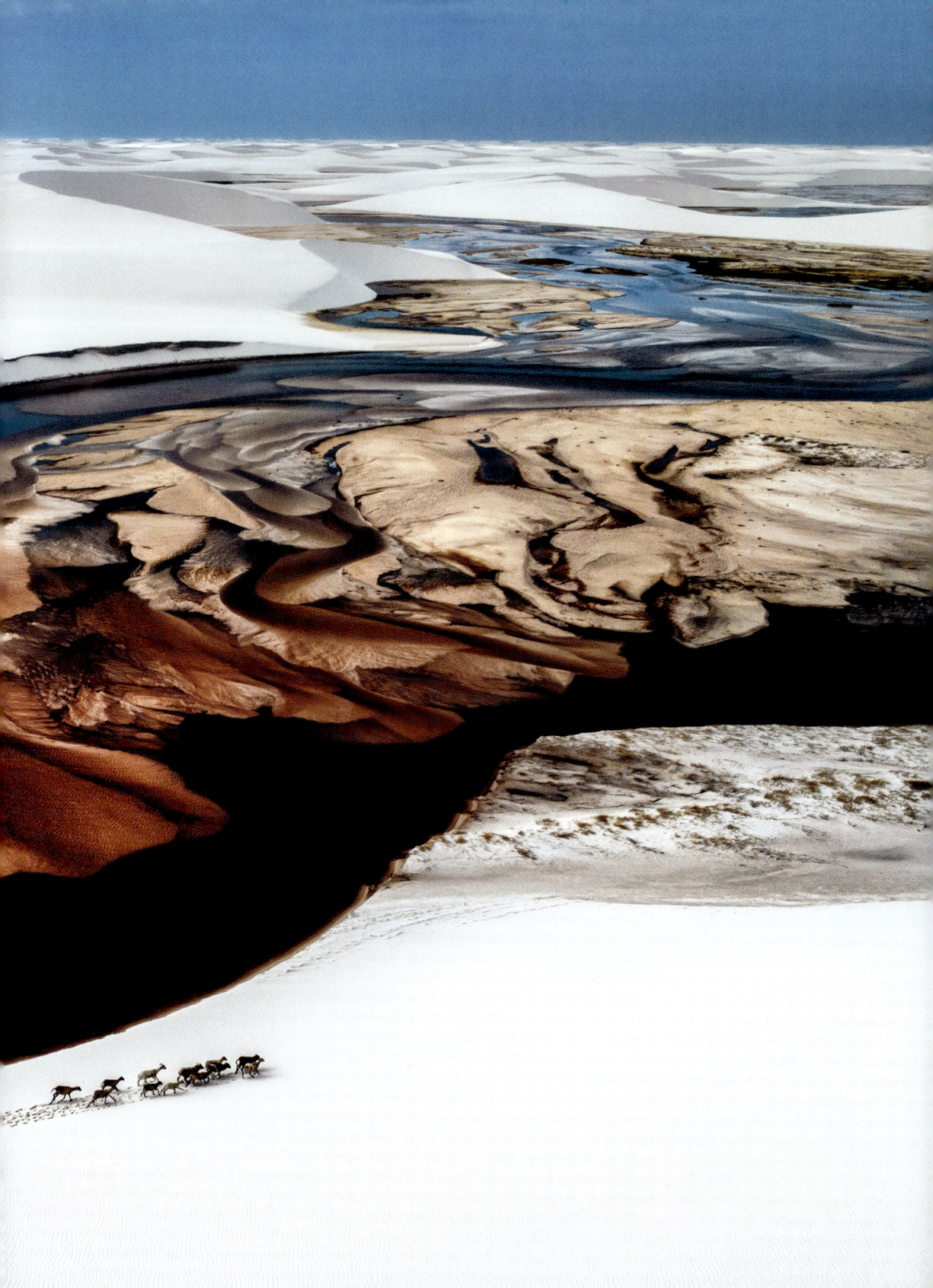

what the magazine wanted; that's what I was hired to do, but I never abandoned my style. My style is me, it's who I am, it's how I shoot. You have to hold on to that, to believe in what you are doing and chase those little voices out of your head (Chapter 5).

A technique I often use to push myself creatively and grow as an artist is something I call my '20-60-20 philosophy'. It is a way to get the shots I need, but also to experiment, to be bold or daring in the way I'm shooting – to break the rules – which I hope will in turn lead to images that are a bit different.

When I'm in the field, I'm in the moment, I'm in the zone. I want to spend the first 20 per cent of my time getting sharp images, in focus, properly exposed – something that the editors at *National Geographic*, or whoever I'm shooting for, want. Even if it's just for myself, I want to get a core body of workable images. Essentially, you're not putting too much pressure on yourself to make every image a home run. So that's the first 20 per cent of your time – just getting something usable on your cards.

After that first 20 per cent, which I move through quickly, I spend most of my time in the 60-per cent zone, where I'm in the moment, using my skillset as an artist, using whatever techniques I've learned. I might be using rear sync flash to shoot motion blur, which demands precise timing and control over ambient light and the subject's movement – too much light, and the blur overwhelms the subject; too little, and you lose the motion altogether. Or I could be taking complex shots where the chance of success is still there, although somewhat reduced. Crucially, I'm pushing myself to the outside edges of my ability, using all my developed skills, all my experience with a camera.

A mistake I see a lot of photographers making is putting on the same lens and photographing the same bear over and over in the same way. It might be a 600mm lens and a bear that's 45 yards (50 metres) away. At the end of the day, they will have shot the same picture many times; same angle, same focal length, same depth of field, same framing of the subject, etc.

Once I have exhausted that 60 per cent and I'm feeling great about the shoot, thinking I've captured some really creative, artistic stuff – incidentally, that 60-per cent zone is where the majority of my best work comes

> " I never abandoned my style. My style is me, it's who I am, it's how I shoot."

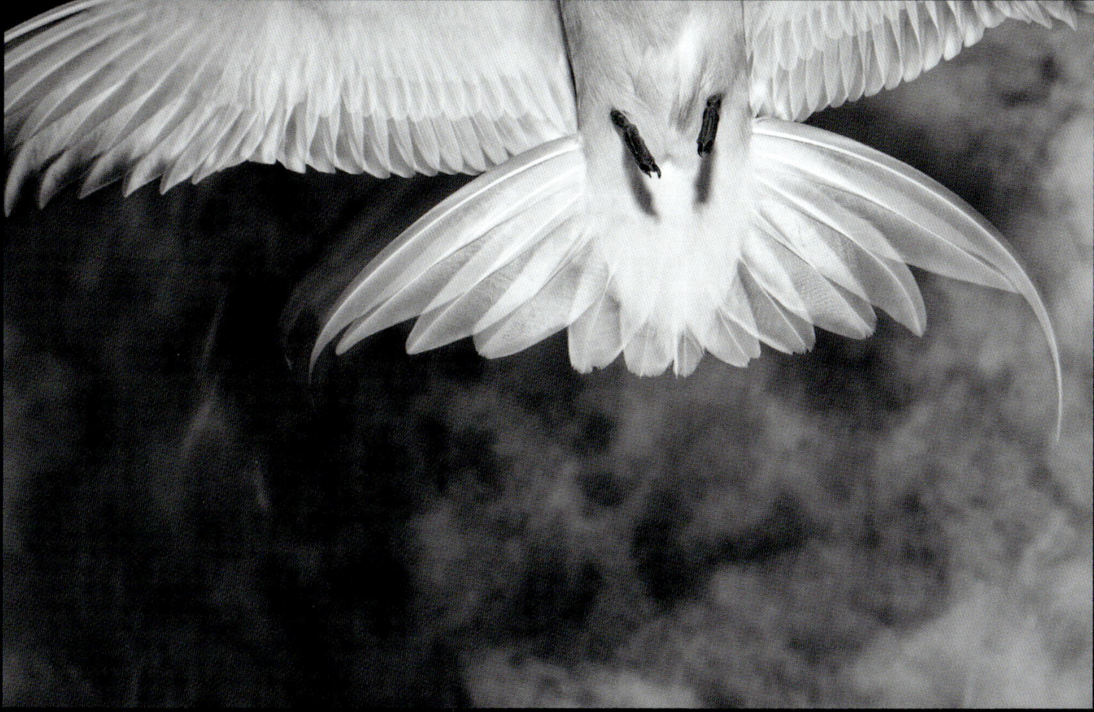

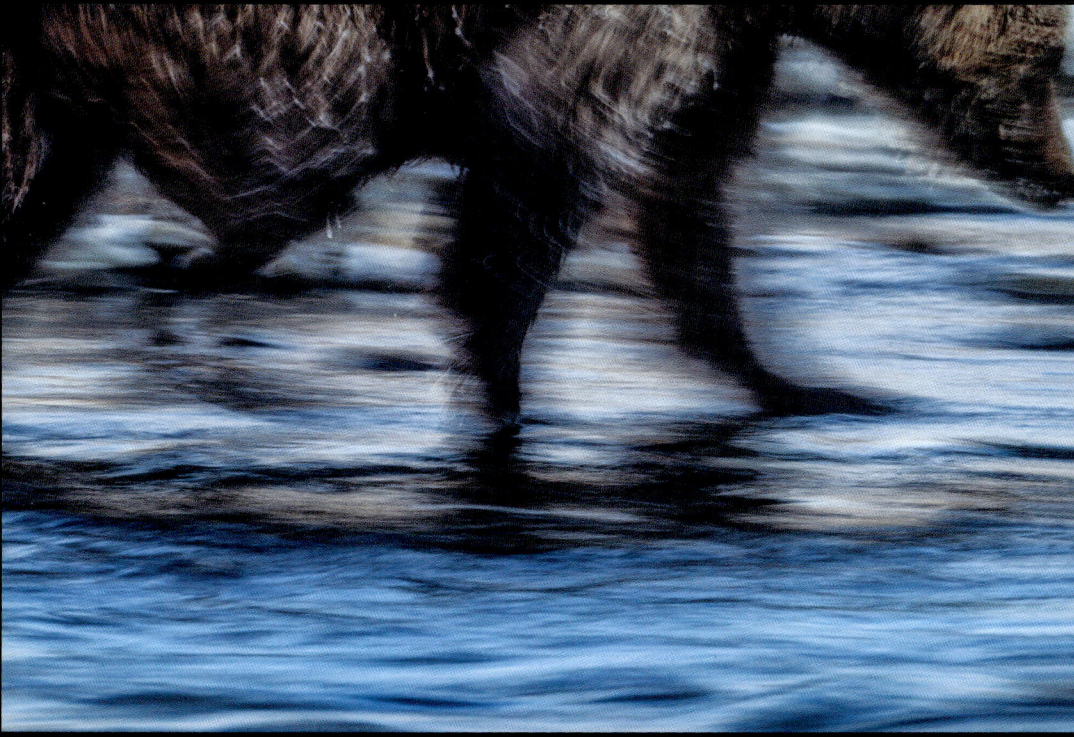

Top: An Arctic tern glides through the frame, Svalbard, Norway, 2007.
Bottom: A grizzly bear with slow shutter, Alaska, USA, 2018.

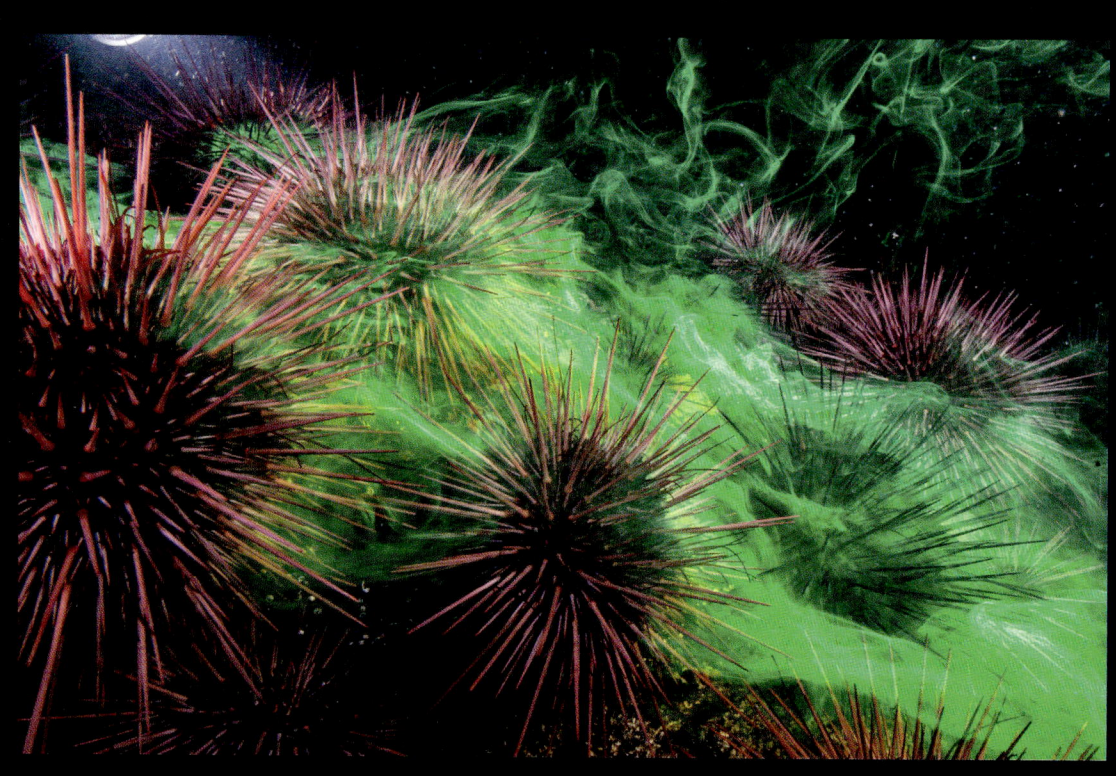

Above: Urchins and scientific dye, Vancouver
Island, British Columbia, Canada, 2005.

from – after that, I'll spend the remaining 20 per cent of my time in the last zone where I just try some 'Hail Marys'. I might be tired, the sun's getting low, and things aren't really working anymore, but nonetheless, I'll keep going for a while longer on the off-chance that something will happen.

I've been underwater in eight knots of current off the British Columbia coast, where all I could do was try something and hope for the best, as there was little chance of getting anything in focus. I didn't have a tripod to steady the camera, of course, and it was pitch-black, but I could see my dive buddy lighting up the scene with his powerful dive flashlight. What did I do? I took a 20-second handheld exposure. That's a 'Hail Mary', where the chances of success are slim to none.

In fact, what came from that moment was incredible, something I could never have predicted: I could see light coming off the flashlight and bending over rocks, travelling with the current. This gave me the idea to use organic dye to track and trace the currents in the ocean. It resulted in an image that ran in *National Geographic*. I wouldn't have got the idea of using the dye unless I had seen the light bending across the rocks.

The best part about spending time in the last 20-per cent zone is that you grow as an artist. You are developing skills that are going to help you later in your photographic journey. And maybe, in time, the techniques that you're testing in the last 20-per cent zone move into the 60-per cent zone, they become part of your regular skillset, and you find you are shooting successful images that push the limits of creativity. That is how you grow as an artist. And that is what this is all about.

"I might be tired, the sun's getting low, and things aren't really working anymore, but nonetheless, I'll keep going for a while longer on the off-chance that something will happen."

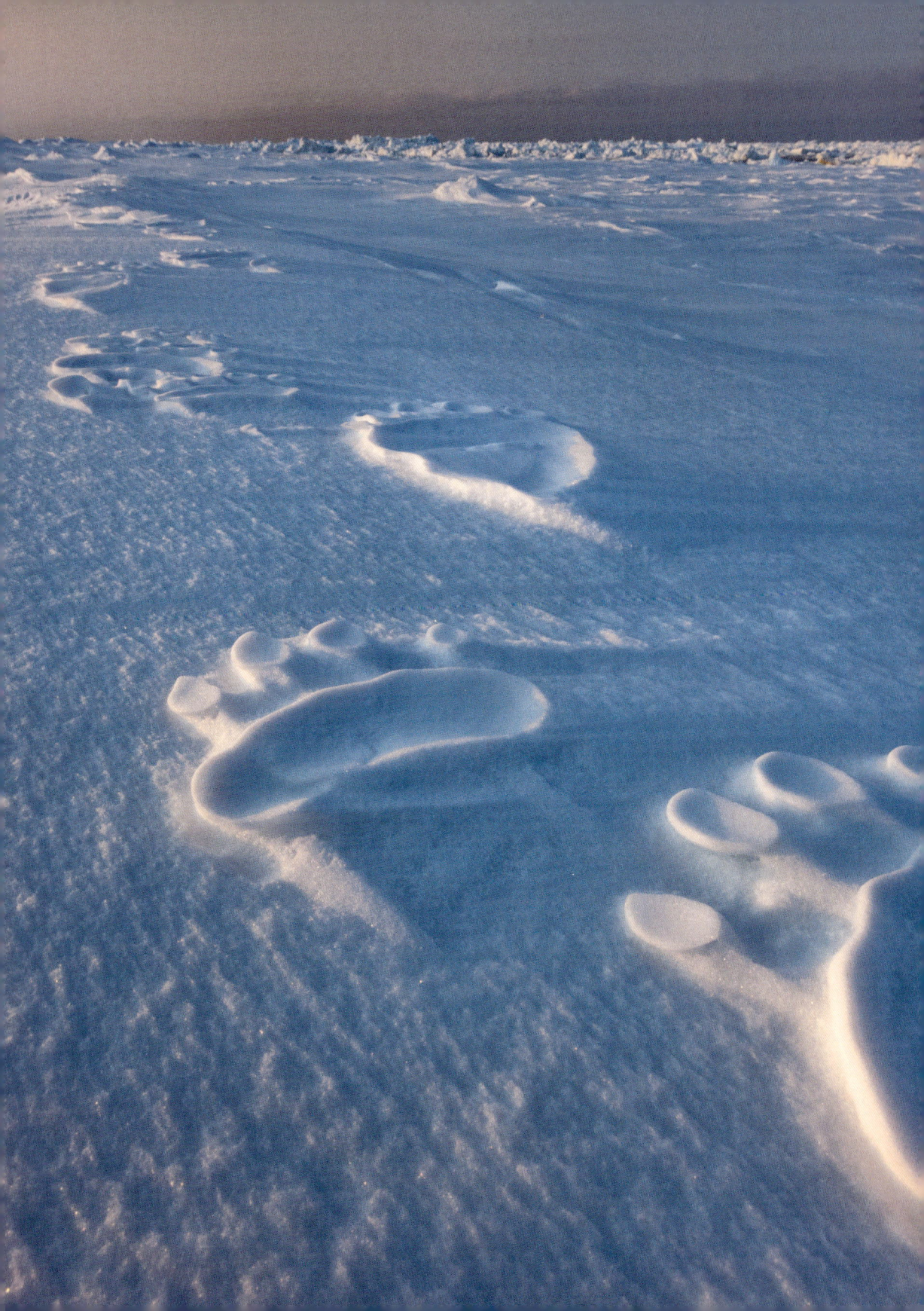

3

A roadmap to success

Set manageable goals

I am not an expert. What I mean is, I am not a career coach. Neither am I an expert in navigating mental health issues. I face challenges in the same way everyone does and strive to find ways to manage the obstacles I encounter.

I always smile when people look at me and say, 'Wow, you're so lucky. Everything has happened easily for you,' or '. . .You get to travel the world and take snaps'. Those kinds of comments irk me, but ultimately, they make me laugh, because my journey has been anything but straightforward. I've encountered many downs as well as ups, and I've had to put in a lot of work to get to where I am today.

I've a toolkit of techniques and exercises that I use to help me keep moving forwards and continue to progress my work. One of the most useful things I find is goal setting – making manageable goals. It's a technique I use whenever I mentor photographers who are starting out, or when I'm talking to someone about photography or indeed anything a person wants to do in life.

Left: *Polar Impressions*, Svalbard, Norway, 2008.

There are lots of great books out there about goal setting, so I'm not going to write an in-depth essay here. I wholeheartedly recommend picking one up – they can be very helpful. Instead, I hope that sharing what I do will help you move a step closer to identifying your own goals and breaking down challenges into manageable pieces.

Early in my career, when I was in my twenties, I wanted *National Geographic* to take notice of me. Nothing was working. I was flat broke. I didn't have the right camera gear, and I didn't have a boat, which I needed to get the kind of pictures I wanted to make. I didn't have money to buy fuel or to hire an assistant.

I complained to my stepdad day after day. He sat there quietly and listened, and finally one night he said, 'You've been talking for several days about why things aren't working, why you're not making it as a photographer. Why don't you try writing down all your problems?' He advised me to list all the things I was struggling with, primarily in photography and my career, but also more generally in life.

And so, I did. I made a list with about 40 points and showed it to him the next day. 'Great,' he said. 'Now, tonight, why don't you stay up for a while and write down 10 solutions for each of those difficulties?' That's a lot of work I thought. It's far easier to sit here and complain. But I did what he suggested. I took each problem in turn and listed all the possible solutions I could think of.

I started writing at around 8 p.m. and I was still going at 7 a.m. the next morning when he woke up. I wrote down hundreds of solutions.

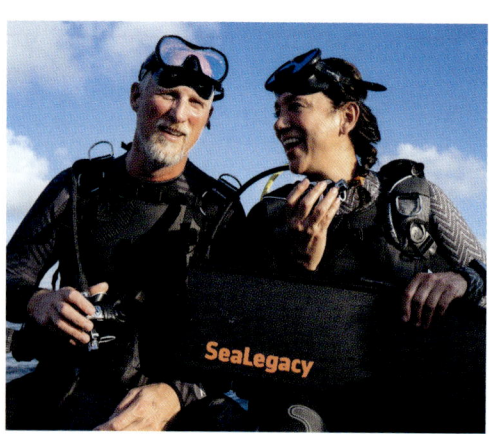

From that moment on, my career changed; everything changed. Nothing became easy, but whenever I was down, frustrated or anxious, I looked at that list, which became a kind of roadmap for success. It helped me to see the way forwards. Now, when I work with young photographers and others, when I see that they are a little stuck or struggling to find their way, I encourage them to get into the task of goal setting. I do this for myself, too.

I start by creating categories or headings for the various facets of my life and work:

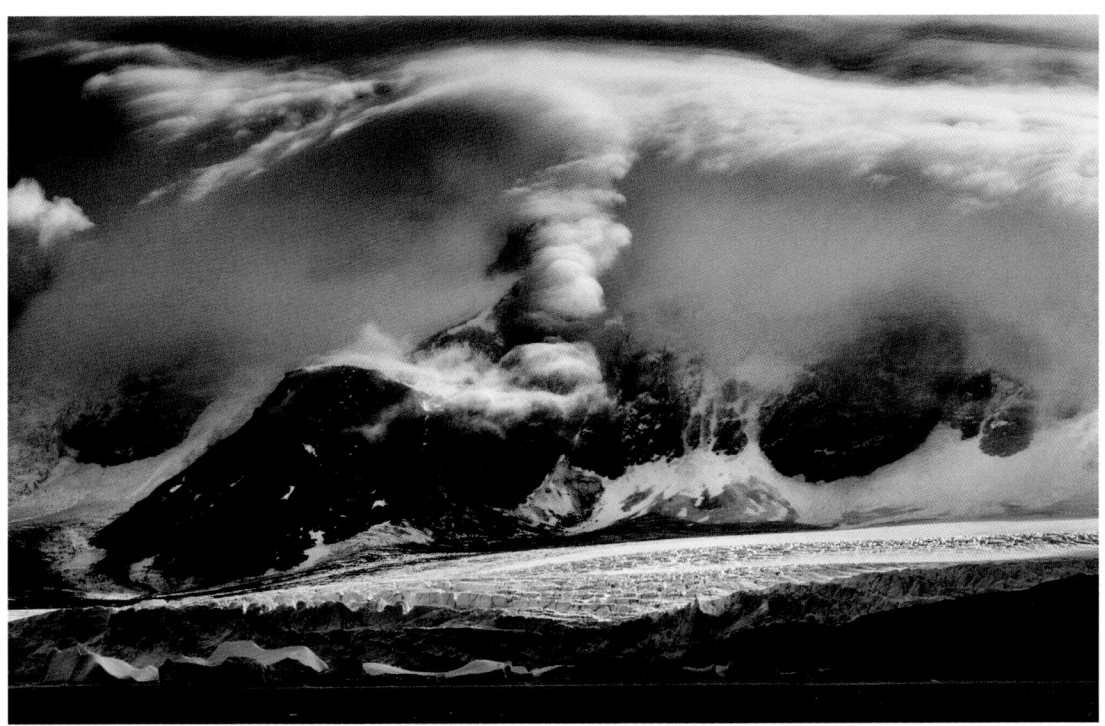

> " List the things you're struggling with . . . and write down 10 solutions for each of those difficulties."

conservation goals and the successes I want to have, photography, income, my fine art business, our non-profit SeaLegacy, relationships and friendships, and so on. I'll break each one down into periods of time – six months, one year, two years, three years, five years, ten years and twenty years.

I don't think about personal shortcomings or other things that might prevent me from achieving those goals. I dream of where I want to be, where I want to go, and then I spend time working out how I can make it happen. That is the key part. It's easy to dream. It's easy to say, 'I want to make however many dollars a year', but making that a reality takes a huge amount of work. You need a roadmap.

If you can, it's helpful to take time away from the day-to-day, to gain some distance and perspective. It's good to get away from distractions, to set yourself free every so often. Sometimes my partner, the photographer and conservationist Cristina Mittermeier, and I will get in our campervan and head out to a lake where there isn't any mobile phone service. We'll spend several days away, dreaming big. We don't bring our computers, but we might take pens and paper and write a ton of notes. We'll think about our respective goals, roadmaps, how we can realize our ambitions. There is a practice called nature bathing, where you mindfully connect with the natural environment around you. For me, nature bathing provides clarity of thought and helps with goal setting, which in turn leads to a vision (or visions) of a path forwards.

When we come home after that time away, having unplugged from society, our heads and hearts are always buzzing with big ideas, passion and a commitment to charge ahead and do the work that we do. It's hugely restorative. We'll do that at least two or three times a year.

You must be able to taste, to feel, to believe in your goals, because achieving them is going to take a lot of work. I'm not trying to scare you away from your dreams. I want to encourage you to go after your dreams, to follow your passions, but know that it's not easy. Dream big, put all your heart into what you're doing, but be prepared to weather the inevitable storms along the way.

With perseverance and patience, you will succeed. Goal setting is one of the best things you can do to alleviate feelings of depression, to calm anxiety, angst, fear (Chapter 3). It is, I believe, the overarching map, the way to energize you to go out and do great work.

And, once you've achieved your goals, the best part is you can set new goals. For me, shooting for *National Geographic*, an early goal of mine, turned out to be a stepping stone on my journey to becoming a conservationist and storyteller. Everything you do is all part of the journey.

"I dream of where I want to be, where I want to go, and then I spend time working out how I can make it happen."

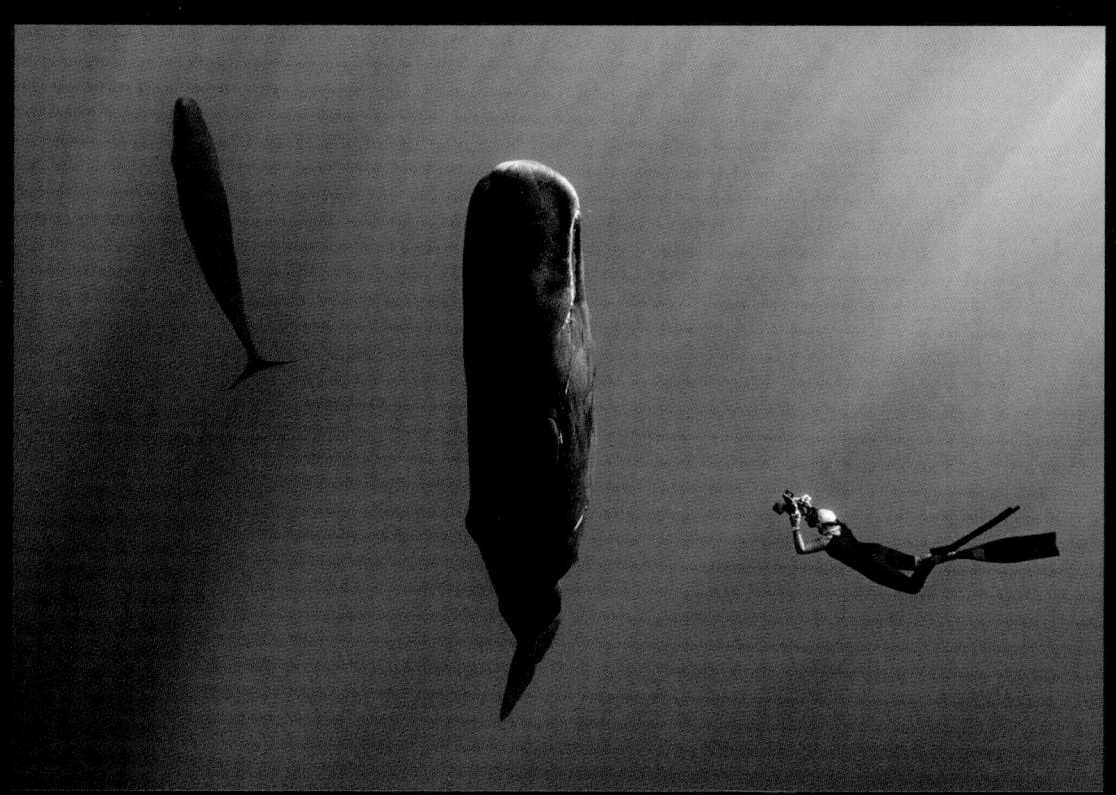

Above: *Matriarch*, Dominica, 2019.

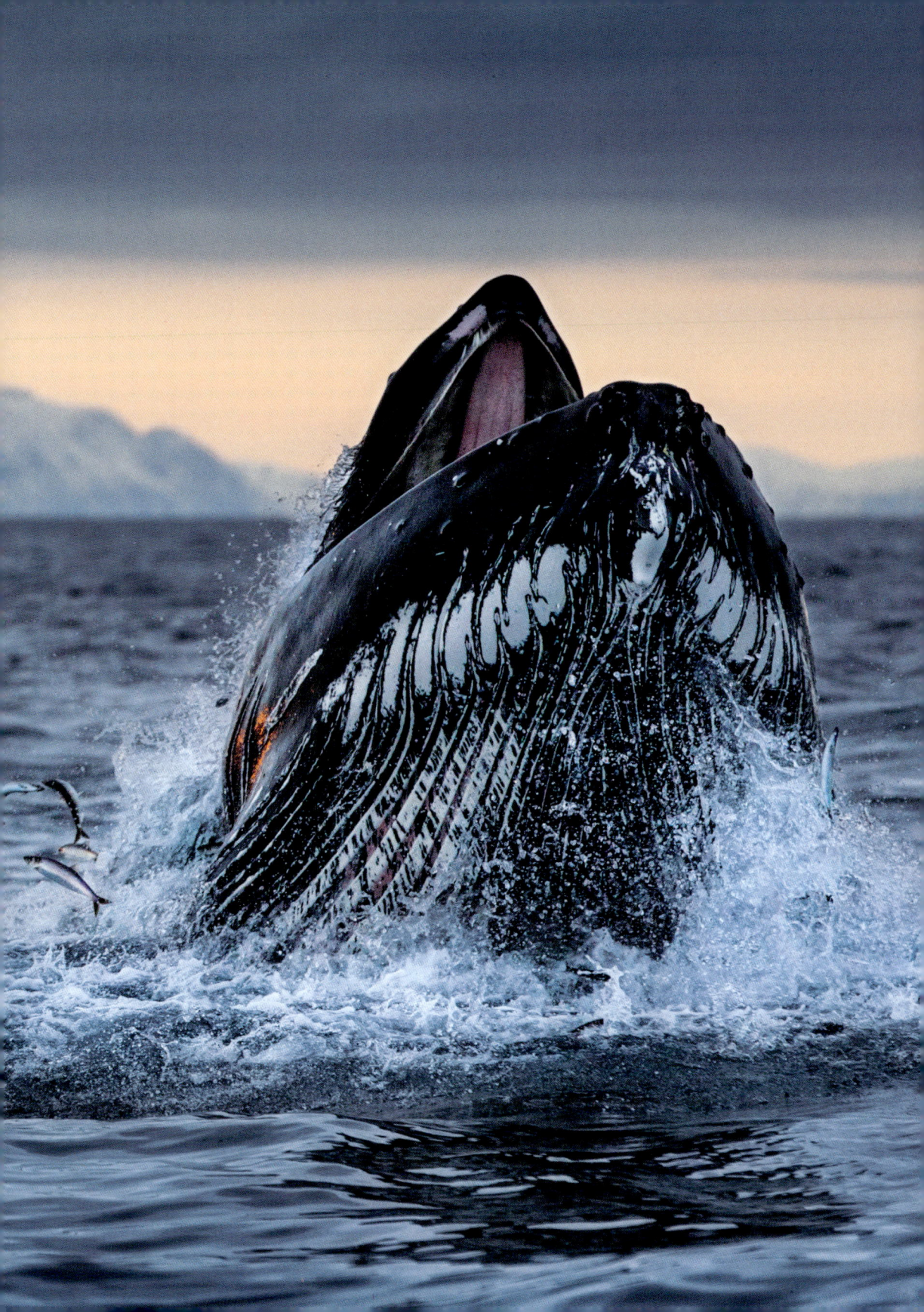

4

Take inspiration from others

Inform your creative practice by dipping into books

Ever since I was a young boy, books have meant everything to me. Growing up without a television or a radio, I would disappear into nature or lose myself in a book. I grew up with encyclopaedias and books by pioneering French oceanographer and filmmaker Jacques Cousteau.

As I grew older and began to develop an interest in photography, I'd study how-to books that explained how to set your aperture, shoot macro, or photograph at night, and how to decide which lens to use for wildlife or how to approach wildlife. Those kinds of books are useful, informative and they help you learn the basics of photography technique, but they don't inspire or trigger an emotional or visceral response. I was desperate to get out there and learn and grow as an artist, to go on a journey and tell stories. Once I had got to grips with the basics of photography, I needed to find my own style, to embark on an in-depth journey to find out who I was an artist; to find my own path.

Certain books were especially influential on me; books where I could devour the incredible work of incredible photographers and feel inspired. Heroes for me at the time included the ocean photographer

Left: *Vertical Feast,* Lofoten, Norway, 2014.

and filmmaker Bob Talbot, who could photograph something as simple as a whale tail in such a beautiful, visceral and powerful way. I also deeply admired the work of Ernest H. Brooks, whose underwater black-and-white photography is incredibly poetic.

Another key role model for me was the nature photographer Flip Nicklin, who ended up being my mentor at *National Geographic* and gave me a copy of his book, *With the Whales*. Flip is one of a kind – the world's foremost whale photographer. He filmed and dived with orcas off the coast of British Columbia when everybody thought it was crazy to do so. He gave us a glimpse into the lives of those animals when most people thought it was nearly impossible to do. Nobody has taken pictures of whales quite like him. He took a 'fly on the wall' approach, whether it was blue whales, beluga whales, sperm whales or humpback whales.

Some people worship actors or celebrities. My heroes were photographers and explorers. The greatest underwater photographer of all time is David Doubilet. It means the world to me to have a copy of his book, *Water Light Time*. When I met David in 2001, I was like a starstruck kid. I could hardly talk, even though I had just been given my first assignment at *National Geographic*. David had done tens of assignments for the magazine. He's an incredibly kind, warm man. I was touched that he took the time to write a personal note to me in the book.

Every picture I look at by David Doubilet, I study for hours. The lighting and complexity of his images are beyond impressive. To think he was shooting in an era of manual strobes, manual exposures and very rudimentary underwater photographic technology. The fact that he shot at such a level, decades ago, using film, is awe-inspiring. He set the bar not just high, but at a level that is pretty much unattainable.

"Some people worship actors or celebrities. My heroes were photographers and explorers."

Photography needs heroes like David and benchmarks like the ones he set. It feels good to know there are people out there shooting at such an inspired level which you can only dream of. It keeps you striving to improve your own craft, your own art.

Another incredible photographer I met in my late twenties was Michio Hoshino. He published a book called *Arctic Odyssey* and another seminal title, *Moose*.

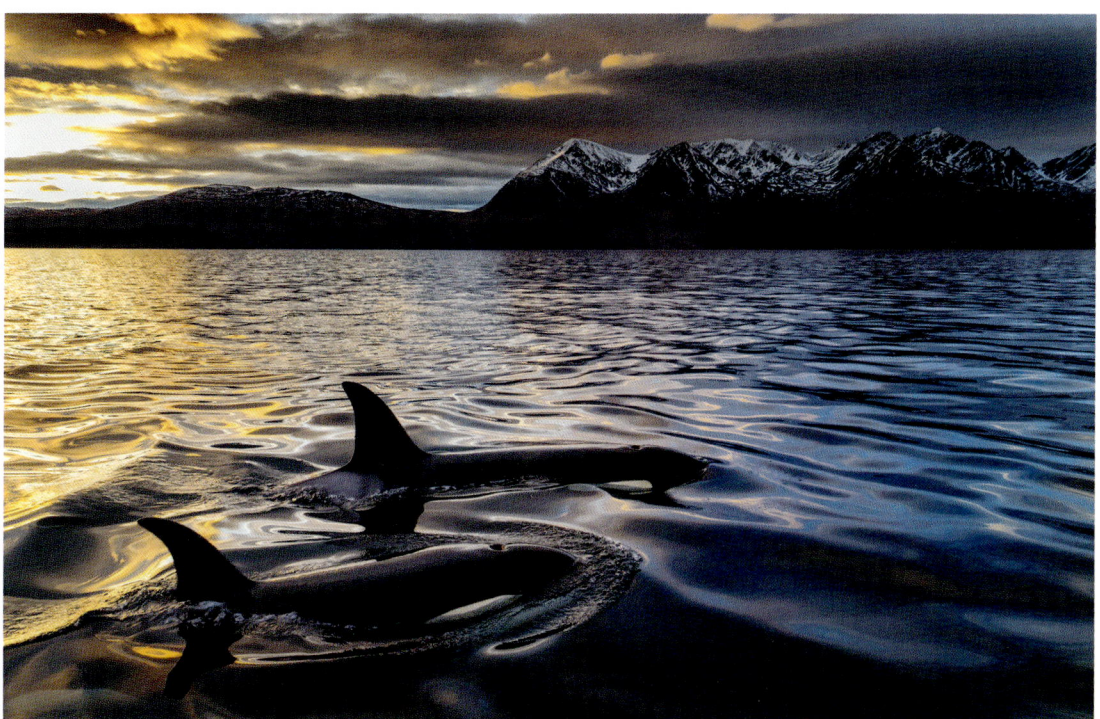

Above: *Norwegian Sunset Cruise,*
Northern Norway, 2018.

Michio was a true artist; he was so creative in the way he composed his images and used light. His pictures feature animals that most photographers dream of seeing just once – grizzly bears, moose and wolves. He captured intimate glimpses into their lives in such beautiful, artistic ways.

I was photographing grizzly bears and wolves in Alaska, and one day, as I was hiking across the tundra, I met a man who said, 'Do you know that Michio Hoshino is in the park?' I replied, 'Are you kidding me?!' I mean, what I would have done to meet Michio. The man said, 'He's driving a red Toyota 4Runner'. Later that day, I saw the vehicle coming down the road. I got down on my hands and knees and started to hail him. Michio pulled over, got out and pulled me up. We started to talk about photography, then we sat down and he showed me *Moose*. Swapping stories with this man, someone who I greatly admired, and having the opportunity to learn from him was like a dream come true.

Of course, you cannot talk about wildlife and nature photography without mentioning the work of Frans Lanting, perhaps the greatest wildlife and nature photographer of all time. He uses such complex lighting and techniques and pushes the boundaries of the tools we as image-makers have at our disposal to come back with images that are on another level. Look at his work when you want to study rear sync flash or macro, or to see the world in a different light.

And then there is the Japanese photographer and filmmaker Mitsuaki Iwagō. In the 1980s and 1990s, he got lost in the ecosystems of the Serengeti. With Iwagō's work, you start to see what it means to not just go to a place, take a few pictures and come home and say, 'Well, I got a picture of a giraffe', but to look at the same pride of lions and cheetahs over a long period of time, study the behaviours and complexities of those animals, become lost in the lives of those species and even get to know individual animals. When his book came out, I realized that to shoot exceptional imagery, you had to go and get lost in the ecosystems you wanted to photograph.

If I have to name a photographer whose style influenced me, it is Jim Brandenburg. I was captivated by the work he made of Arctic wolves on Ellesmere Island in Canada, namely, its sensitive and creative nature. At that point, I was still in the phase of my journey where I was just hoping to photograph an animal full frame with its eye sharp, while Jim and others were coming back with incredibly complex compositions of moments I could only dream about. The images were so advanced that my young brain wasn't yet able to envisage anything of the kind, but they were instrumental in helping me develop my creative vision.

" Find photographers you admire. Study their work, break down their images in every possible way you can think of."

So, find photographers you admire. Study their work, break down their images in every possible way you can think of, from the shooting angle to the lighting, to the equipment and how they got those moments, because that's how I got my start: I studied the work of my heroes.

Sometimes I read books just for fun – funny books that help me to switch off. It's good to let your brain have a rest every now and then, so you're not always thinking about photography. I might take a book with me when

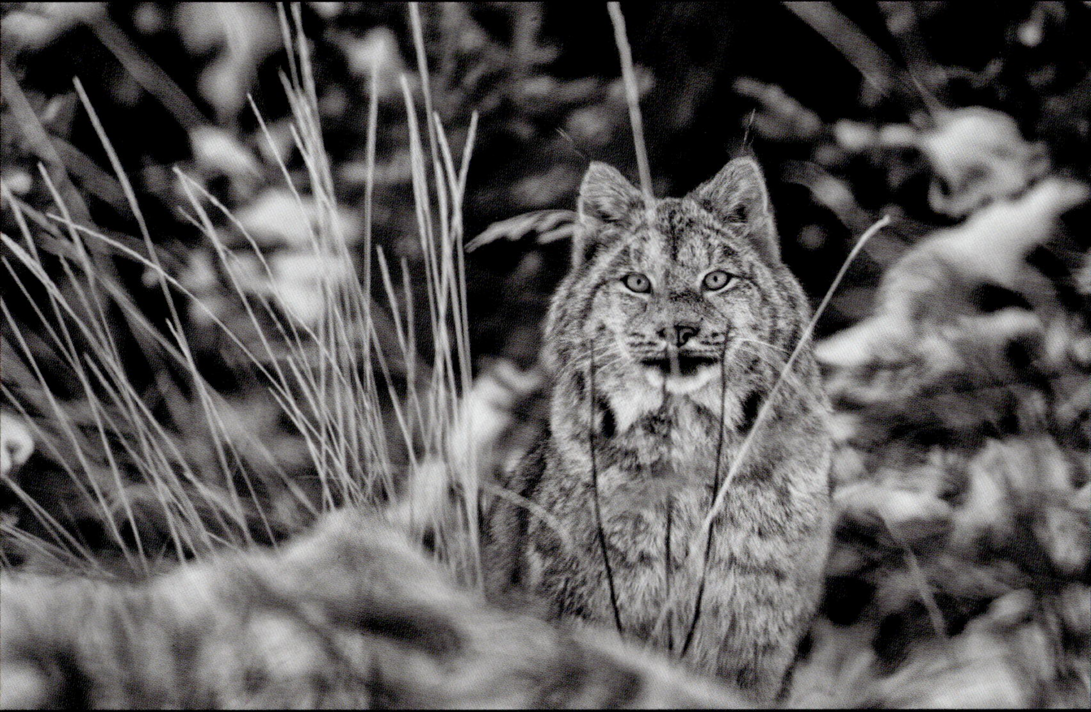

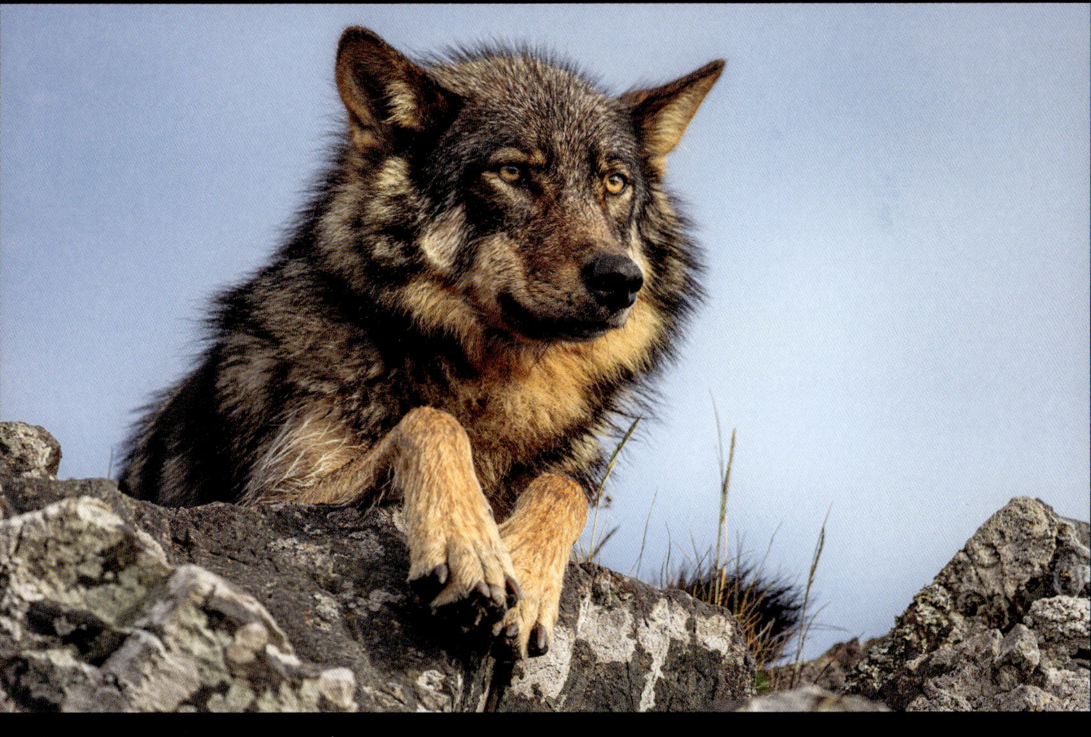

Top: *Stealth*, Northwest Territories, Canada, 2011.
Bottom: A sea wolf keeps a look out, British Columbia, Canada, 2011.

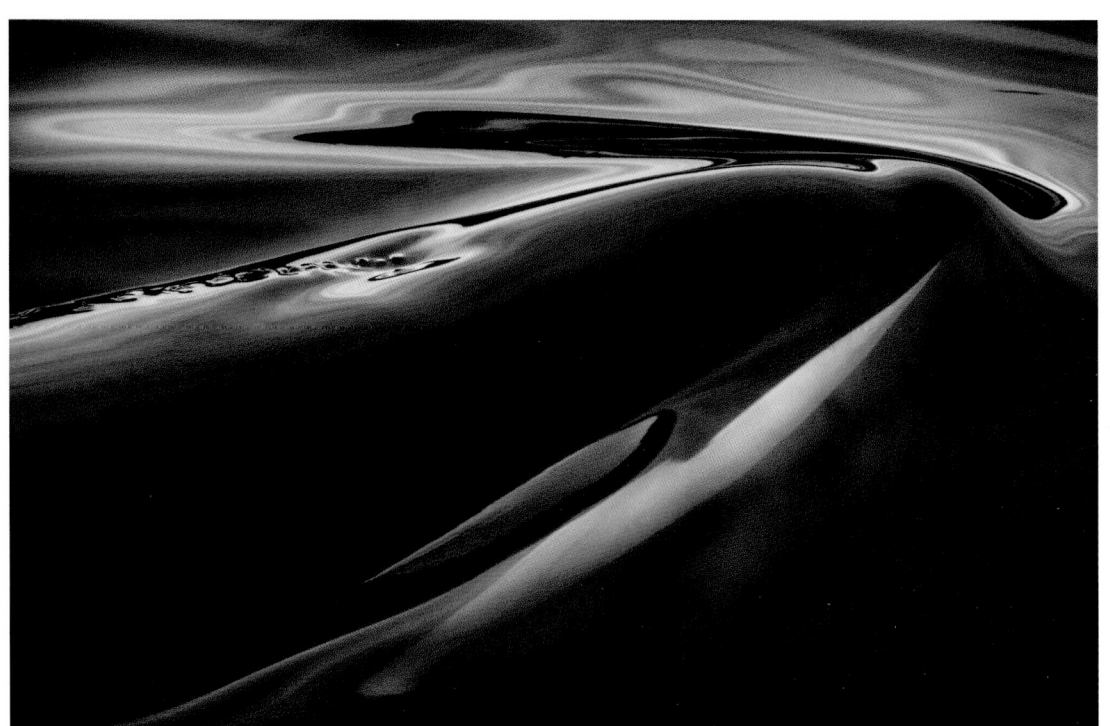

Above: Killer Tension, Alaska, USA, 2015.

I go out on to the sea ice in the Arctic and get lost in what that book has to say. Other go-to books include those about great explorers such as Robert Falcon Scott and Sir Ernest Shackleton – I could read those kinds of books all day long. They are the truly tough characters who I'm inspired by.

Most important of all is a book by Rachel Carson called *Silent Spring*. There are no pictures, but when you start to read, you see the power and the strength of an individual. Through her writing, Carson not only drew attention to the terrible harm caused by DDT and other pesticides, but she also successfully challenged the industry on its use. Her work contributed to a ban in the United States.

Whether it's Carson or oceanographer and conservationist Sylvia Earle, or primatologist Dr Jane Goodall, these are the warriors who have been on the front lines of conservation their entire lives; selfless, hardworking, dedicated people who are brave enough to speak out – to take on big industry, sometimes against the odds – and who, in the end, effect change.

For me, everything I do is about storytelling and conservation. I want all my photography to be at the intersection of art, science and conservation. The images need to be beautiful, powerful and evocative, but also based on science and fact. The work must have purpose. As such, I'm constantly reading about conservation initiatives and thinking about how I can add value to my storytelling and photography to fight for a better planet.

So, immerse yourself in books that cover a broad cross-section of topics. Learn the techniques and then seek out the work of other photographers who inspire you, people who will help you to grow as an artist.

" I'm constantly reading about conservation initiatives and thinking about how I can add value to my storytelling and photography to fight for a better planet."

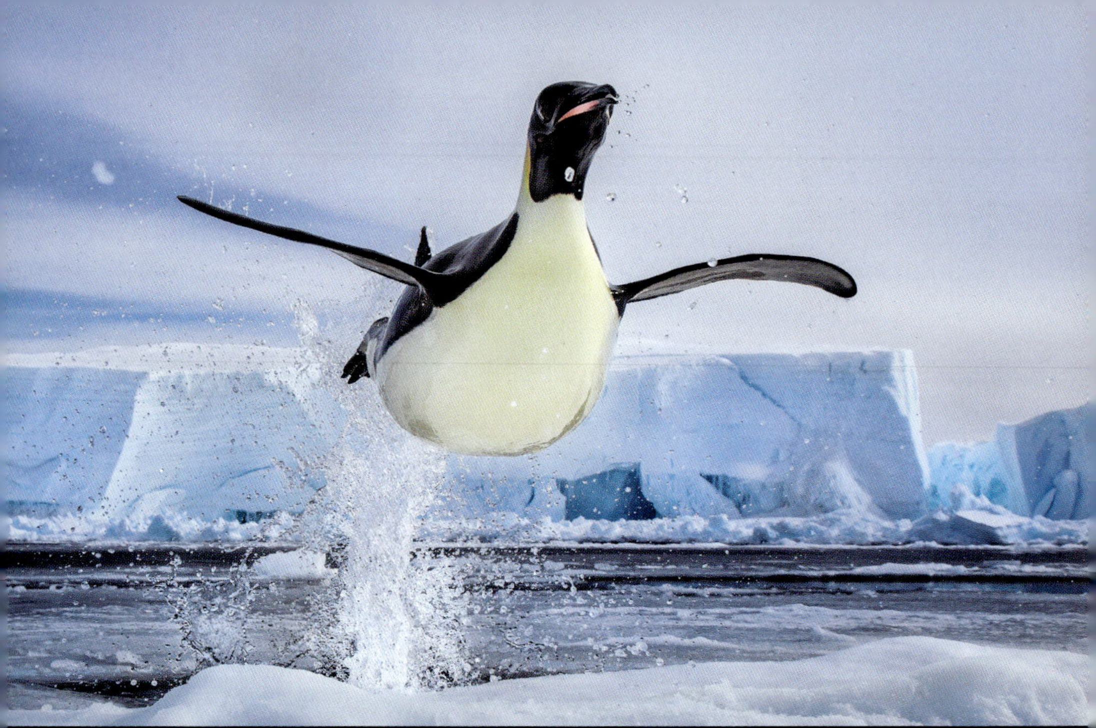
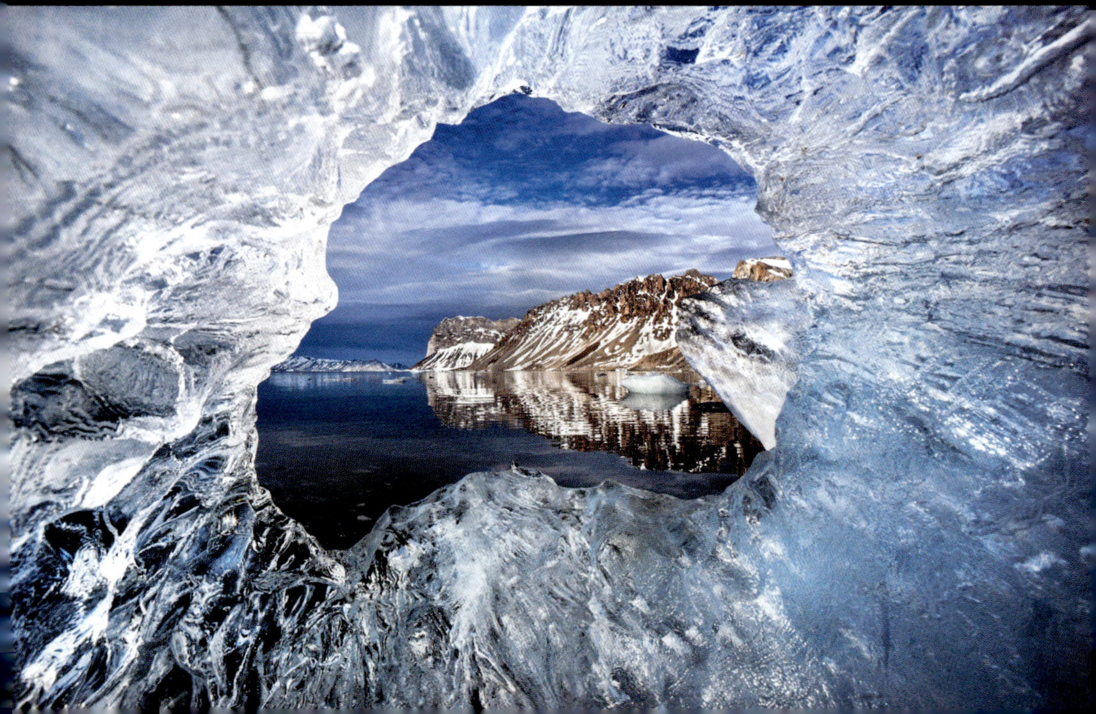

Silence your inner critic

Overcome doubt and the fear of failure

L ike many photographers and creatives, I deal with anxiety, depression and feelings of insecurity that are always knocking at the door. It is not easy to make it as a photographer; it never has been. When you set big goals, you're going to encounter a lot of things trying to bring you down. And most of those things are inside your head.

It's terrifying to set a goal to try and achieve something in the world. Little voices will pop up and jeer, 'You're going to fail!' Those voices occur because you may well fail, and in a sense, niggling voices are just trying to protect you.

When I was deciding on my life goals and going out to chase them, people were constantly telling me that I was going to fail. I had a boss who was always telling me to 'put the camera away' and 'stick to being a biologist' because that's 'all there was for me' in the world. After I left that job, he would often pop into my head. Various characters would appear in my mind, telling me I wasn't going to make it. It got to the point where the voices were constant. I had to find a way to make them go away.

Top: *Freedom*, Ross Sea, Antarctica, 2011. Bottom: A window of ice, Svalbard, Norway, 2007.

So, when a voice showed up, I did a fun, tongue-in-cheek exercise. I would imagine the negative character wearing Mickey Mouse ears; I'd turn them into a big cartoon character in my mind. Perhaps I'd devise a scene from a *Bugs Bunny* episode. I would imagine taking a wad of dynamite, lighting it, shoving it in the character's mouth and watching it explode. The massive 'explosion' was silly, but crucially, it made the little voice disappear.

When I was working as a biologist, I felt frustrated with the work we were doing. At times, I was full of rage, as some of the work I found to be ethically questionable. Later, after I'd left to pursue photography full-time, I went up to the High Arctic to refresh my mindset. A light aircraft dropped me off, and I wouldn't see another human for three months. My brain was consumed by anger, negative thoughts and frustration, not least towards the people who told me not to go on this trip. 'Why would you waste so much money going on a trip like this? You're going to fail.' So much negativity was swirling around in my head. I was lost and in a dark place.

One day, while I was out on the tundra, things got so bad I found myself screaming at the top of my lungs. There was nobody else around, just birds, bears and wolves. I've got to deal with this, I thought. Here I am in paradise, full of anger. I began focusing on my breathing and on happy, positive thoughts. Every time a negative thought came into my mind, I pushed it away. I started setting the clock. Whenever a negative thought lingered, I had to start the clock again.

My goal was to go for ten days without having a negative thought. I came across this concept in the book *Awaken the Giant Within* by the coach and motivational speaker Tony Robbins, which I'd read some years earlier. It took me thirty-five days to achieve ten days of uninterrupted positive thinking. After thirty-five days focusing on feelings of positivity and gratitude, on all the great things in life, and how fortunate I was to be on this journey, I felt euphoric, excited and grateful.

That's when I embarked on my goal setting for life. I took out a notebook – I only had one on me – and started to write on the pages in

> " Various characters would appear in my mind, telling me I wasn't going to make it. It got to the point where the voices were constant. I had to find a way to make them go away."

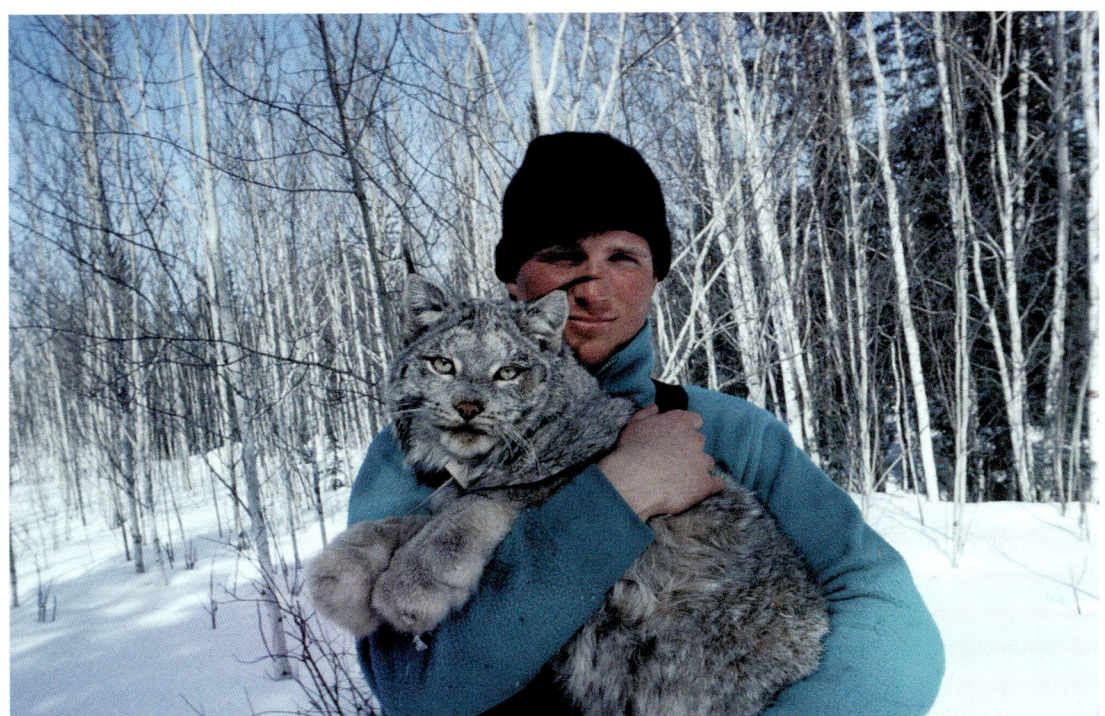

Above: Paul with a wild
Canadian lynx (taken
by Mark Sabourin), Fort
Providence, Northwest
Territories, Canada, 1992.

big, bold letters. By the time I'd reached the end of the notebook,
I was writing in tiny letters because I was running out of space.
I went back to the top of the notebook and started writing in the
margins, and then on cardboard boxes in the little camp I was staying
in – anywhere, because my head was exploding with ideas. I had to
release all that negativity to free up my mind to dream, to be filled
with passion and excitement.

I still have that notebook. It's strange looking at it now, as it tells
the story of my career path – how I got to where I am today.

It's crucial, I believe, to get rid of, or to at least dial down the little
voices saying you won't succeed, and to battle the negativity inside
your head or work towards reinforcing a positive view of yourself,
because before you know it, you could find you are depressed or
full of anxiety about where you are in life. Those feelings can leave
you feeling paralyzed creatively, or you could end up shutting
down completely.

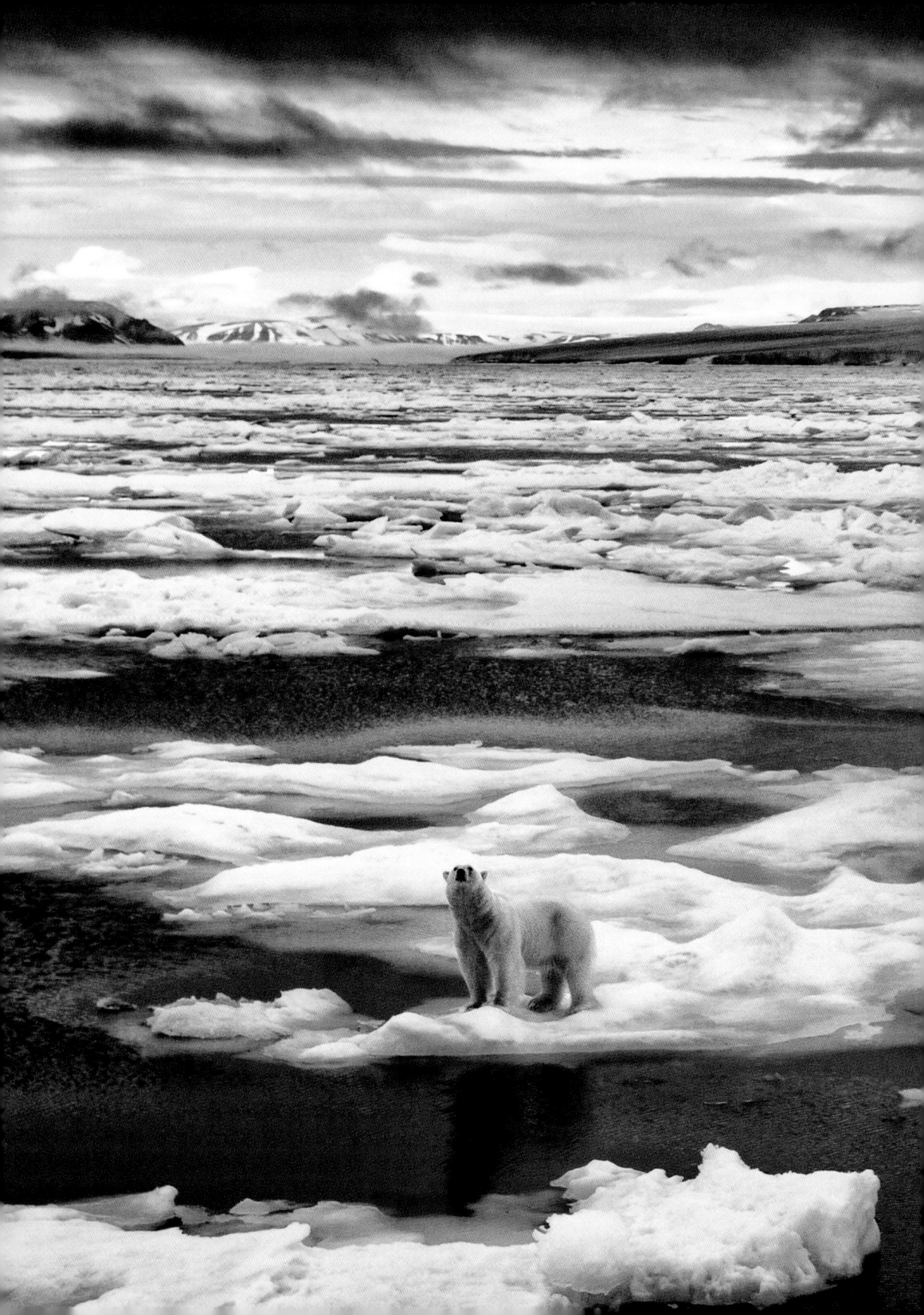

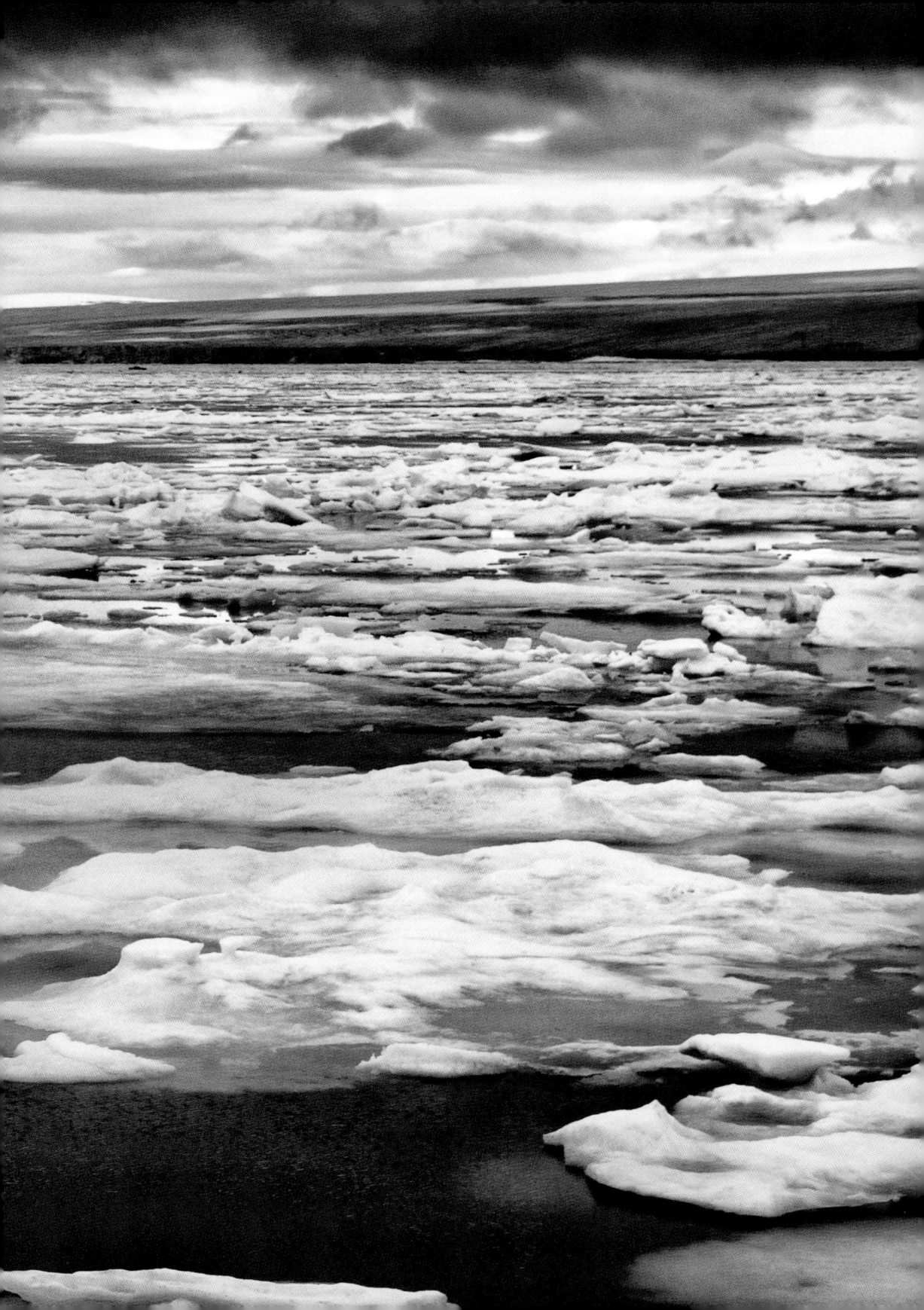

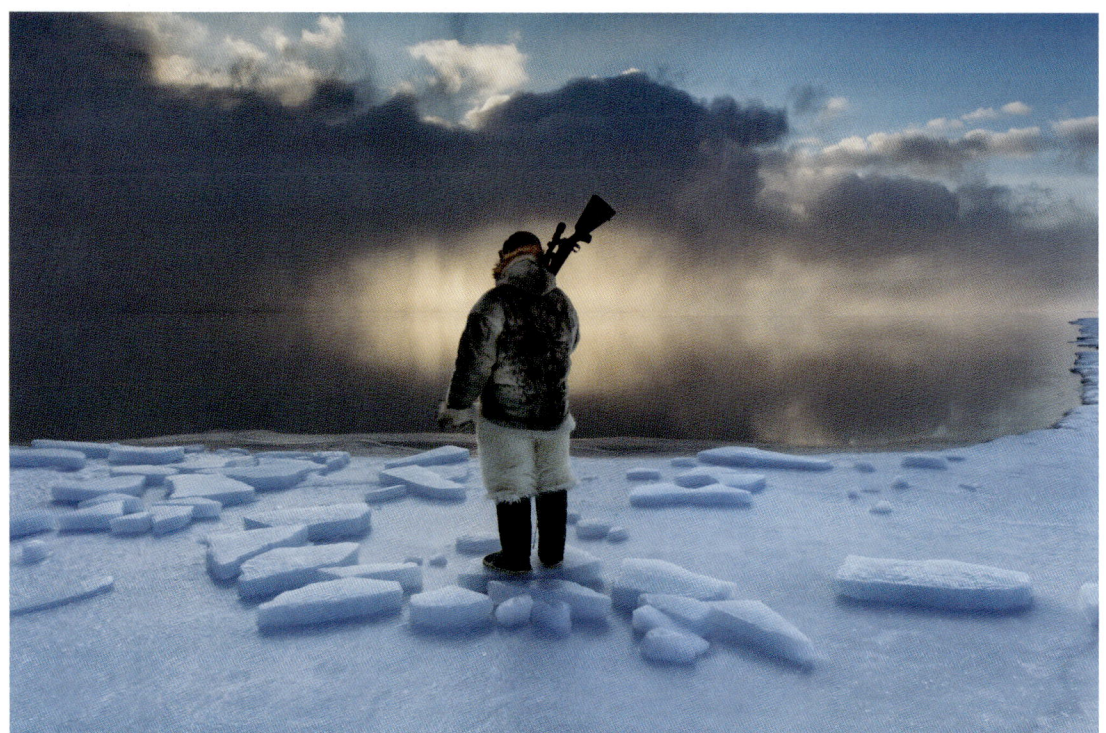

Previous spread: *Vanishing World*, Svalbard, Norway, 2006. Above: An Inuit hunter stands on the edge of the ice, Qaanaq, Greenland, 2015.

I have a mental toolkit that I use when I'm prepping a shoot and out in the field. As photographers, artists, conservationists, storytellers, we're a little like mechanics with our respective toolkits, telling our stories, doing our work.

Inevitably, before you embark on an expedition, you're going to have a whole bunch of noise in your head. A lot of little voices will start screaming at you: 'the weather's not going to be right', 'your equipment's going to let you down', 'the animals aren't going to show up'. Or even, 'why bother at all, why don't you just stay home on the sofa where it's safe?' That's a surefire way to guarantee you'll never know if you would have failed or not.

You have to find a way to push through the noise and get yourself mentally prepared, pack your gear, and get on with it. Learn to know and accept that the little voices are coming, as they do for everything in life. They're going to bubble up, but you can teach yourself to be ready for them when they do.

It's worth saying that as a wildlife and nature photographer, I fail about 95 to 98 per cent of the time. That's a huge amount of failure. Imagine waking up every morning and saying to yourself, 'Today, I'm going to shoot the best images of my life. I'm going to shoot *National Geographic*-worthy images or images that are going to be beautiful pieces of art and will hang on the wall,' knowing that there's going to be a 98-per cent failure rate. That's tough. You need to develop a sense of mental toughness to combat that.

Mental toughness comes into play before, during and after an expedition. I'm good at toughing out a shoot – being on my own, coping with being hungry, enduring freezing conditions, dealing with my emotions, sitting in the pouring rain, managing when equipment fails. With practice, you too can become mentally tough, which will help you to cope with whatever a shoot or indeed a life in photography throws at you.

The bottom line is – and it's about being realistic rather than negative – there's a very good chance you're going to fail during any given expedition. You're going to fail to make those images that you've dreamed about or sketched out, but that's okay. It's about doing everything you can to *not* fail, but being ready to fail, and when you do, picking yourself up and going again.

No matter what you do in life, you have to try to enjoy the journey. If you say to yourself, 'Unless I succeed on this trip, I am going to be miserable', then you're probably going to end up being miserable most of your life. In photography, we fail all the time, and that's part of the process (Chapter 17). When you do succeed, when everything comes together, it tastes so sweet because you've been through a lot of hard times to get to that moment.

"It's about doing everything you can to *not* fail, but being ready to fail, and when you do, picking yourself up and going again."

I try to remind myself that I'm lucky: I'm in control of my time, I get to pack my own gear and head off and experience incredible places and moments. Whether success comes on any given occasion or not, it is a gift to go out there and make art, to tell your stories and make a difference.

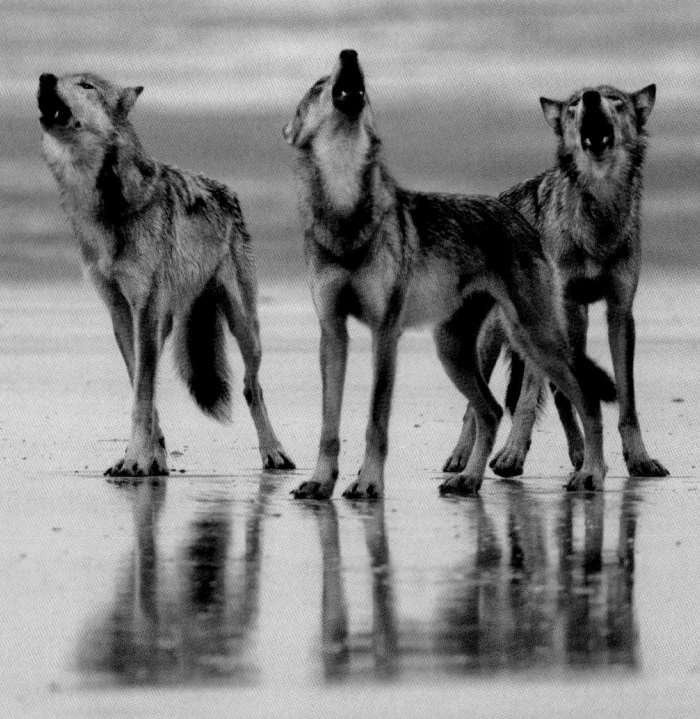

Inside Paul's kitbag

Know your kit

I am going to make a confession: I'm not a gear junkie. I don't obsess over manuals. I love to learn from other photographers who are studying what is possible with the latest equipment, but I don't get hung up on every last spec. It's important to know your camera and to be able to move fluidly between settings and lenses, but ultimately your kit is just a series of tools, a means to produce the images you want to make.

I have my own 'toolkit' – a collection of things I do – that has helped me along the way. One of the most important is to memorize the functionality of my camera system. Whether it's an underwater housing, a lens or a camera, I get to know that system inside out.

With a new camera, for example, I'll take it out, read through the manual and go through everything several times. Using that camera will become second nature. For example, I'll get to know my Sony A1 so well, I could change the settings in the dark, without looking. (Other ways of doing this are blindfolding yourself or just looking away as you play with the settings.) I'll practise rolling the shutter and f-stop, or changing from single autofocus to continuous mode. I'll know how many clicks it takes to go from 1/15th of a second to 1/250, and f/5.6 to f/11.

Left: *Sea Tribe*, British Columbia, Canada, 2020.

When you're in the heat of the action, or you're working in the dark, perhaps photographing the aurora borealis, you need to know all the dials on your camera and how to use them without looking. You don't want to be sitting there staring at your camera and wondering, 'How do I change such and such again?' You want to be lost in the creative process. I make sure I'm confident operating my camera gear because I don't want to be thinking about it when there's something incredibly beautiful happening in front of me. So, get to know your camera.

If you're just getting into photography or you've been doing it for a while and you're trying to rethink your kit, you could not be at a more exciting time in the industry. Heavyweight manufacturers such as Sony, Nikon, Canon, Leica and Zeiss are all vying to produce the best products. As a result, we're spoilt for choice.

Nowadays, almost any top lens you buy is going to be great. Even so, I try and keep my kit simple. I don't carry around hundreds of dollars' worth of glass just so I know I have every lens with me.

When I'm out in the field, I only need three lenses, maybe four. Generally speaking, my widest lens will be a 16–35mm, maybe a 12–24mm if I'm after something specific. A 16–35mm is a great lens – very wide, and sharp. Then I'll have a 24–105mm. It's a small, compact, sharp piece of glass. I might have a 100–400mm lens. I tend to avoid carrying a 400mm prime lens and save that weight for a 600mm super telephoto instead for extreme close-ups.

If I'm trying to be extra efficient and simplify my kit, I'll take three lenses and two bodies – a 24–105mm, 100–400mm and 600mm with a 1.4x converter, which becomes the equivalent of an 840mm lens. That way I have everything from 24mm to 840mm covered in just three lenses.

" If I'm trying to be extra efficient and simplify my kit, I'll take three lenses and two bodies – a 24-105mm, 100-400mm and 600mm with a 1.4x converter, which becomes the equivalent of an 840mm lens."

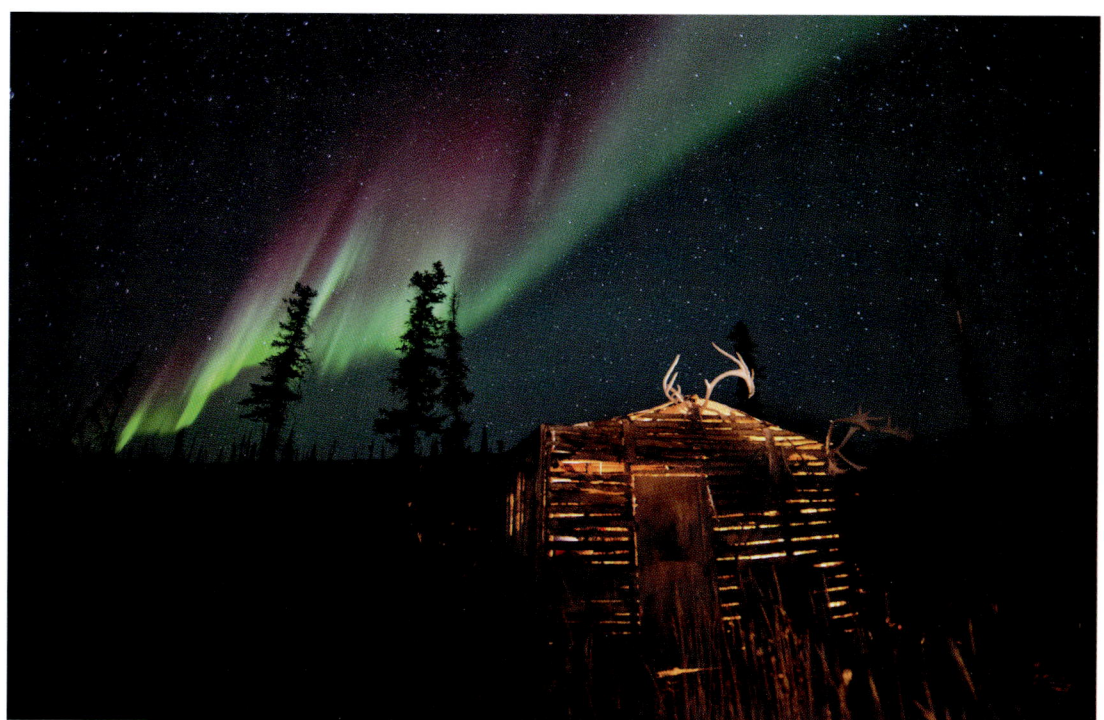

Above: Hunter cabin, Yukon,
Canada, 2011.

When I'm in marginal light conditions and I have to handhold my camera, I know that I need to use a fast enough shutter speed to avoid camera shake (which results in less than acceptably sharp images). To calculate the appropriate shutter speed, I use the reciprocal rule – this means using a shutter speed that is equivalent to the focal length of the lens, i.e. with a 50mm lens, I would use a minimum shutter speed of 1/60. When using zoom lenses, I apply this rule to the maximum focal length, for example, 1/125 for a 24–105mm lens.

I generally use longer telephoto lenses with a tripod for stability. I have used my 600mm lens at 1/8 or even 1/4, but only because it's on a tripod, which mitigates the risk of introducing blur at those slower shutter speeds. The longer the exposure, the more potential there is to introduce blur from any movement of the camera.

When you come to any situation, you need to work backwards – ask yourself: 'What shot do I want to make? What is the best camera for the job?' You might have sketched out the shot, done your research

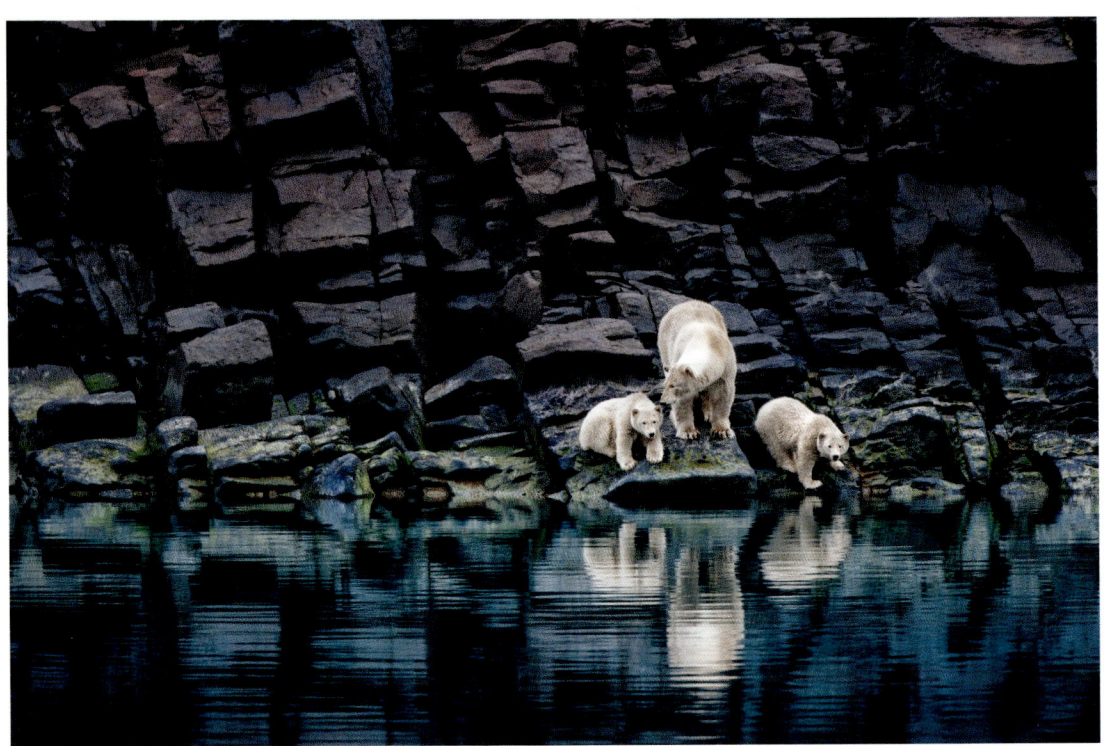

Above: *The Long Summer*,
Spitsbergen, Norway, 2007.
Overleaf: *Sea Wolf of the
Great Bear*, British Columbia,
Canada, 2011.

– you know what you want to do. Then you decide what tool is most suitable. If I want to take a shot of a wolf in its surroundings, for example, and I know that 'X' is the right lens for the job, that's the lens I'll choose.

When I'm photographing wildlife, I'll often start with my 600mm lens. There's a reason for that: I don't want to get close to the animal; I don't want to disturb it or change its behaviour. The animal has a chance to see me from a distance, to smell me, to hear the clicking of my camera, to see my body in motion; it can see that I'm not a threat. From there, the animal starts to relax and get into its routine.

As the animal starts to do its thing and gets a little closer to me, I might switch lenses. If a coastal wolf, for example, starts to walk down the beach towards me, I might switch to my 100–400mm lens. As that wolf changes direction and walks 10 feet (3 metres) away from me down the beach, I can very quietly and smoothly reach down and pick up a camera with a 16–35mm lens.

In summary, I have my core lenses, which include a 16–35mm, 24–70mm, 100–400mm and a 600mm. That's my key set for wildlife and nature. But what about other 'speciality' lenses? We all want to get them, and why not? They're exciting and fun. But they need to be used at the right time and in the right way.

A macro lens can be good to have to hand – who doesn't want to do macro photography in wildlife and nature? The extreme close-ups of macro photography can transport the viewer into a completely different world.

Then you have fisheye lenses. Attach one of those to your camera, and the whole world looks warped and weird and wonderful. No matter where you point that lens, the image looks amazing. Generally, though, the rule with fisheye lenses is that they belong with the fish. My editors at *National Geographic* would remind me of that all the time. Even if you are thinking of using a fisheye lens for underwater photography, I encourage photographers to use it sparingly.

Choosing the right lens is about being able to respond quickly as situations change and not just stick to what you know. When a photographer gets nervous, when an amazing scene opens up in front of you, the temptation is to go wide because so much is happening. A true artist will step up and respond to the elements of the scene. They won't go wide by default. Consequently, they're more likely to come back with something exceptional.

Finally, I like to keep a couple of fast lenses in my bag. Fast lenses are useful when you're shooting night scenes – stars and the Milky Way and so on – and need to use a slower shutter speed. A 14mm f/2.8 lens is great for shooting aurora borealis, and a 20mm f/2 or similar is nice to have (that shallow depth of field comes in handy).

" I'll often start with my 600mm lens. There's a reason for that: I don't want to get close to the animal; I don't want to disturb it or change its behaviour."

Lenses are important, of course, but be selective about what you are using. Get your core group – the lenses you can take anywhere that will enable you to accomplish almost anything. As you grow as a photographer and develop special interests, think about the lenses that will be useful to add to your kitbag, but when you're starting out, don't rush into buying lots of expensive lenses that you think you need.

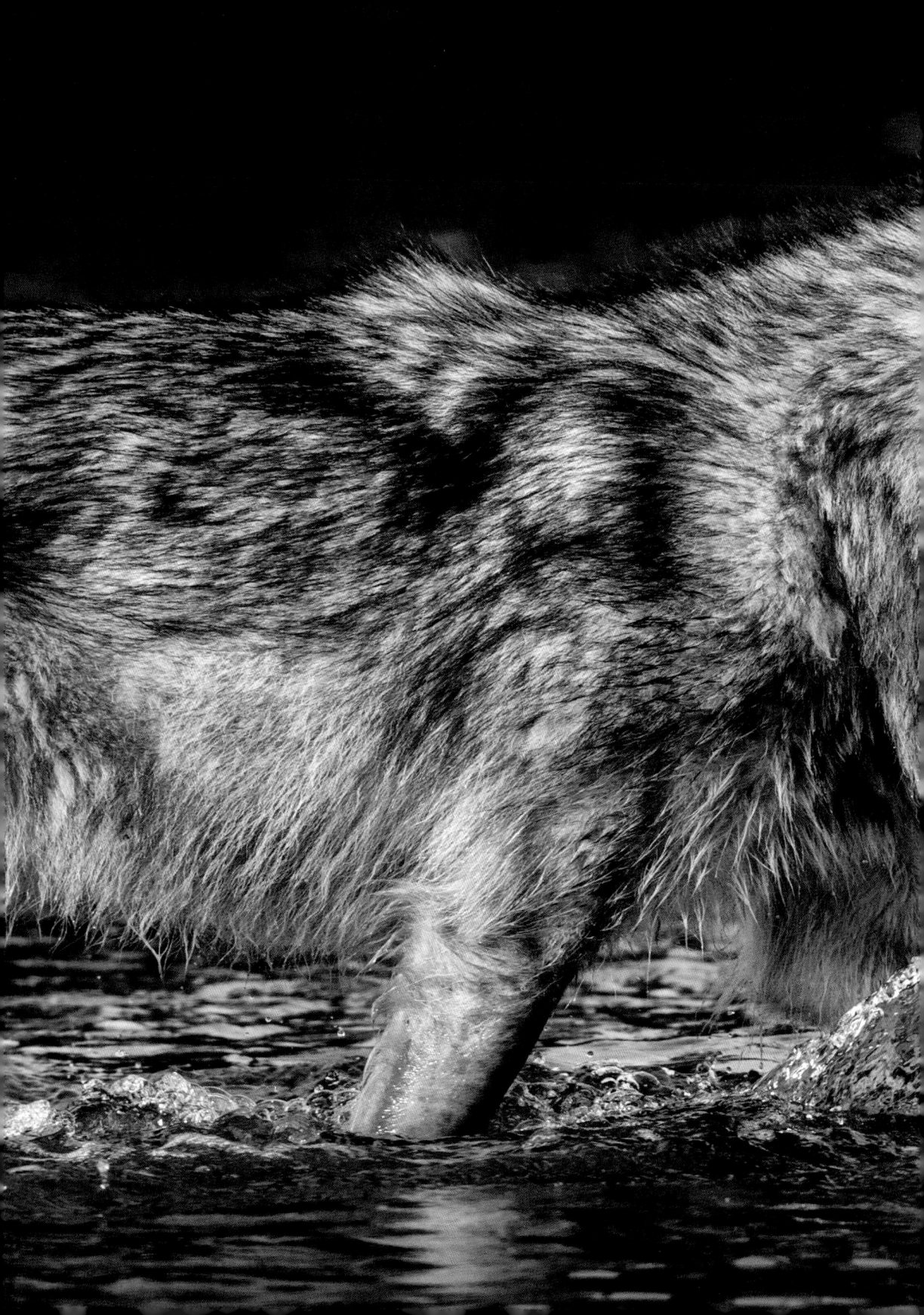

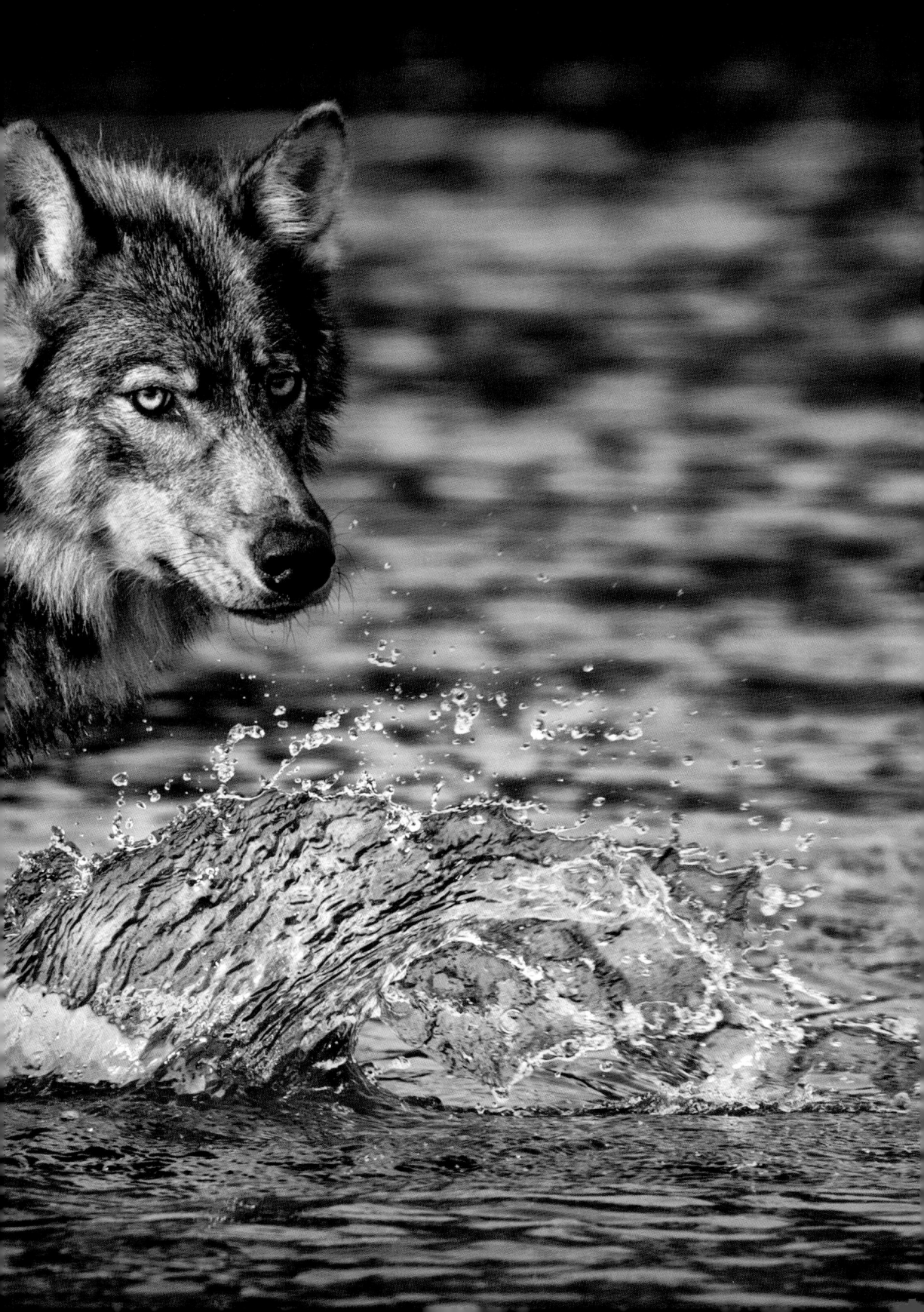

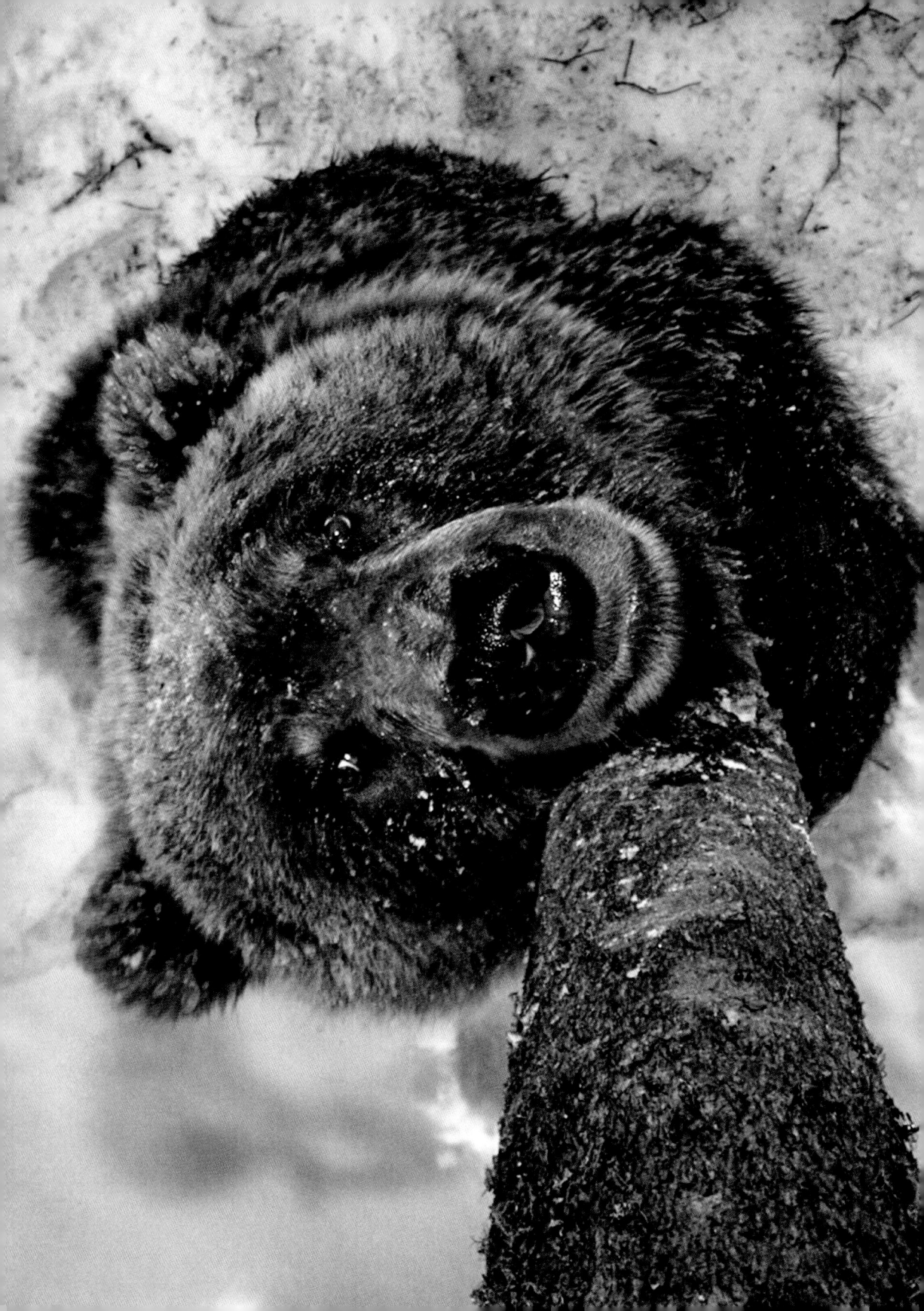

Know your subject

Understanding animal behaviour and habitats

T o convincingly photograph an animal in the wild, to create a standout image, takes a deep understanding of the animal's behaviour. That understanding, that knowledge, comes from research.

If you do a major assignment for a magazine such as *National Geographic*, no stone is left unturned. You reach out to every scientist, conservationist and NGO to gather as much information as possible before sketching out your ideas and executing the assignment. The same goes for any project you undertake – research and image planning should be a fundamental part of your preparation process.

It's often said there are two types of photographers: those who take pictures and those who *make* pictures. A photographer who takes a picture will go somewhere, lift their camera and capture a moment. *Making* a picture is different. If you say, 'I want to photograph wolves howling under the aurora borealis,' you need to research the time of year the aurora is at its best. Maybe you need to research the tidal conditions at that time of year, what the moon is doing, the solar storms to see when you have the peak in the aurora, where the wolves are at that time of year. Or ask yourself, 'Is this the right location?' You can see the difference right away: shooting a very complex, carefully thought-through image is very different to raising your camera and taking a picture of something in front of you.

Left: *Bear Scents,*
Yukon, Canada, 2012.

The former requires a lot of research, and research is key to most of the work I do. I rarely go for a hike with my camera and take pictures. I envisage concepts for images I want to make that I hope will live on forever – images that I will sell as fine art prints, use in books, in my lectures, for conservation storytelling for our non-profit SeaLegacy, and other non-profits. Those are the images I am interested in making and that I encourage you to make too – images that go on to have a life of their own and hopefully become etched in people's minds.

I really wanted to photograph emperor penguins in Antarctica. Around four feet tall (1.2 metres) and weighing 90 pounds (40kg), these huge birds rocket to the surface, and as they do, they release millions of micro-bubbles from their feathers. This helps to reduce the friction between their body and the water. They can double or even treble their speed as they shoot to the surface to avoid being preyed upon by leopard seals.

When I heard about this phenomenon, I thought it would be a brilliant photograph or series of photographs. I knew it would be incredibly difficult to pull off, but I started to do the research: do all emperor penguins always do this? Where exactly are the penguins at certain times? Who are the scientists working with these creatures? Who am I going to work with? What are the risks of being in the water with leopard seals in this area?

I needed to factor in everything I could possibly think of that would be involved in making the images. Then I started to sketch them out in my mind. 'What do I want the pictures to look like?' I could do a full frame shot of a penguin releasing bubbles, but the shot I really wanted was of a penguin rocketing out of the depths, racing towards the surface and releasing bubbles as it went, looking small against beautiful rays of light – something that captures the ecosystem, the penguin's habitat, and its behaviour, but also shows the bubbles coming off its feathers. In other words, an image that tells a story of the animal in that moment.

> " I will visit a location several times. The first time I go somewhere is my 'scouting' trip – my 'sketching' trip."

Whether I'm planning to make a single image or shoot a body of work, I will visit a location several times. The first time I go somewhere is my 'scouting' trip – my 'sketching' trip. I shoot hard, I work hard.

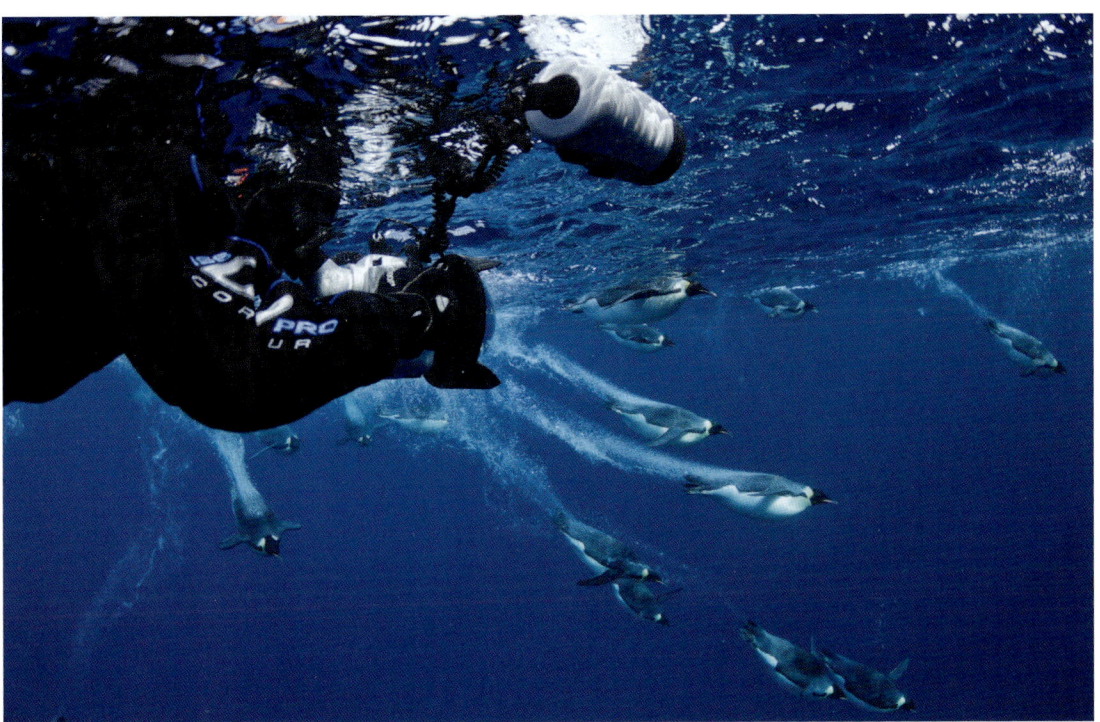

Above: Paul photographing
emperor penguins (taken by Göran
Ehlmé), Ross Sea, Antarctica, 2011.
Overleaf: *Evolve*, Ross Sea,
Antarctica, 2011.

At this point, I've done all my research, I've set myself up for success, and I begin to photograph. I shoot and shoot and shoot. This is when I do my highest volume of shooting, but despite this, I know it's unlikely I'll have shot the situation as well as I could have if I'd had multiple cracks at it.

So, I'll go home and look at all my work. I'll edit it. I'll let the work sit for a while and I'll come back to it with fresh eyes. I'll keep going through my shot list, looking at my sketches and at the body of work as a whole, knowing I'm in the fortunate position of being able to go back. Perhaps I need to refine the time of year I'm shooting at or the time of day. Maybe I need to get different photographic equipment – different lenses, different camera bodies. You often never quite know what's required until after you have done that first expedition.

I'll go back a second time, and usually that's when I get lost in the creative process of making images – images of which I'm really proud. I'll go back a third time if I need to.

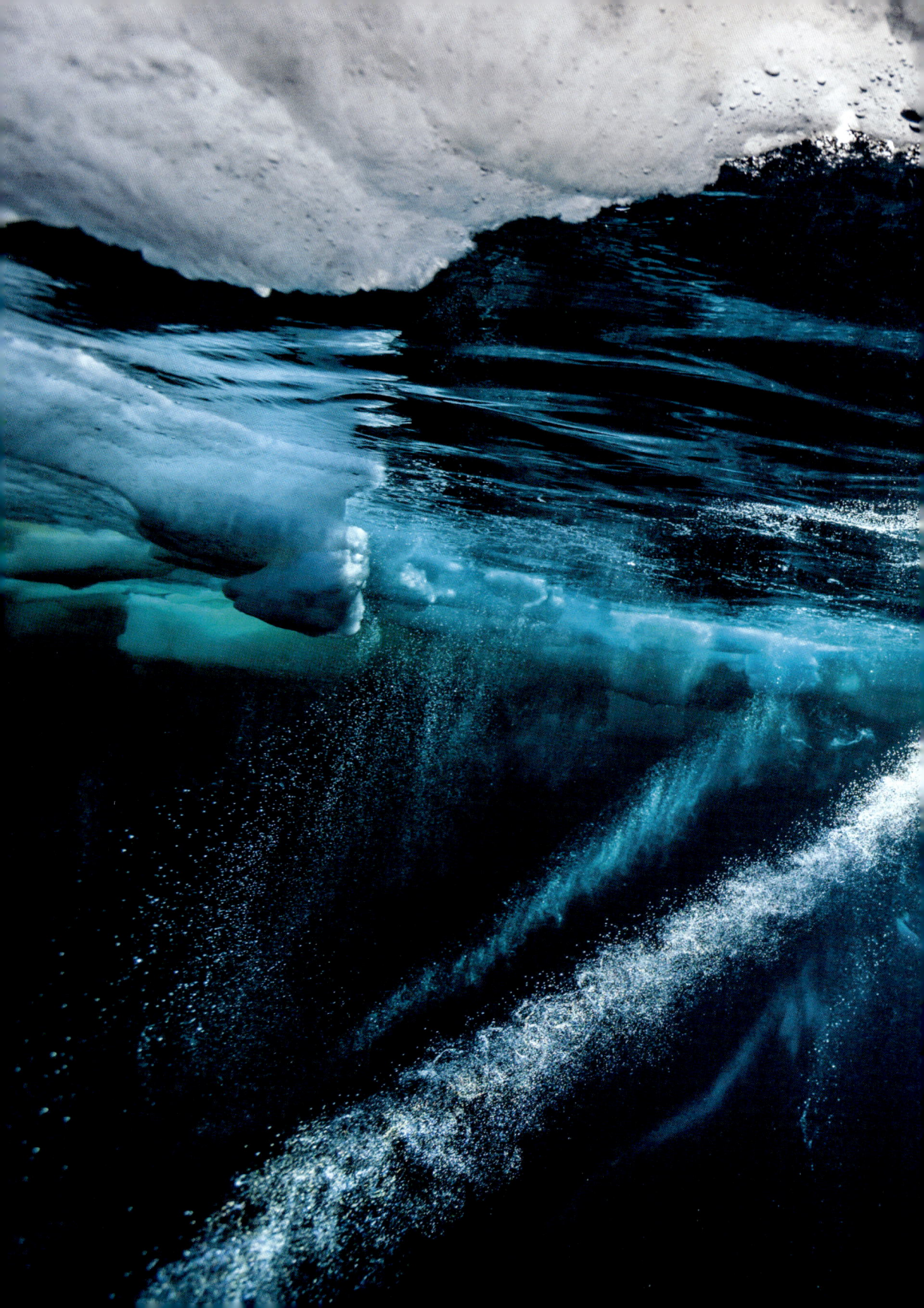

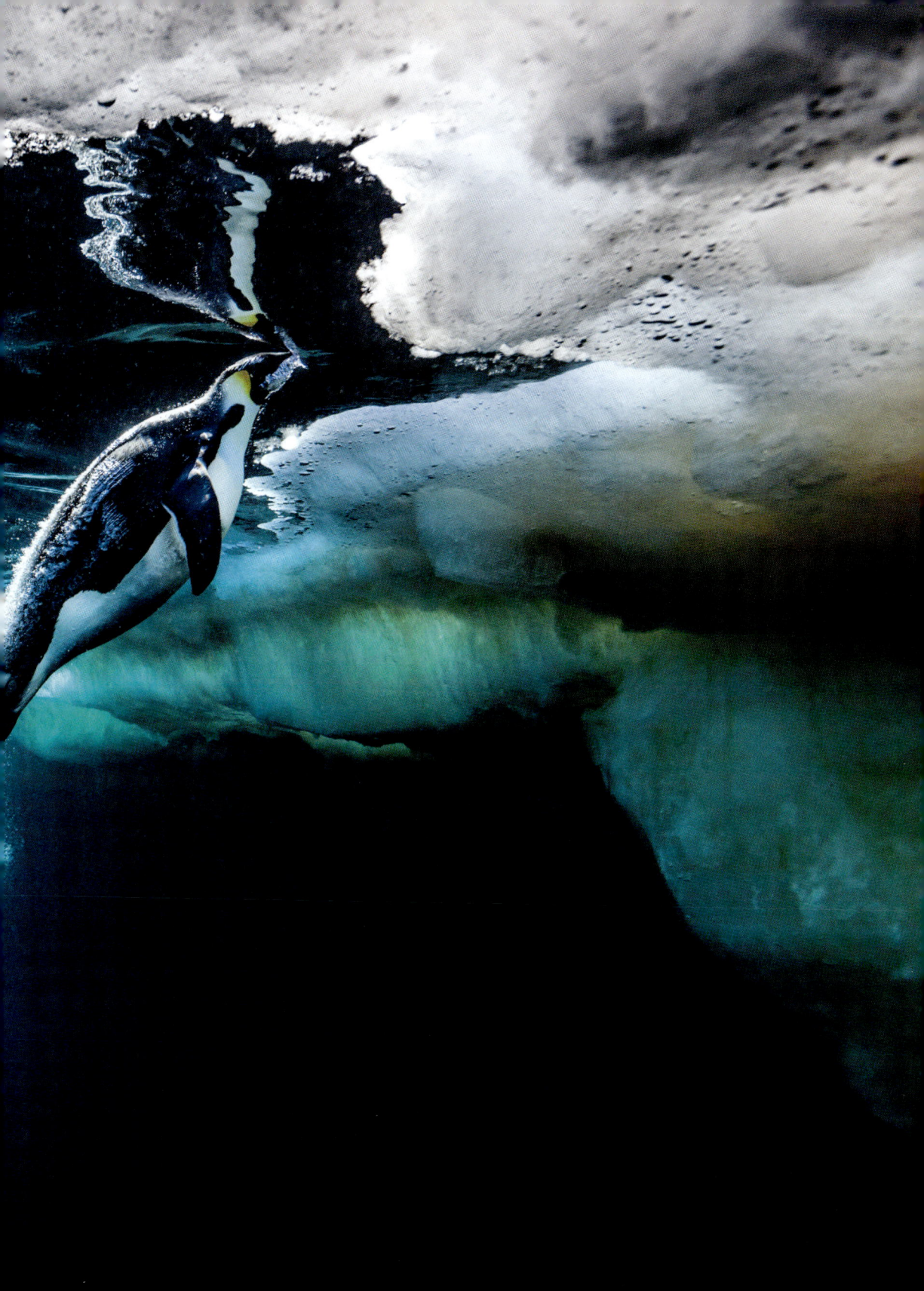

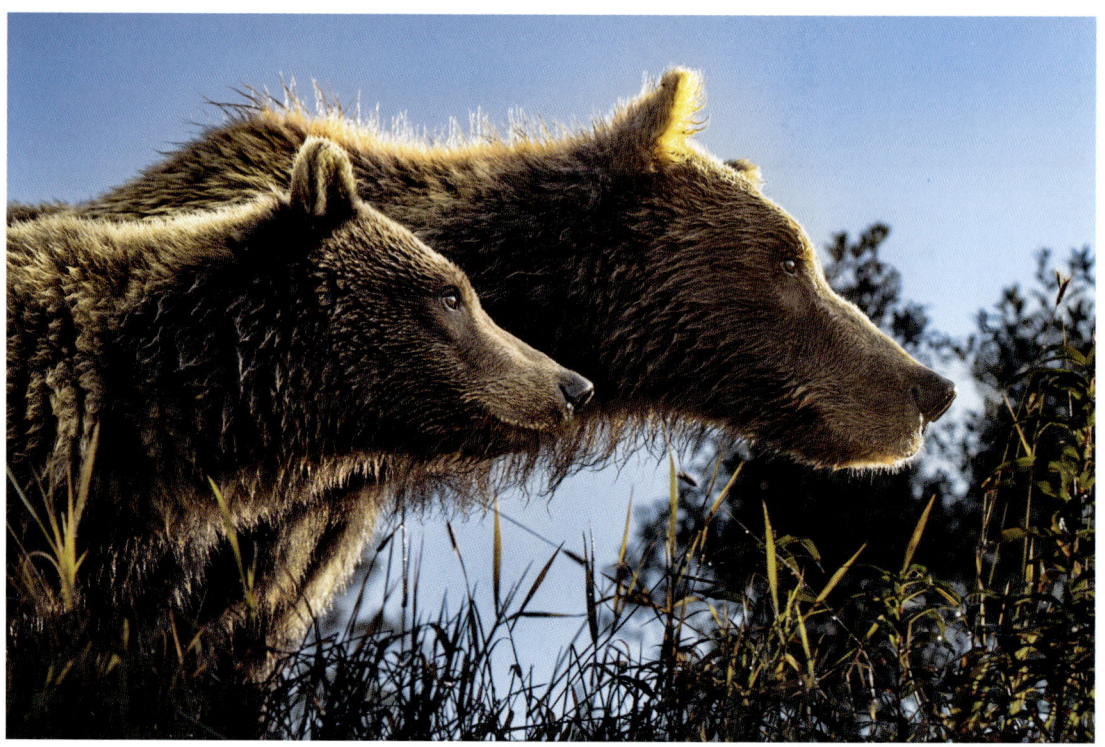

Above: *Golden Bond,*
Katmai, Alaska, 2018.

Even with an idea of the shot in mind, rarely do you know exactly what picture you're going to make. And you don't often get it on the first try. It is a process, an evolution. The beautiful thing about photography is failing (Chapter 5), although the times when things don't work out are not really failures so much as learning experiences (Chapter 17). As an image-maker, you're constantly evolving and growing, honing your craft (Chapter 2).

That initial expedition is also essential for research purposes. Perhaps you have an idea, a dream, a vision, which you've sketched out, but you've gone to the location and those animals aren't there anymore. Maybe that entire herd of caribou has migrated to another area. It doesn't mean you keep going until you're financially broke and exhausted. You may need to change direction. It's important to learn how to know when you need to evolve, to shift, to try something else – that's a crucial part of the craft of photography.

Growing up where I did – in the Arctic, with the Inuit, surrounded by wildlife – taught me the importance of doing research to understand the behaviour of a species, to avoid disturbing the animal.

I was doing a shoot on grizzly bears in an area of the Canadian Arctic where the animals weren't used to seeing people. I was working with renowned bear behaviourist Phil Timpany. I wanted to get the most natural imagery of the bears doing wild things and I didn't want to interfere with their day-to-day. I hate disturbing animals. Besides, a disturbed animal shows up in your photography: it looks terrible when an animal is nervous or stressed, when the bear is tense and staring at you – it doesn't make for great photography. To have relaxed animals doing wild things – that's what excites me.

I asked Phil what I needed to do to make a success of the project. 'We are going to sit in the exact same spot, every day for a month,' he said. 'You can't move; you can't fidget. You have to sit there, and the bears will decide if they want to come near you.'

The bears were a little timid for the first few days, but by the end of that month, they were coming within a few feet, sitting down next to us and just hanging out. By doing my research and talking to one of the best bear behaviourists in the world I was able to go in and get the natural images of grizzly bears I so dearly wanted. The images went on to help protect the Peel watershed in northern Yukon. That conservation win took research, patience, humility (Chapter 14) and listening to experts and following their lead.

Whether you're photographing a rabbit in your backyard, a fox down the street, a coyote over the next hill or a giraffe in Africa, the same guidelines apply: Do your research to set yourself up for success. Go knowing the sun angles, the moon angles, the light, the conditions, the weather, the behaviour of those animals, their patterns and rhythms, but let the animal dictate the encounter. If you do that, you'll see a beautiful world unfold in front of your lens.

" Even with an idea of the shot in mind, rarely do you know exactly what picture you're going to make. And you don't often get it on the first try."

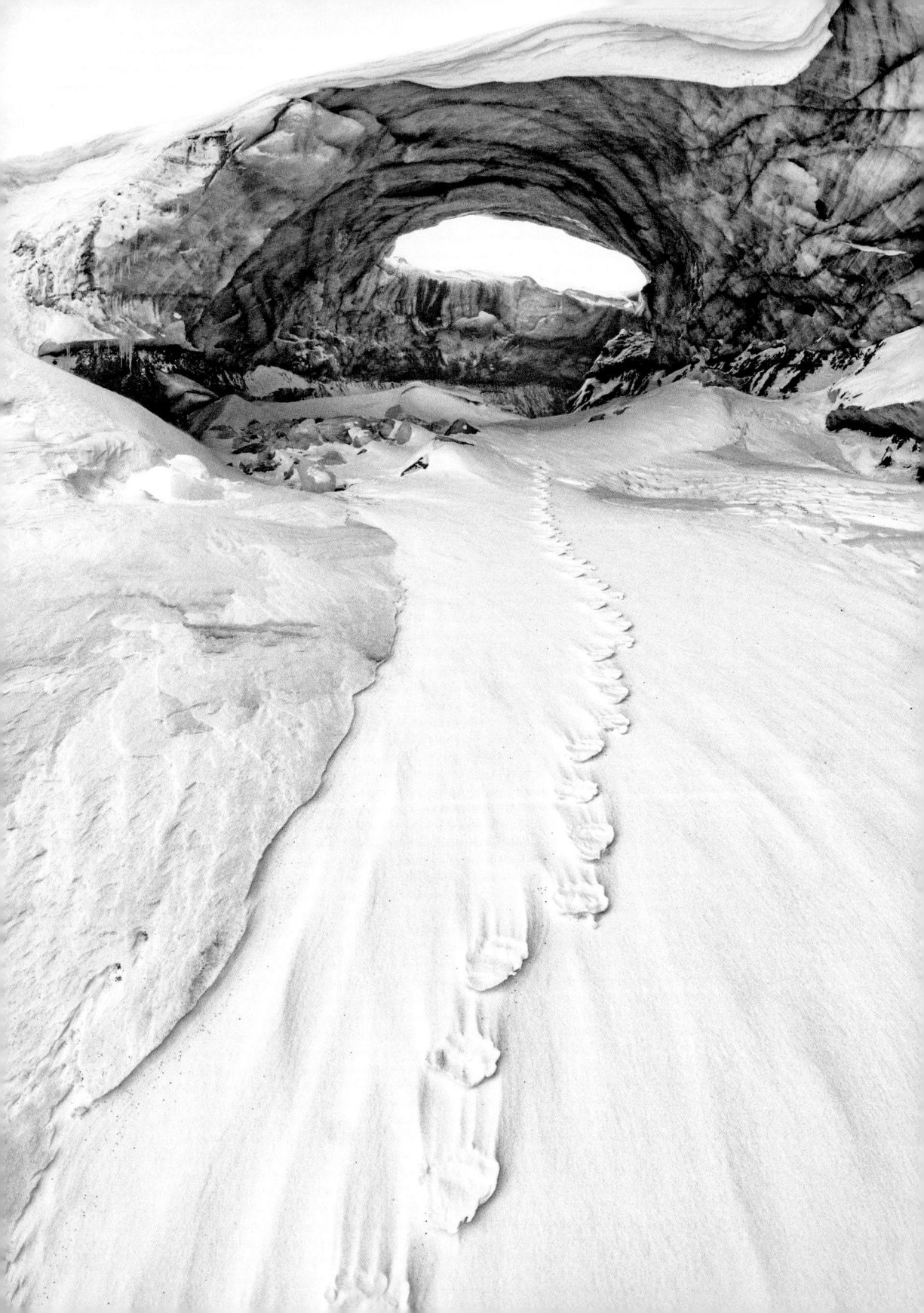

Fine-tune your composition

Techniques to try

When it comes to composition, I don't believe in having or following rules – for example, using the compositional technique of the Golden Ratio, where points of interest are aligned with the 'Fibonacci spiral', or the rule of thirds, where you divide your frame into a grid with nine equal parts and place your point of interest within one of those squares or at the intersection of two lines. To me, those are composition suggestions, not 'rules' or 'laws' you must follow. It's fine to have them at the back of your mind, if they help you or if you want to try them out, and sometimes they can work well, but my advice is to not get hung up on them.

Despite not advocating using well-known compositional 'rules', I do have a few guidelines, if I can call them that, which I keep in mind when I'm shooting. I like to use elements of the composition to guide the viewer's eye, and I try to ensure the image is cohesive.

Maybe the viewer's eye is drawn to a river and diagonally moves through the image, and they notice how the mountains, forest, rocks and foreground perfectly frame a little speck – an animal of some kind – walking across a beach in Alaska. Everything in the image works together beautifully; it feels right – it feels good to look at.

Left: *Bear's Lair,*
Svalbard, Norway, 2008.

I try not to put my subjects in the middle of the frame. I don't want the viewer's eye to go straight to the middle and then not travel throughout the rest of the image. Of course, there are times when placing your subject in the middle is your only option. When you're up against it and you just need to get the shot – perhaps there is an eagle diving through the air or a wolf running across the beach – you could put the animal in the middle as you're tracking it, to get something down, and then crop to move the animal out of the middle. But generally, my feeling is to avoid the centre.

It's also important to keep the edges of your frame in mind. When I'm out in the field and something is happening quickly, I'll grab my camera, bring it up to my eye and start shooting. As soon as there's a brief second where I can afford to pause for a moment – maybe the animal looks away from me – I'll scan the entire frame and mentally clean it up, paying special attention to the edges. I'll be saying to myself, 'yes, great, that works', or 'no, I don't like that twig there, or that tree, I'm going to zoom in a tiny bit more to get rid of such and such distraction'.

So, scanning the frame and looking at the edges is important. But again, you don't want to become so obsessed that you forget to look at your subject. Get into the shooting – shoot the moment – and then, as you're photographing, fine-tune the framing, refine your picture.

Another thing I try and do, and in a way, this comes back to my 20-60-20 philosophy (Chapter 2), is to shoot everything. By this I mean, when I'm photographing, I try and cover a subject in many ways – I'll shoot it ultra-wide, from a medium distance, and tight.

Let's take an example of a polar bear on sea ice. I might use a 100–400mm lens to begin with so that he fills most of the frame. But here I'm just shooting 'ID' shots. Really, the scene is all about the iceberg behind him, the beautiful light bouncing off the sea ice, and the wind blowing across the scene.

"When it comes to composition, it's okay to experiment, to play. Varying your depth of field is one way to do this."

To capture this, I'll attach a wide-angle lens to my camera and reframe so the bear is in the corner of the frame. Now I've got a beautiful scene with a beautiful sky and the bear all working together.

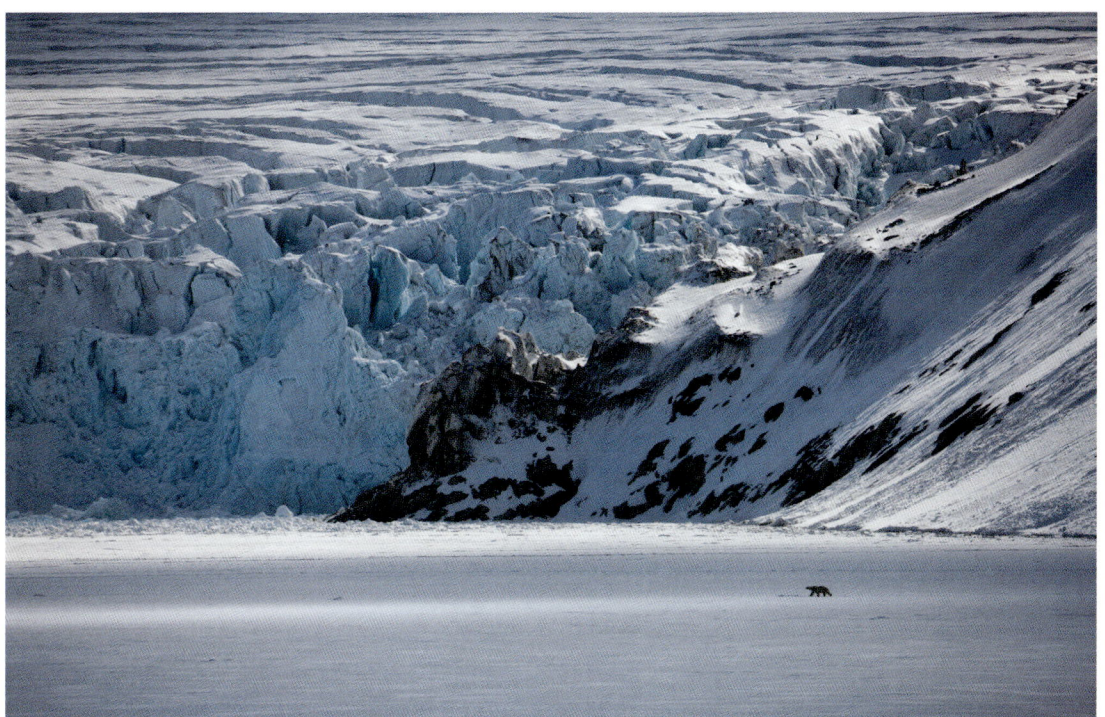

Above: The massive landscape of a fjord dwarfs a lone polar bear, Svalbard, Norway, 2007.

I'll then try and make that bear as small as possible. When I can make the animal into a tiny speck, I am capturing an image that conveys 'a sense of place'. Those images are about a beautiful scene and the animal is there for scale, to guide the viewer's eye, and to make the image more interesting.

I'm also always looking for patterns in nature. It could be patterns of waves across the ocean, ripples from an animal gliding through the water or the footprints of a bear on sea ice. Look for repeating patterns. They are appealing compositionally – they help an image flow. I also like to look for odd-number patterns. Two is sometimes strange, six sometimes doesn't feel quite right, but three and five for some reason work.

When it comes to composition, it's okay to experiment, to play. Varying your depth of field is one way to do this. Depth of field shapes how we experience a scene – sometimes you want every grain of snow sharp to show the expanse, other times just the glint in an eye to let

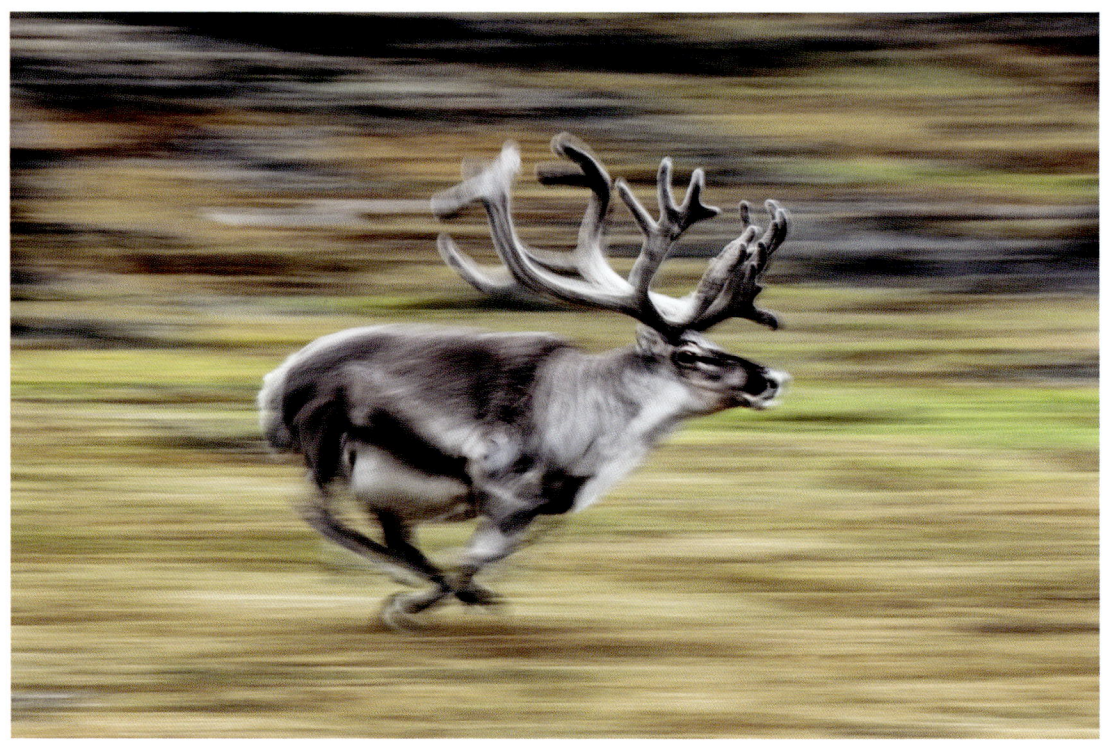

Above: *Reindeer Express*,
Svalbard, Norway, 2007.
Overleaf: *Ice Waterfall*,
Svalbard, Norway, 2014.

the rest fall away. I use a range of depth of fields depending on the look I am after. If I want to have a shallow depth of field to accentuate something in the foreground, I'll shoot at f/2.8 or f/1.4. If I want to do a starburst, it's probably f/16.

The best thing you can do to get to grips with the creative possibilities of depth of field is to go out and practise. Make portraits of a friend at f/16 down to f/1.2 and look at the differences between backgrounds. See what you find more pleasing. Find your own aesthetic, your own style (Chapter 2).

When it comes to depth of field, and you're trying to get a great image, remember that digital camera sensors are so high-quality nowadays, and lenses are so sharp, you can afford to back off a little bit, knowing it's possible to crop in later. For example, if I'm photographing a narwhal, or something I'm unlikely to see again, if it's a once-in-a-lifetime opportunity, I'll zoom out a little and get the shot, knowing I can crop in later.

Shutter speed is another tool in your toolbox that you can get creative with, play with, have fun with. Shoot everything from 1/30th of a second to 1/8000; notice the difference, see what happens. If your dog is running in a field, photograph it at 1/15, 1/8, 1/4 and study the pictures.

I love to handhold my camera and do a lot of 1/30 second exposures. I like having motion in my images. I like an area of my animal to be sharp, but for there to be a lot of blur in the image. It makes that image come to life; it gives it energy. It feels like the animal is going to walk off the page or the wall. A little bit of motion blur can be beautiful. Don't be the person who sits there with a 600mm lens, shooting everything full frame at 1/2000 all day long.

Another compositional technique to try is rear sync flash. I used it a lot during my early days at *National Geographic*, and it comes in and out of style. Rear sync flash is essentially using flash and freezing a moment on top of an image. Try setting your camera to, for example, 1/8, and get somebody to run down the hallway, outside, wherever. Take your shot, and the flash pops at the end of the exposure. You'll have an image that is blurry, and then the flash freezes an image on top of the blurry image.

When I was starting out in photography, I was learning various compositional techniques. But I was shooting with film, and it was expensive. I wasn't getting instant feedback and instant knowledge, of course. We're fortunate that now, with digital cameras, we can immediately see and study the difference between images shot in different ways – between a shot at 1/8, 1/15, 1/30, what it means to shoot front or rear sync flash, and so on.

Once you have a digital camera, it doesn't cost anything other than your time to go out and play and enjoy. So, practise, practise, practise. Find a technique or a style or a look that you really like, so that when you are in those real moments, you have that technique at your disposal.

" Shoot everything from 1/30th of a second to 1/8000; notice the difference, see what happens. If your dog is running in a field, photograph it at 1/15, 1/8, 1/4 and study the pictures."

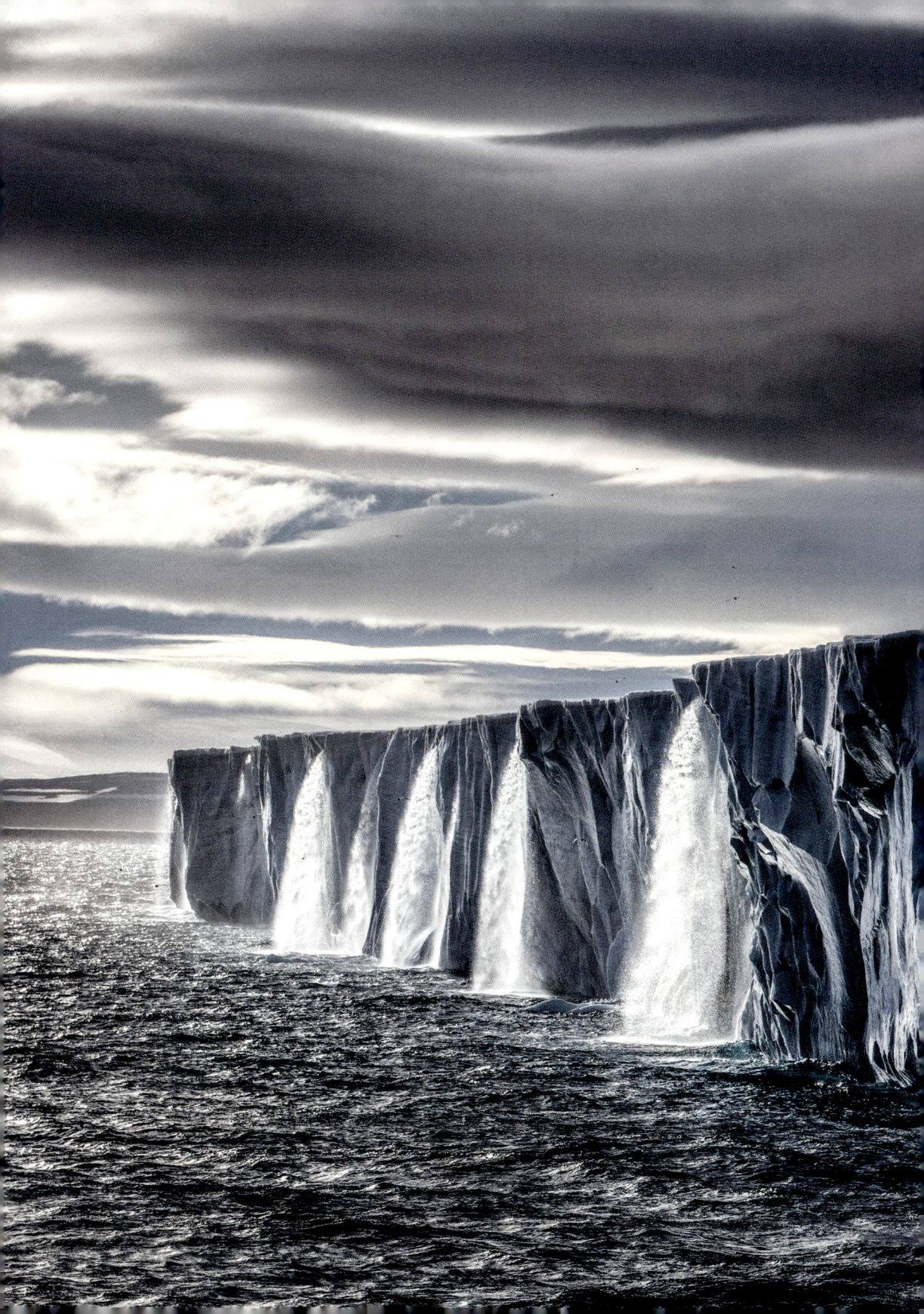

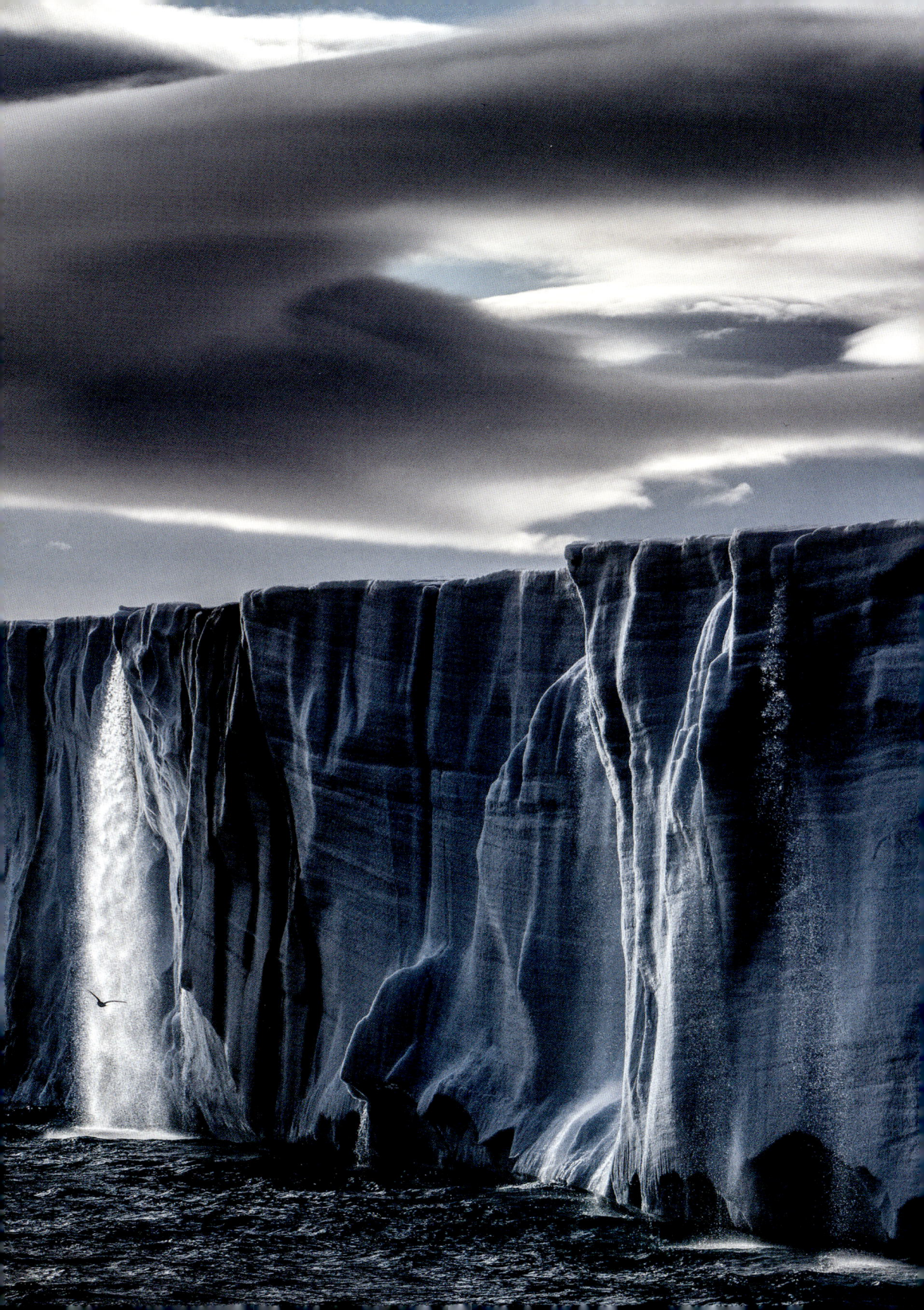

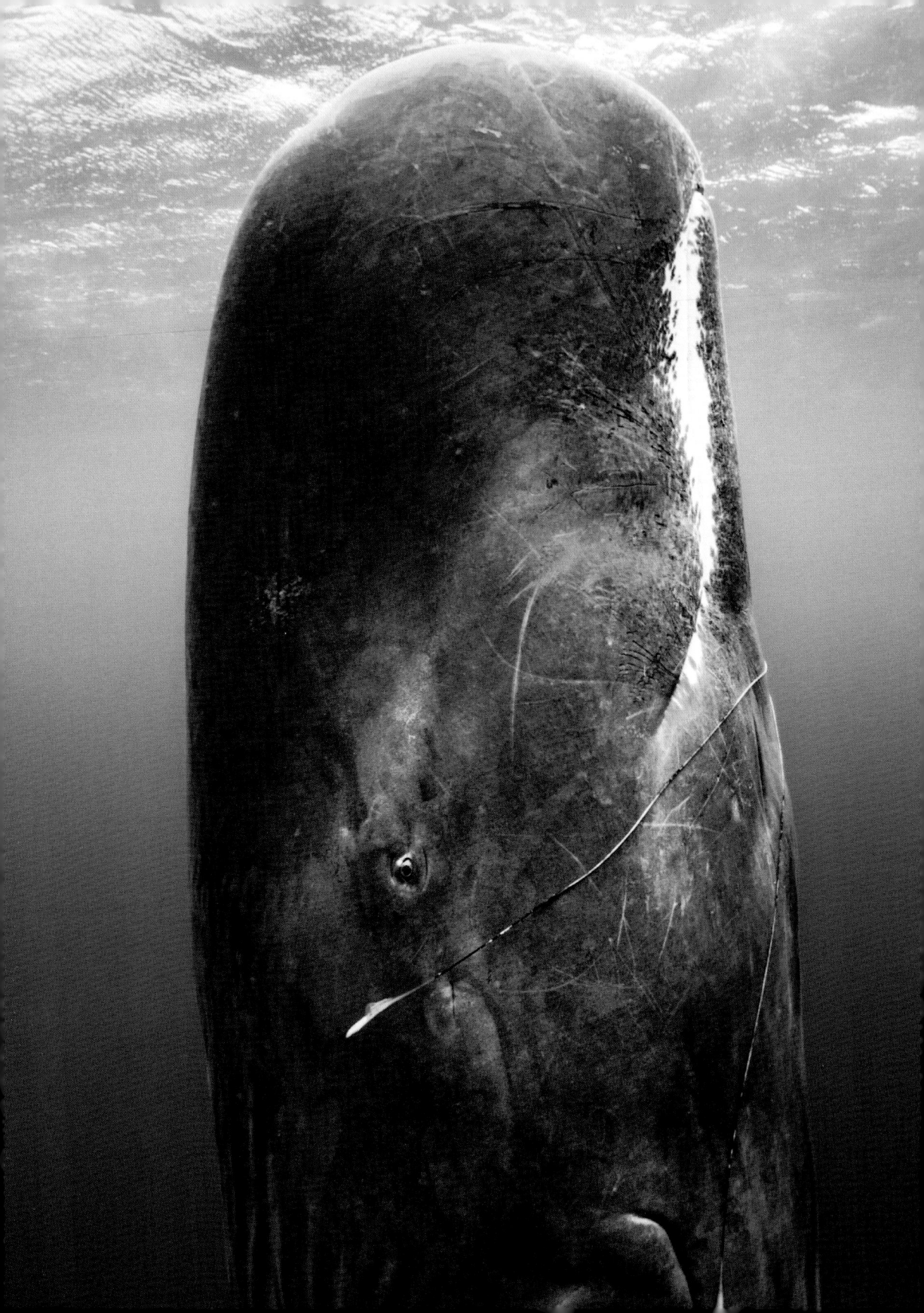

9

Create images with impact

Take your pictures to the next level

I'm always looking for ways to elevate my images – to create photographs that go above and beyond, that stop viewers in their tracks or stay in their minds for a long time afterwards. I want my images to strike a chord, to say something, to be meaningful.

The more I think about the way I make pictures, the more I'm realizing that my standout images are perhaps not quite as premeditated as I thought they were. There is a lesson there, I think: you need to get in the ballpark, to be in the game, and then relinquish some control – turn off your analytical brain and get lost in the creative process, in what's in front of you.

One of my favourite images I've ever taken is at the intersection of art, science and conservation. It's the image on the previous spread I call 'Ice Waterfall' depicting the Nordaustlandet island ice cap in Svalbard, Norway. I was photographing and filming polar bears, and the captain kept saying, 'we have to stay on the ship', because hurricane-force winds were coming. We had to get to a place where we were safe before the approaching storm arrived.

Left: *Feast from the Deep*, Dominica, 2019.

Katabatic winds, downslope winds that can reach more than a hundred miles an hour, were visible in front of the glacier face. As we took the ship around a corner, I looked back and could see dozens of what looked to be waterfalls pouring off the face of the glacier.

With the light source – the sun – behind us striking the subject directly from the front, I took a couple of shots with a telephoto lens and then some tighter shots to show just how much water was pouring off the glacier face – to give an idea of how much water there is when temperatures reach the high-60 degrees Fahrenheit (16–20°C), even though it's 600 miles from the North Pole.

As the ship drifted along, I saw the first waterfall had become backlit with the movement of the sun, then the second and the third, and I realized we needed to tuck in behind a little bay to see all the waterfalls becoming backlit.

Sometimes, as photographers, we need to force ourselves to zoom out with our eyes. As I was looking at the waterfalls, I noticed little birds flying along the ice face. I was looking at this scene unfolding, with many different elements working together: incredibly beautiful lenticular clouds, the ice face, waterfalls, the ocean sea water lapping at the base, and the tiny speck of a bird that, in that moment, intersected with a waterfall and brought everything together. The bird gives the whole scene perspective and scale.

It's one of those moments where it's good to not overthink what you're doing. You go to ISO 400, f/8, get your focus right and just shoot. ISO is just your camera's way of seeing in the dark. The higher you push it, the more light you pull in – but you trade some clarity for that boost, especially when you're working in the shadows or chasing light at the edge of day. I'm a fan of zoom lenses because they allow you to move quickly, to react, and on this occasion, I was able to zoom out a little and watch as the scene came into perfect balance.

The Arctic waterfalls photograph is my best-selling fine art print. It also says 'conservation' – it is a reminder of the fragility of ice ecosystems. These are the kinds of images I strive to make and have always sought to create – images that are not just compositionally pleasing, but that have something to say.

"Sometimes, as photographers, we need to force ourselves to zoom out with our eyes."

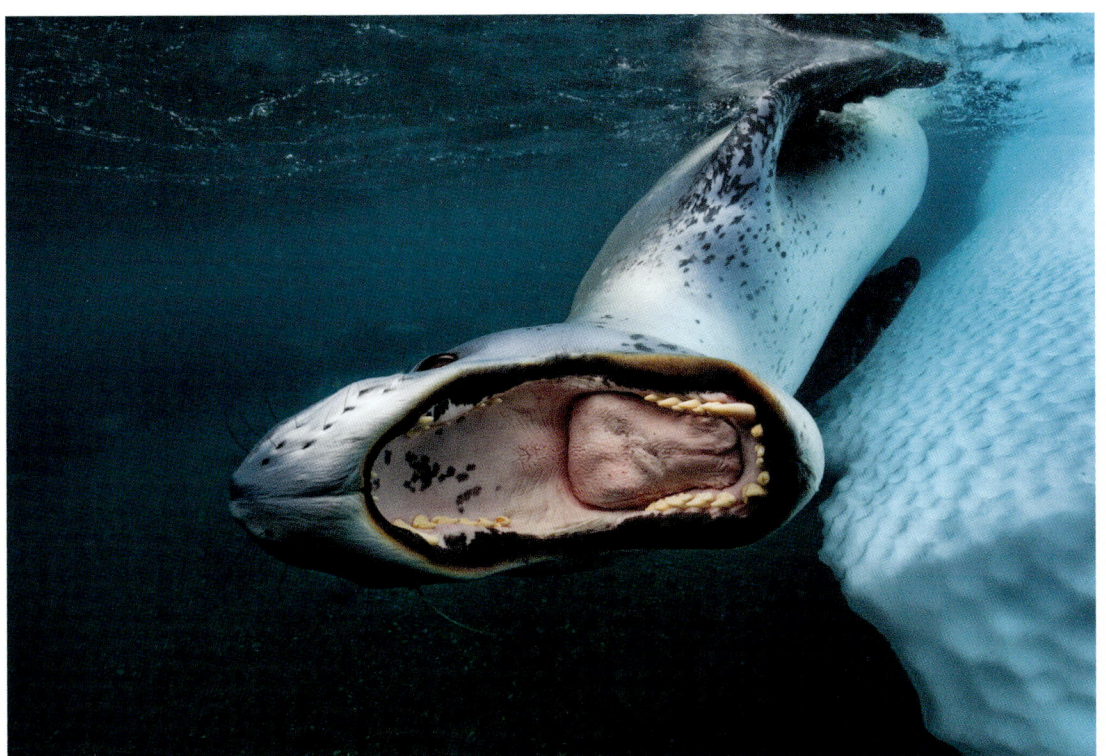

Above: A leopard seal positioning himself against threat, Antarctic Peninsula, Antarctica, 2017.

Sometimes, getting an image or series of images that are 'next level' requires nerves of steel – that has been my experience on more than one occasion at least. The images I took during an encounter with leopard seals are to this day among my most well-known, but also hard-won.

Despite the many challenges, this encounter was among the greatest of my life. Leopard seals have long had a bad reputation. Explorer Sir Ernest Shackleton's team was attacked by one, and other people have been on the receiving end of attacks in recent years. I was intrigued that an animal could have such a bad reputation and wanted to find out more about these Antarctic predators. I submitted a proposal to *National Geographic* to go to Antarctica and get in the water with as many leopard seals as I could over a one-month period, to try to find out if they really deserved their notoriety.

My friend Göran Ehlmé is a great BBC cameraman and has experience with leopard seals. He joined the expedition to introduce the leopard

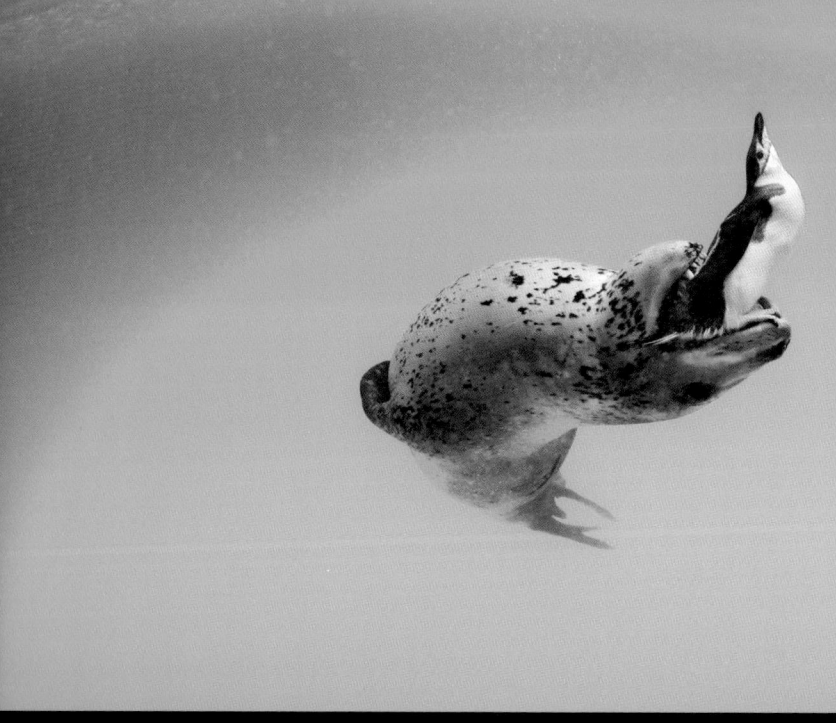

Above: A leopard seal with a penguin, Antarctic Peninsula, Antarctica, 2006.

seals to me. To obtain the best journalistic coverage possible about the animal's behaviour, I had to work with the best.

We rented a 45-foot (13.7-metre) sailboat, hired an experienced crew and sailed across rough seas to get to Antarctica. The waves were 30 feet (9 metres) high, and the wind was blowing 50 knots (58mph/93kmph). After 48 hours of this extreme, rough crossing, we finally had some calmer weather, and two days later, we arrived in Antarctica. I'd never been so happy to see land in my life.

We gathered our camera equipment and let down a 12-foot-long (3.7 metre) inflatable boat. I thought we were going to spend weeks looking for leopard seals, but as we came round an iceberg and into a bay, we were greeted by a monstrous female leopard seal.

Females are 30 per cent larger than males, the average length and weight of a male leopard seal is around 9–11 feet long (2.7–3.4 metres) and up to 660 pounds (300kg). Right away, the leopard seal swam off, grabbed a penguin and came over to the boat. She started smashing the penguin against the side. This was my introduction to leopard seals in Antarctica. She was longer than our boat and probably weighed over a thousand pounds. Her head was twice as big as a grizzly bear's.

Göran turned to me and said, 'Now is a good time for you to get in the water.' I told him there was no way I was getting into the water. 'I'll do it tomorrow,' I said. 'Paul, you've come all the way here, you've been complaining there's not enough budget or enough time, that you won't be able to deliver the assignment; stop talking and get in the water. Go and get your pictures.'

My entire body was numb (and not just from the cold). I knew he was right. *National Geographic* publishes pictures, not excuses. Trembling, I put on my dry suit, grabbed my gear and eased myself into the water.

" You've come all the way here . . . Stop talking and get in the water. Go and get your pictures."

There she was – a massive leopard seal, just a short distance away. Objects appear larger underwater, and this animal looked like a small whale. She dropped the penguin and came racing over to me, her mouth wide open. She began lurching at me. It was terrifying.

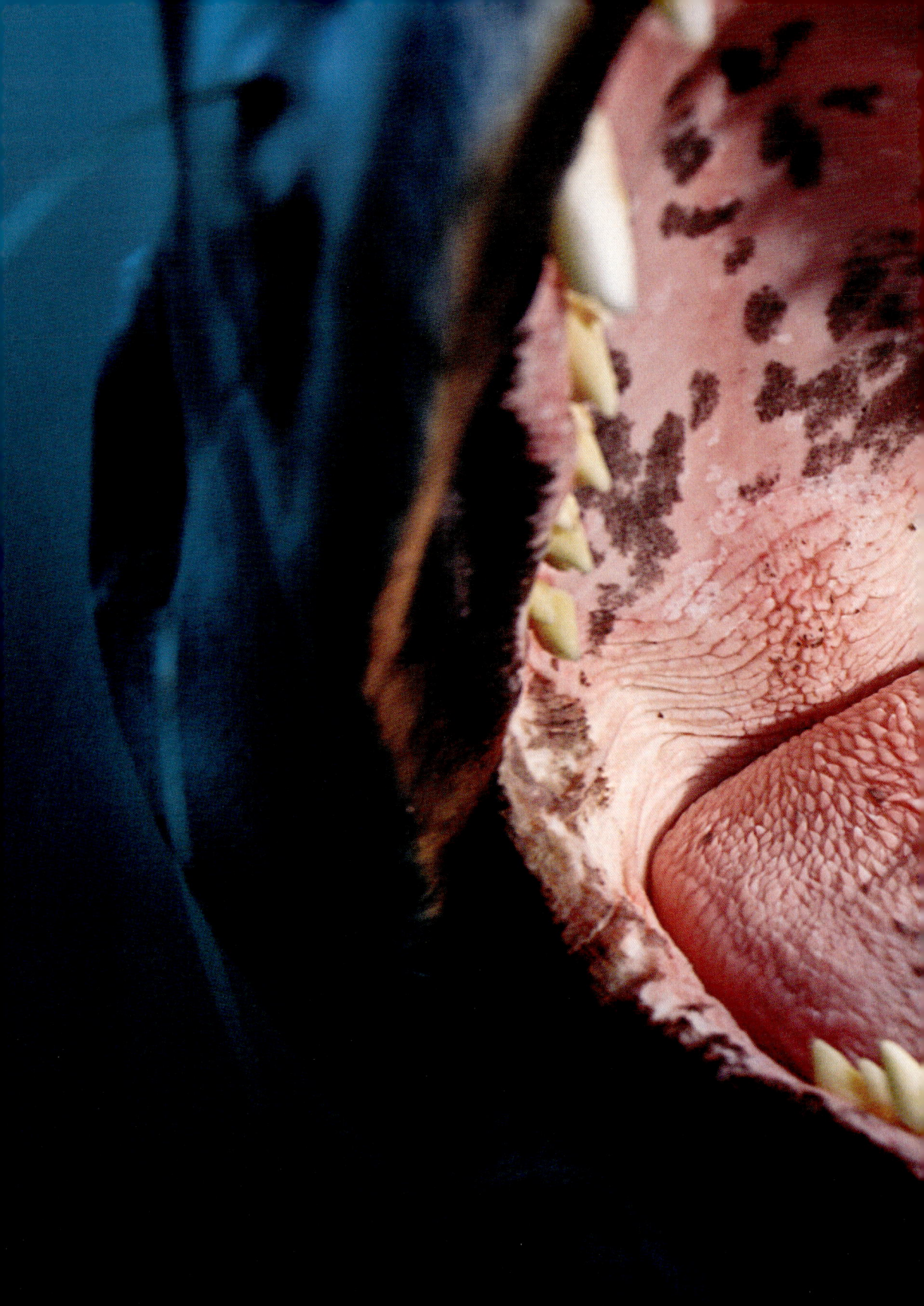

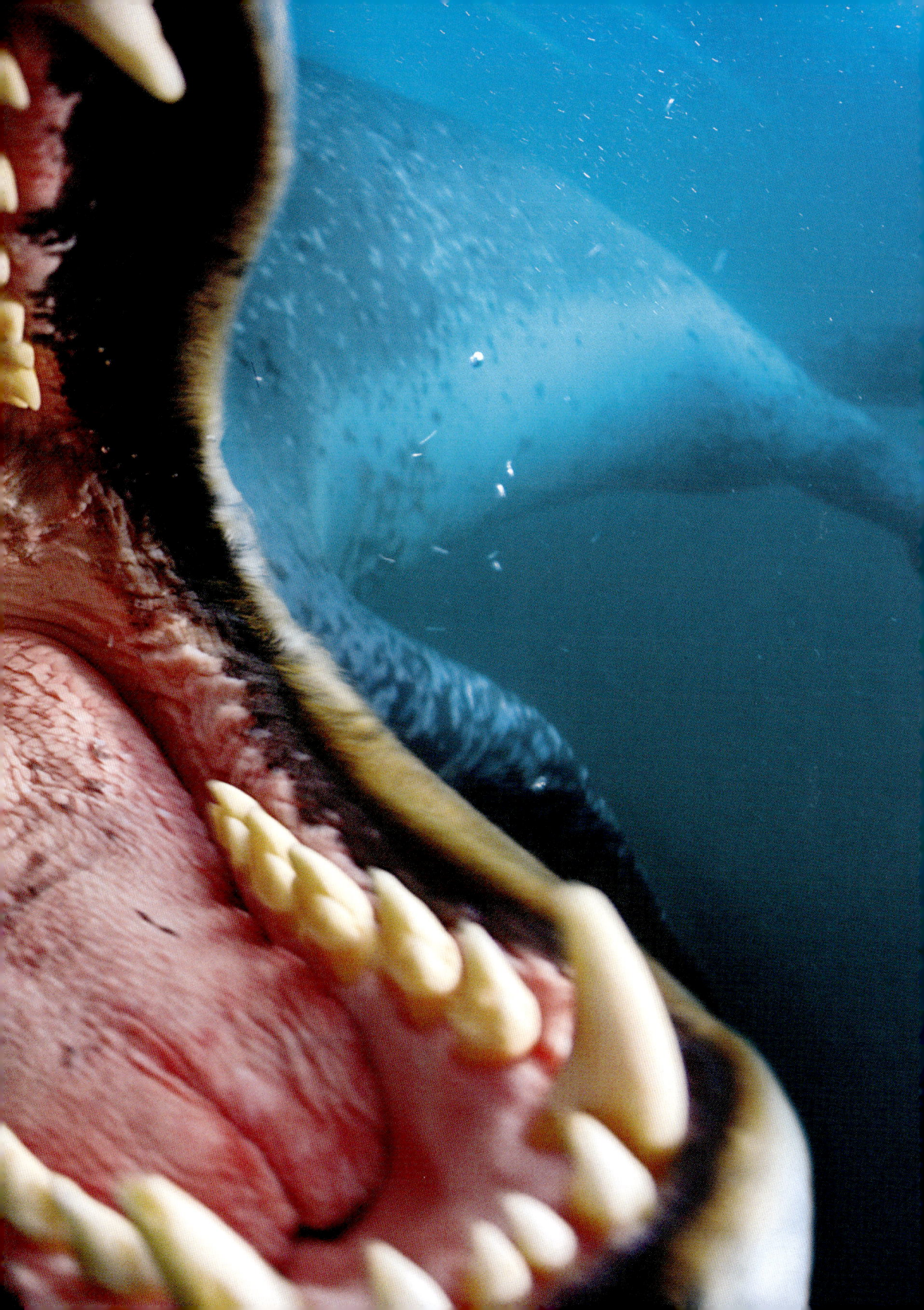

Previous spread: Inside a
leopard seal's mouth, Antarctic
Peninsula, Antarctica, 2006.

There I was, staring down her throat. At one point, my camera housing was inside her mouth. I had to make pictures, so I set my strobes to half power and got to work. After a few minutes, she went away, and I thought the encounter was over, but she came back. She'd caught another penguin. It was as though she was trying to feed me.

This went on for some time. Indeed, every time I got into the water over the following days, the leopard seal was there to greet me.

It was the most incredible experience. At night, I sat there, looking at my images, tears running down my cheeks, thinking about what I'd encountered. I couldn't sleep. Sometimes I just started laughing because of the unbelievable absurdity and sheer brilliance of it all.

I call it my deathbed story. I've been lucky enough to have seen and experienced a lot of incredible moments in nature, but the leopard seal encounter is at the top of my list to this day, and it probably still will be when I take my last breath.

These stories are fun to tell, but most of all, they remind me what it takes to create images that go the extra mile. If you step out of your comfort zone and push yourself physically, mentally and creatively, it's possible to come away with images that stand the test of time.

" There I was, staring down her throat. At one point, my camera housing was inside her mouth. I had to make pictures, so I set my strobes to half power and got to work."

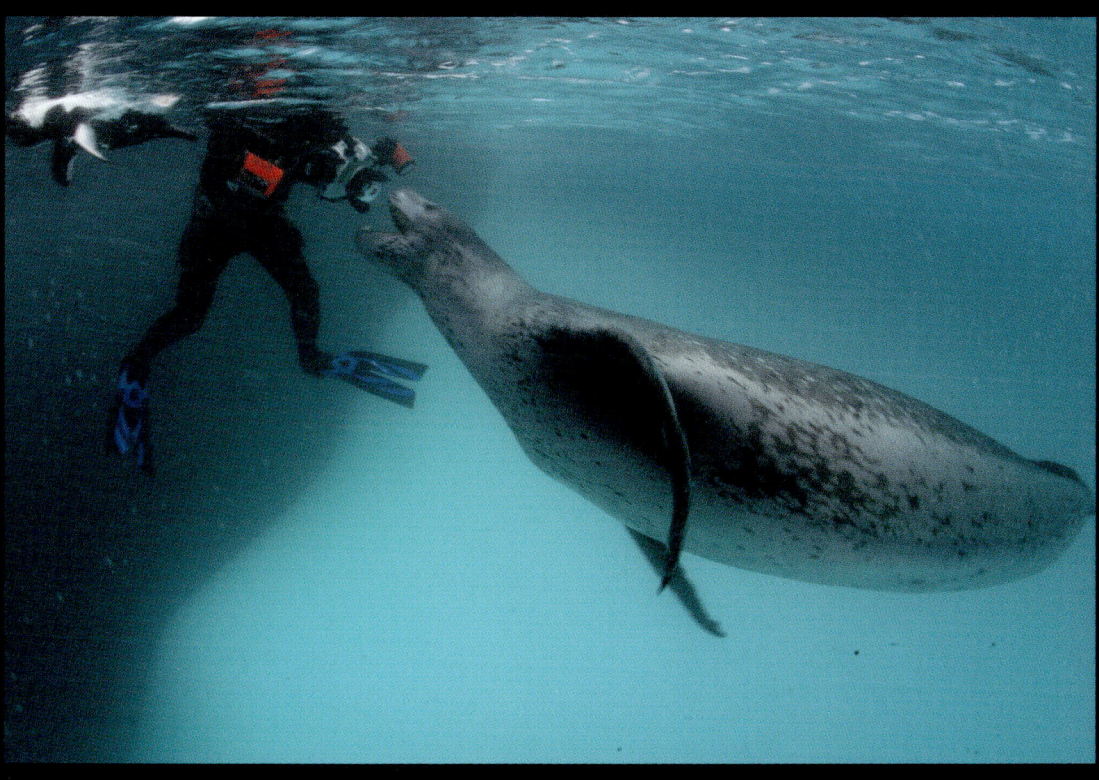
Above: Paul getting devoted attention from a large female
leopard seal (taken by Göran Ehlmé), Antarctica, 2006

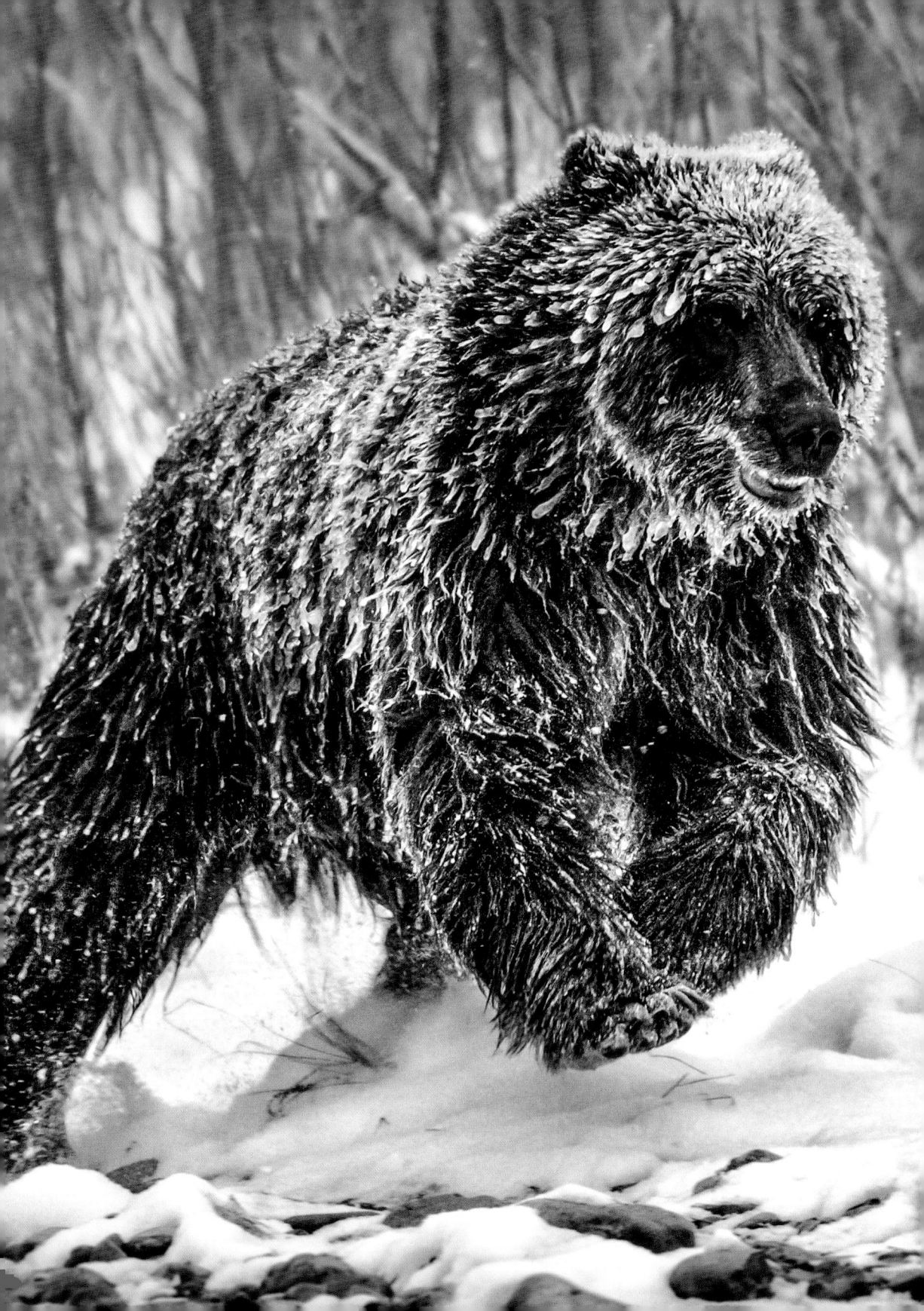

10

Out in the field

Quickfire tips

W hen it comes to working in the field and setting myself up for success, I've tried a lot of different approaches, some of which I'd like to share with you in the hope they might help you too.

When I'm shooting, I always remind myself of the left brain, right brain theory: that there are two 'sides' to our brains – the left 'analytical' side, and the right 'creative' side. When you're using the latter, you're seeing the world in shapes, colours, patterns, diagonals, converging lines and so on. You're not thinking too much, you're lost in the creative process.

I'm using my creative brain when I 'sketch' with my camera. It's just my eye, my lens and the scenery in front of me. Working like that, you're exploring ideas, trying things out. You might be learning about the area where you're shooting in the knowledge that you will come back later that evening or the next day and shoot some more. Or you might sit and wait for the stars to come out, or put your camera on a tripod and do a beautiful time exposure. There are a bunch of different things you can do when you're in that creative space, but you need to allow yourself to come into an area and start to feel, and sketch, and not think too much. Giving yourself permission to experiment is key.

Left: *Cold Pursuit,*
Yukon, Canada, 2010.

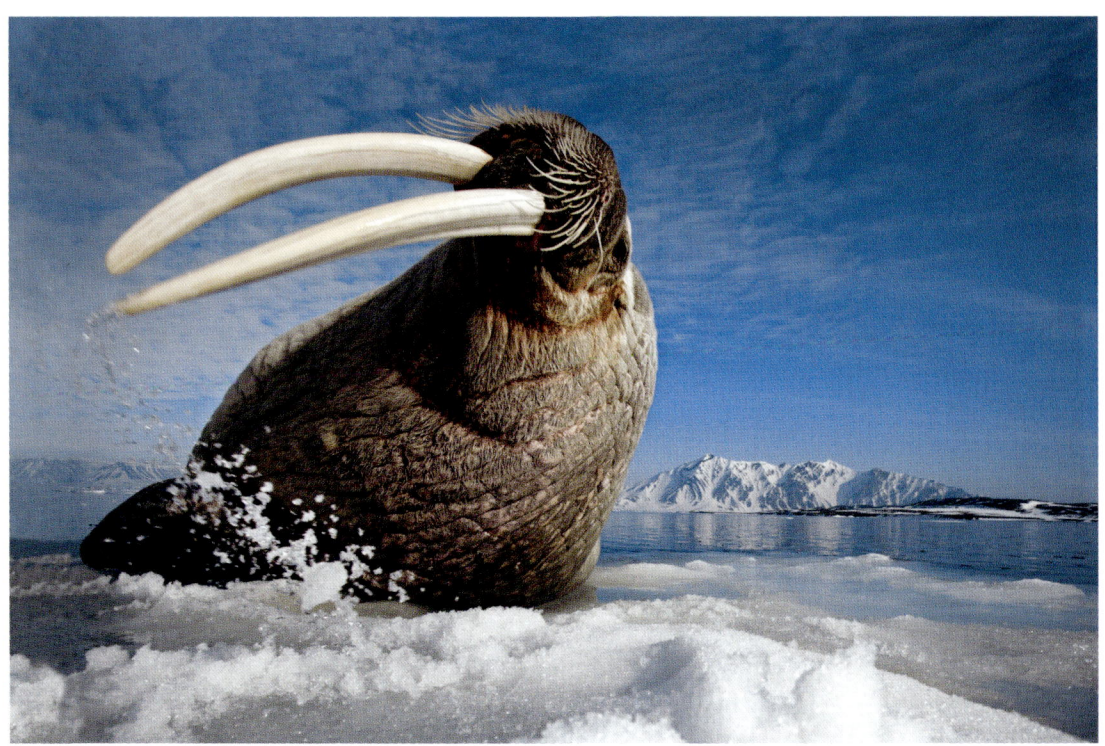

Above: A walrus rests on
sea ice, High Arctic, 2005.

I encourage you to do the same when you're scoping out new locations and setting up a shoot. You've spent time thinking about camera menus, got to know your kit inside out, practised switching dials and changing settings, and so on, so when you're surrounded by beautiful towering Douglas firs in the rainforests of British Columbia, you're able to get lost in the artistic and creative process.

Keeping the camera stable is an important area of field work too, of course. When I was using Fujifilm Velvia 50 film, everything was about tripod, tripod, tripod. Today, working digitally, I bring tripods with me on expeditions, but I find I am using them less and less. And I certainly don't obsess about using one.

It helps if you have quick reactions. An animal might be walking towards me, and I can be down on my stomach quickly, shooting a low-angle shot, looking up at and elevating that animal in the frame. In that scenario, if I'm able to properly support my camera and lens on the ground, a tripod isn't necessary.

If you are using a tripod, make sure it has a ball head that you like working with. There are some complex tripod heads out there, and using them can be fiddly and frustrating. You could also consider purchasing a video tripod head, so you can move fluidly between video and stills, which gives you options. Video heads are made for motion. They are more fluid and allow for smoother pans and tilts – essential when tracking a bear through tall grass or following a whale breach.

There are many ways to support your camera, though, you just need to think creatively. Beanbags can be useful for stability, or even a nearby branch or mound of earth. Think about how you are holding your camera to minimize movement. I like to rest the tripod plate in the palm of my hand and use the rest of my arm and shoulder for extra support. I can pull my arm into my chest, and everything's quite stable. Holding the camera in that way gives me control over my f ocus and the ability to zoom, and I don't rock the camera. I might be shooting at 1/8 with a 16-35mm lens and getting good results.

I also like to use back-button focus, especially when photographing moving animals – a wolf, for example. This is where the autofocus function is assigned to a separate button on your camera instead of the shutter release button at the front/top of the camera. The AF-ON button on advanced digital cameras is designed for this purpose. By separating the functions of shutter release (taking the picture) and autofocus (AF), the camera will not be constantly refocusing every time you press the shutter release. This avoids unwanted refocusing and defocusing as you take pictures and gives you more accurate control over where your point of focus is.

> " Think about how you are holding your camera to minimize movement. I like to rest the tripod plate in the palm of my hand and use the rest of my arm and shoulder for extra support."

Give it a go. Try it in a few different scenarios. Before long, I'll wager that all your cameras will be changed to back-button focus.

I'm also a fan of the silent shutter. I was slow to come round to mirrorless cameras until I noticed the noise my camera was making in the field. I was clacketing away at 10 frames a second. When you're around wildlife, being able to shoot silently is a game-changer.

Another piece of advice I give to mentees is something I'm sure you've heard before, but it's worth saying again: always be ready and prepared. A good habit to get into, I find, is to set your camera to your standard 'home' settings at the end of a day's shooting. When I put my cameras away at night, I leave them at ISO 400, f/8 and on back-button focus, so when I pick up my kit first thing, I'm ready to go. I keep the batteries charged and have an extra set of batteries to hand. I always keep fresh memory cards in my cameras.

Imagine you're walking along a river, not expecting to see much, and suddenly the most incredible moment unfolds in front of you. A spirit bear or a wolf walks out into the scene, for example. You grab your camera, but it's set to a five-second exposure, or the 'wrong' focus setting, or the 'wrong' ISO – you might be on ISO 3200, but you really want to be on ISO 400. You lose time, or worse, miss the moment entirely. So, getting into the habit of coming back to those 'home' settings is important.

I always keep my lenses and camera bodies in the same spot in my kitbags, so I know where they are and can grab them quickly and easily, and there are always tripod plates on the long lenses – you don't want to be searching for those. Keeping your kit organized and accessible is key.

If you get into good habits, when a scenario is unfolding, you'll be able to respond more efficiently. You don't want to be locked up in your left brain trying to find the lens you need or trying to find a memory card or a battery. It's easier and frankly more fun to be ready, and will likely lead to a rewarding experience.

> " When I put my cameras away at night, I leave them at ISO 400, f/8 and on back-button focus, so when I pick up my kit first thing, I'm ready to go."

A final quickfire tip is, when you're out shooting and you're achy, tired and feeling weak, I encourage you to keep a bottle of 'Try Acting' on you. It's something we always take with us on a shoot. When somebody on the team starts to complain they're cold, hungry or tired, one of us will pipe up and say, 'Take some Try Acting' – it's a tongue-in-cheek reminder to tough it out.

Being a photographer sometimes means pushing through your own personal boundaries of discomfort. You won't always be comfortable when you're working in the field, but when you stick it out and get a shot you're proud of, the success will taste even better.

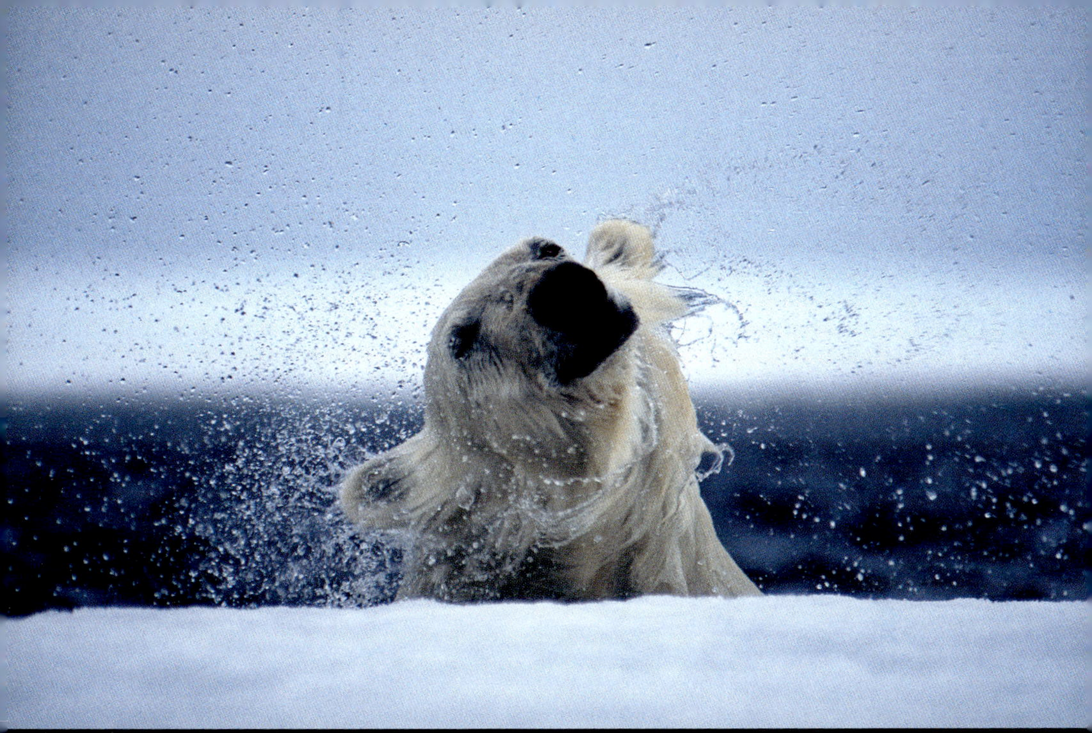

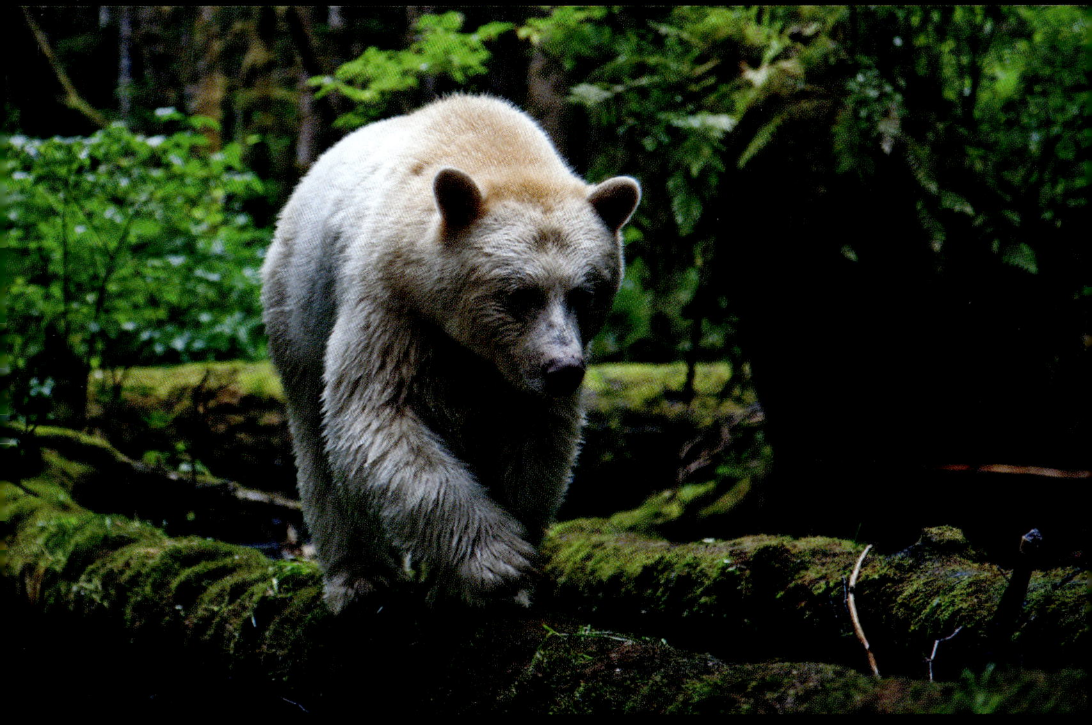

Top: *Emerging*, Nunavut, Canada, 2006.
Bottom: *Pipeline Through Paradise*, British Columbia, Canada, 2010.

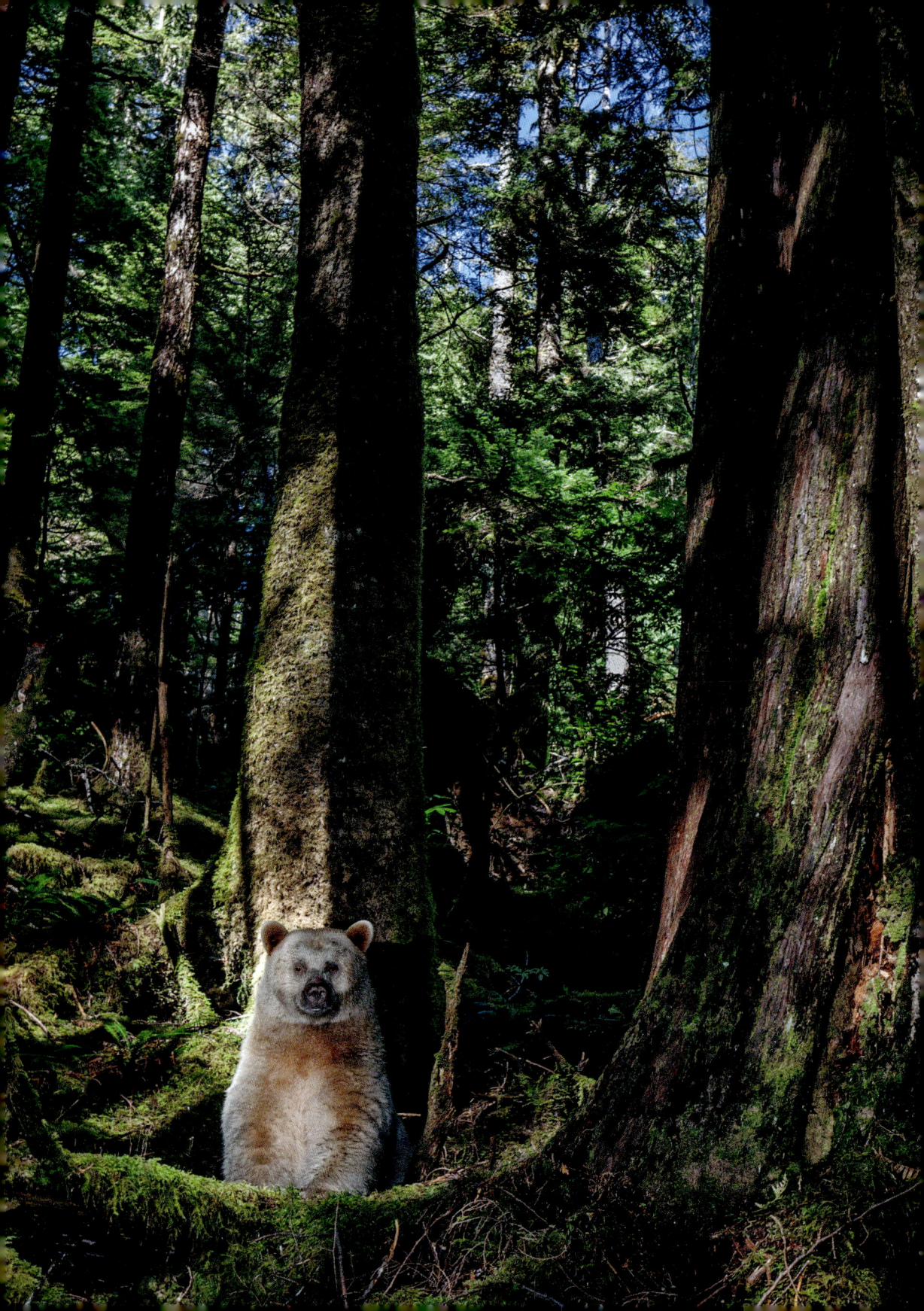

11

Kickstart a personal project

Coming up with ideas

As photographers, artists, storytellers, conservationists, we need to free up the creative sides of our brains, get lost in dreams and visions, and go out and make the best images possible of the subjects we choose – subjects we deeply care about – to drive effective and lasting change.

When it comes to creativity, my goal is to shoot amazing pictures that tell a story, that draw in the viewer, and make them care about or take notice of important issues. Most importantly, I want to have 'conservation wins'. So, how do I get creative? How do I come up with ideas? How do I kick a project into action?

The key for me is having the right mindset. Being active is an important way I get into that headspace. Indeed, a lot of my best ideas arise when I'm moving – I might be out hiking or on my paddleboard or swimming. If I'm doing something that doesn't require too much skill, I can get into a rhythm for an hour or several hours. What is crucial is the breathing, deep breathing – I'm oxygenating my brain and fuelling my body. I'm feeling good, I'm feeling alive. I'm not thinking too much. I'm not on my phone, or on my computer. That's when the best ideas come to me.

Left: A ghostlike spirit bear rests under a forest patch, British Columbia, Canada, 2010.

What we're talking about is a form of meditation, being present. I love to climb mountains and take in the landscape. I'll study the mounds, trace them with my eyes, and work on my breathing. Learning to breathe deeply is something that will help you in almost everything you do, not just when it comes to taking pictures. Breathe in for four seconds and out for eight. Do that 10 times and you'll start to feel a deep sense of relaxation. When you enter that state, big ideas are more likely to enter your mind.

I also find brainstorming to be a useful process. It is a lot like goal setting (Chapter 3), but you take the brakes off and start throwing ideas around. Who do I want to work with? What projects do I want to be involved with? What photos do I want to make? Where do I want to go?

Brainstorming is invigorating. It's fun to get a group of people together, put a subject out there and throw ideas around. You start to feed off each other and generate incredible ideas. I also highly recommend picking up a copy of the brilliant book *Jump Start Your Brain* by Doug Hall, which is all about improving your creative thinking.

When I think back to my twenties and early thirties, when I was getting established in photography and wanted to shoot for magazines, I thought, 'It's no use, all the good stories have been photographed, there is nothing left to shoot', or, 'Everything I want to shoot is in extremely remote locations and I don't have the right gear', and so on. I quickly recognized those as unhelpful, negative little voices, and realized I didn't have to listen to them. When you look around, stories are everywhere, and they're always evolving.

I went from thinking 'all the stories have been shot' to 'how am I going to photograph even a tiny fraction of the things I want to photograph in the short time I have on this earth?'

" Keeping it local is a great route to take, at least while you're learning the ropes and getting an idea of the kind of stories you want to tell, and how."

The truth is, you don't have to travel far to find great stories. Look around and you'll come across plenty on your doorstep. A lot of people who are starting out in photography think, 'Okay, I want to be a photographer. I really love the work of Thomas D. Mangelsen, for example, so I'll go and buy a telephoto lens, fly to Africa and do a story on lions.' That is a terrible way for photographers to think. You'll end up spending all your money on equipment and an

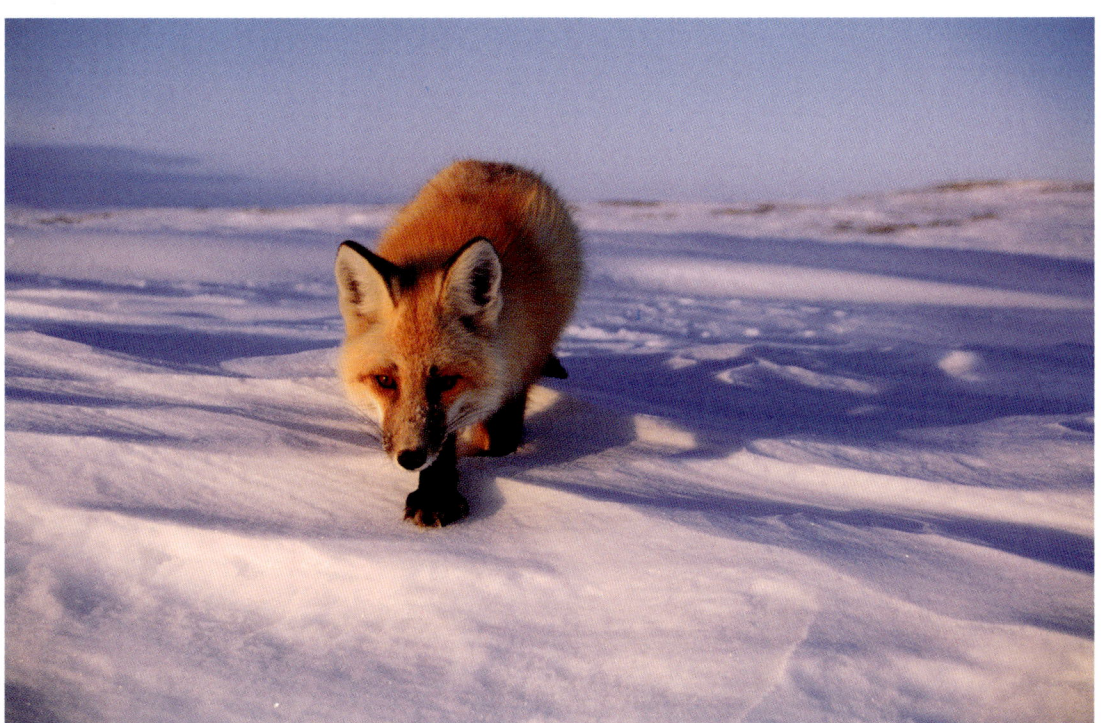

Above: A red fox crouches on the snow, Canadian Barren Lands, Northwest Territories, Canada, 1995.

expensive trip, only to photograph a subject that's been done by a lot of the greats. You're trying to shoot something as well as they have, and it often won't be as good because they're the best for a reason. And now you're broke. You could have bought a camera body and a couple of lenses and shot a masterpiece in your backyard instead.

So, keeping it local is a great route to take, at least while you're learning the ropes and getting an idea of the kind of stories you want to tell, and how. Give yourself a fighting chance to develop your skillset. You can practise the 20-60-20 philosophy (Chapter 2) with your dog, or a fox that's living on a nearby street.

I used to photograph foxes near my town in the Northwest Territories. I learned a lot about photography from doing that. I learned what to do when there is a beautiful red fox in front of me, about depth of field, composition, how to decide whether I'm going to shoot 'sense of place' images or extremely tight images on just the animal's eye (Chapter 8), or whether to create some motion blur on the animal. Then, when you are finally in the moment, when you have a real off

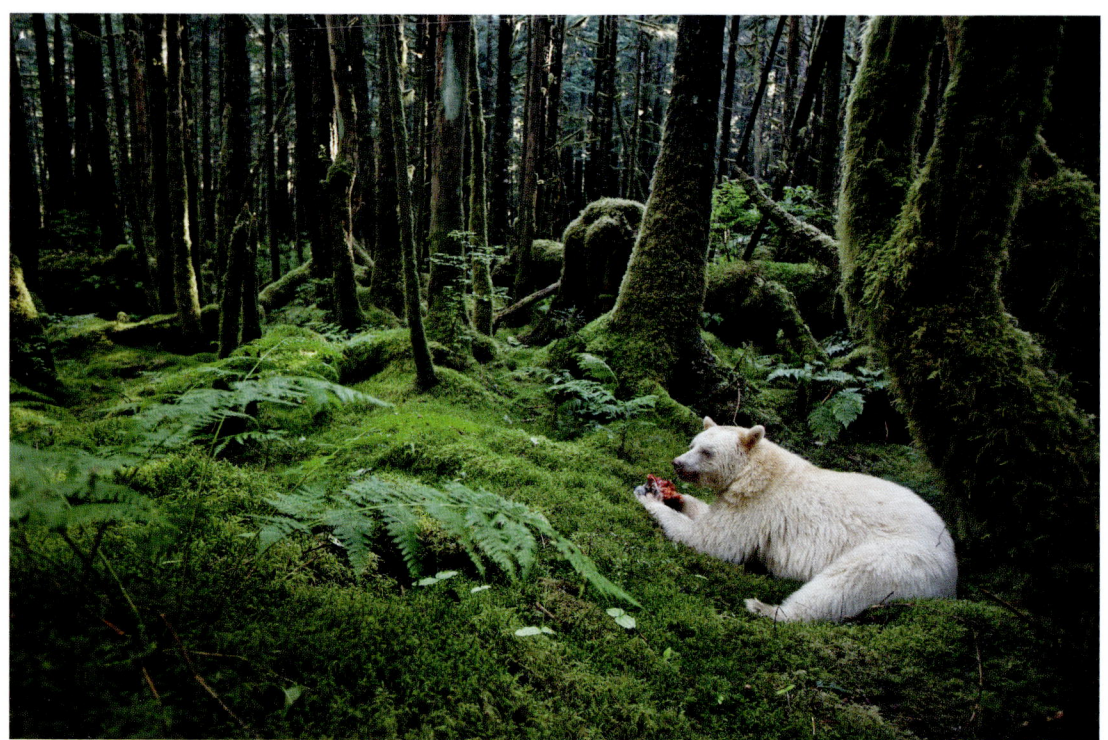

Above: A spirit bear eats a pink salmon, British Columbia, Canada, 2010. Overleaf: *The Waiting Game*, British Columbia, Canada, 2010.

the chart moment unfolding in front of you, you're not going to be flustered and panicking: you've got the necessary skills, the ability to produce powerful imagery, because you've been practising on every subject you've been able to get your hands on.

But remember, it's not just about great images; it's about great storytelling (Chapter 12). I am constantly looking for local stories that will not cost very much to do but will bring value to the conservation community. When my partner Cristina Mittermeier and I heard about the Enbridge Northern Gateway Pipelines that were going to go right through British Columbia and potentially displace bears and destroy salmon runs, we didn't have to go far to make a story.

The proposals had started generating a lot of concern, so we were fortunate to get some funding. *National Geographic* got involved, film crews came on board, and Cristina, who founded the International League of Conservation Photographers, brought along some photographers. Local NGOs got involved too. Lots of us joined together, and from there, it was a case of, 'Okay, what story do we want to tell? What is our end goal here?'

If the goal was to protect the coastline as the First Nation Elders stipulated, it was a case of thinking and working backwards. What species would help me to talk about the entire ecosystem in the affected area, to ultimately gain world attention towards this habitat, and in turn, keep big oil out? What iconic species would help me to do that?

I immediately thought of the spirit bear. Also known as the Kermode bear, the spirit bear is an American black bear with a rare recessive gene that makes it appear white. If we could get world-class material of this animal – video, stills photography, stories – we could give that to the media. We could also create supporting imagery of wolves, salmon, eagles, grizzly bears, the habitat, underwater life, invertebrate life, and so on. With such an incredible cross-section of material, it would be possible to create a narrative that showed just how rich the area was and what we stood to lose.

The conversation began with the spirit bear, though. I did research, talked to local First Nations, to scientists. I gained as much knowledge as I could and made a shot list (Chapter 7): spirit bears in the forest, in the water, salmon and spirit bears, eagles and spirit bears, wolves and spirit bears, aerial shots and so on.

I sketched, visualized, made notes. I had around 300 shots in 10 categories. From there, I took four or five images from each category and drew them on paper. I narrowed down the drawings to 10 of the most beautiful and striking images that could tell the story and storyboarded those 10 images as if they were going to appear in *National Geographic* (Chapter 12).

We had six to seven good days of shooting over two seasons, and one epic final day. On that day, I photographed a beautiful male spirit bear in the rainforest. I ran down to the beach where an aircraft was waiting for me and flew to Vancouver. Cristina had gathered hundreds of people for a press conference. Because of that collective effort, we had a conservation win; the project was cancelled.

I always ask myself, 'Where can I make a difference with my camera, with my ability to tell stories, with my skills? What matters to me?' I then go after the story or project, resolutely, and with humility.

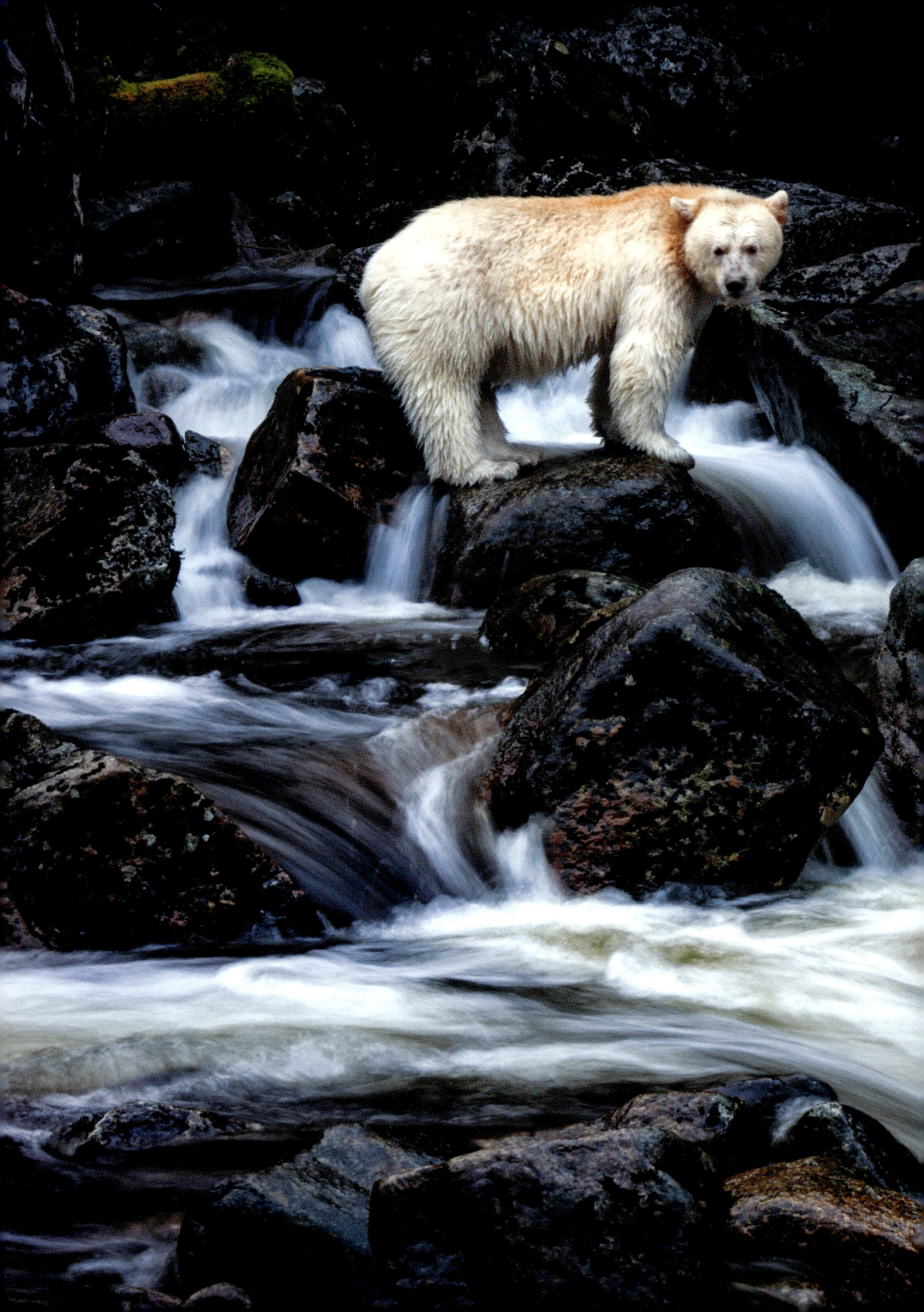

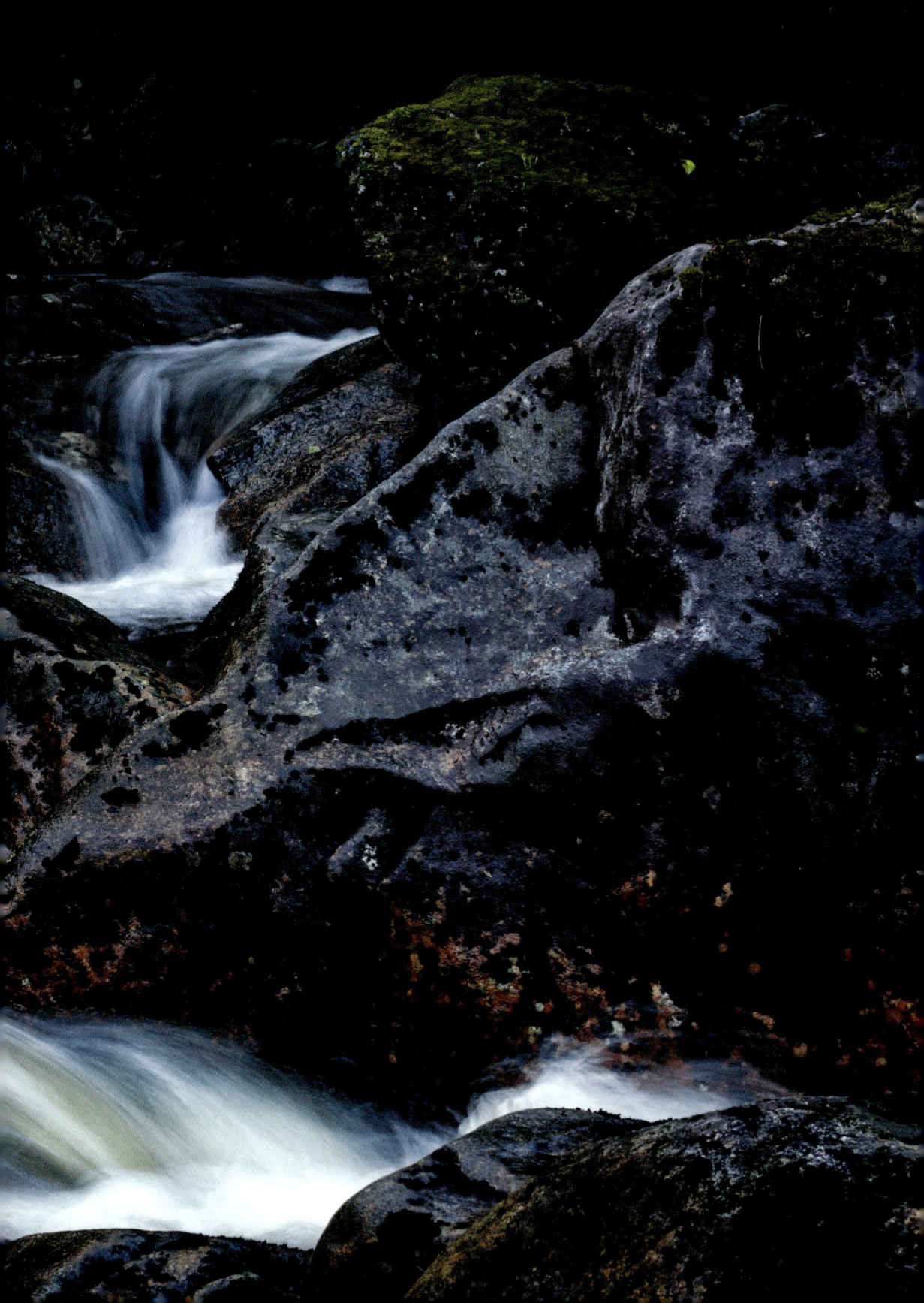

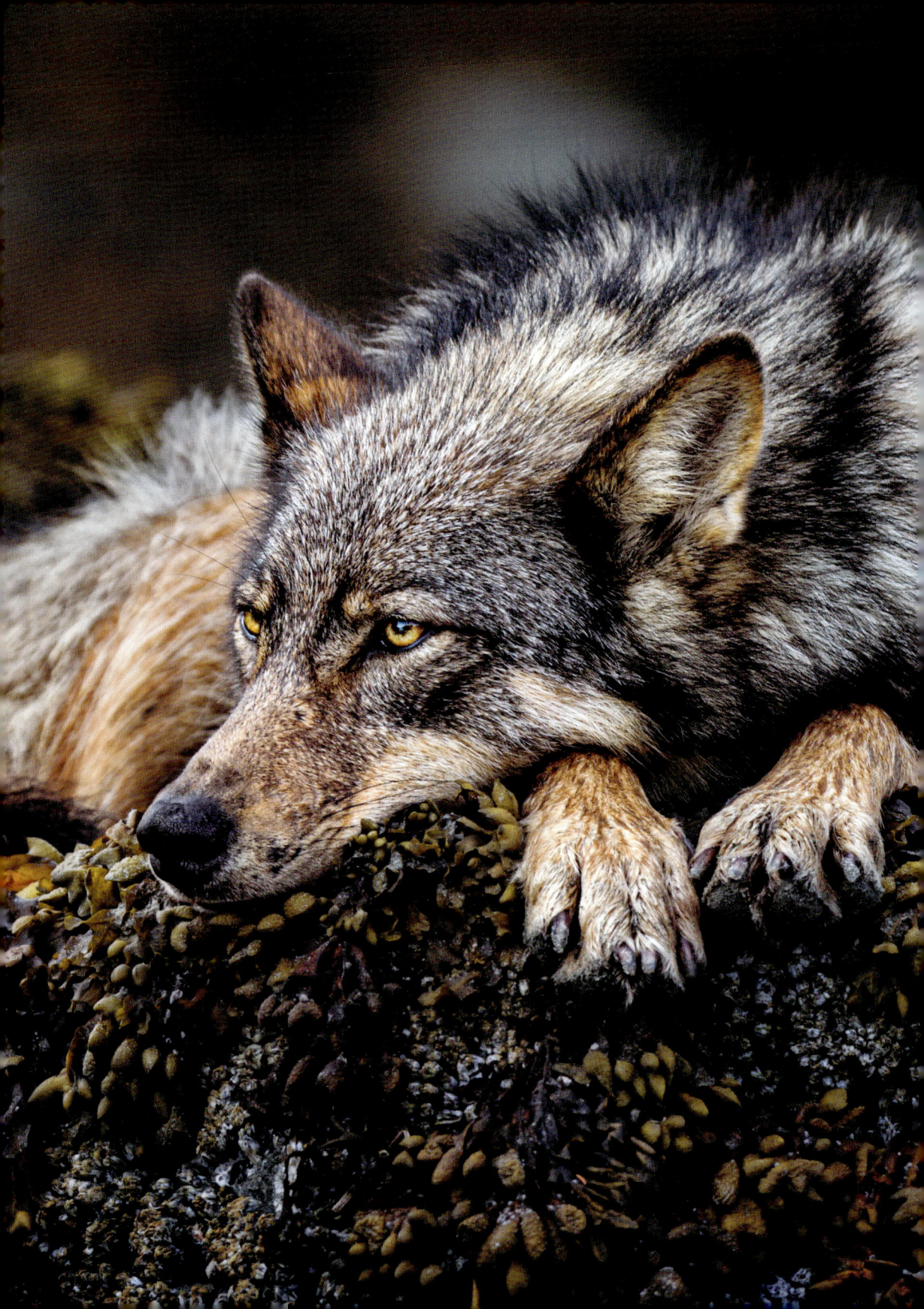

12 The art of storytelling

Create a photo essay

An important lesson I learned from shooting my first assignment for *National Geographic* is that you need to believe in yourself. Self-belief will only get you so far, though. You also have to learn what it means to tell a story.

Anybody can go out and shoot a perfect picture or imitate another photographer's work, but to go out and shoot a new, creative body of work where the images collectively tell a story, and at the same time – equally importantly – give the writers space to tell the story effectively, takes skill, hard work and a lot of practice.

I equate shooting an assignment or a photo story with baseball. You need home runs. When a person is sitting in a doctor's office, flicking through magazines, and you want them to look at your story, you need to stop them in their tracks. You need to punch them in the gut, grab them by the heart, and say, 'Hey, this is my story, and I want you to read it'. To do that, you need to shoot a number of 'home run' images – images that stay with you, that you work especially hard for.

In the assignments I did for *National Geographic*, I was always most proud of the first three double-page spreads, where every picture was, 'Wow, wow, wow'. Those opening images had to be powerful. From there, you insert a handful of 'storytelling' images, which still need

Left: *On the Rocks*, British Columbia, Canada, 2011.

to be beautifully shot, well-lit and evocative, but they are more what I call 'point' pictures – images that create structure, that help to shape the narrative. Then there is the finale, the final flourish. As readers are leaving the article, you want to include one or two double-page spreads of pure poetry – beautiful images that stick in the mind.

That's generally the flow and pacing I follow. It needs to be *boom* – powerful, full frame, interesting. It must grab people, drag them into the story, and then keep their interest with captivating storytelling moments. So, lead with strong imagery and do the same going out. That way, you give readers a captivating story bookended by very powerful photography.

With practice, as you become more used to editing your images (Chapter 16), you'll develop a sense for what makes for a strong opening image or images, and likewise, ending image or images. You'll also be able to more readily spot images that are strong contenders for storytelling 'point' pictures.

As with any photo story, there is an element of trial and error – you'll need to swap various images in and out to see what works best for the narrative flow of the work. It's helpful to keep a record of the various combinations, so you can compare.

Creating a compelling photo story requires skill in terms of deciding the best order of images, but you need to have a strong pool of images to choose from. And that is down to the judgments you make in the field (Chapter 10). Making good decisions is all about learning to read the situation you're in and being responsive. For example, if a wolf walks out of a forest, I might put on a long lens, perhaps a 100-400mm, and get a full-frame shot of it. Maybe I'll zoom out a little to show the wolf in its surroundings. If the wolf is jumping from rock to rock, I might use a focal length of 400mm.

"It must grab people, drag them into the story, and then keep their interest with captivating storytelling moments."

These are not Earth-shattering images, but they're useful to have, to tell a story of the animal in that moment. If the wolf starts walking towards me, that's when things get interesting. It's tempting to use a wide-angle lens and keep photographing the same image over and over, but being brave and switching lenses can give great results. I'll use the longest lens I have to get as close up as I can, and

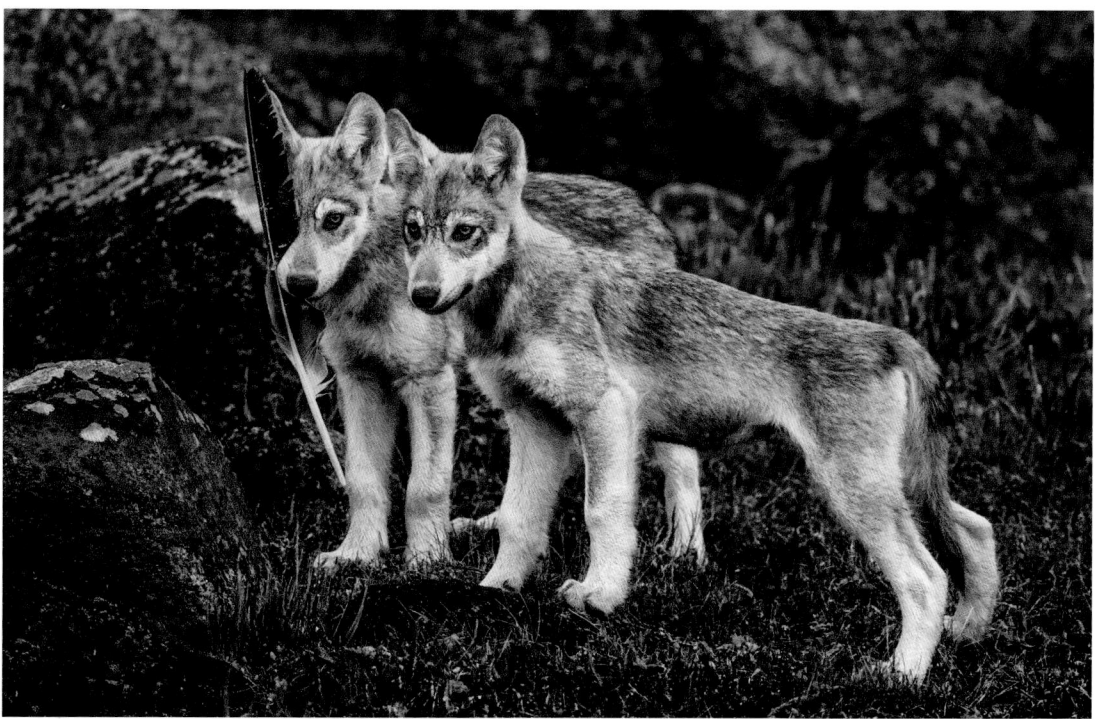

Above: *Playtime*, British
Columbia, Canada, 2011.

then I'll focus on its eye or frame the shot so that its nose is ever so slightly off-centre, and I'll use that to lead the viewer's eye through the image to the animal's eyes.

Whether you're shooting a big, beautiful, wide-open vista with the animal small in the frame – a sense of place image – or tight, you're using the same compositional skills and sense – for example, not putting your subject or the horizon line in the centre.

When it comes to the orientation of your image, shooting landscape images is more natural, of course, than shooting vertically because of the way we hold a camera. Almost all the photographers I know who shoot journalistically or who shoot at the level of *National Geographic* rarely shoot verticals.

Interestingly, almost every time I've had a cover in *National Geographic*, it has been a horizontal image that was cropped to make it vertical to fit the cover space. Similarly, you can take a horizontal image and make it a vertical for social media, of course (Chapter 20).

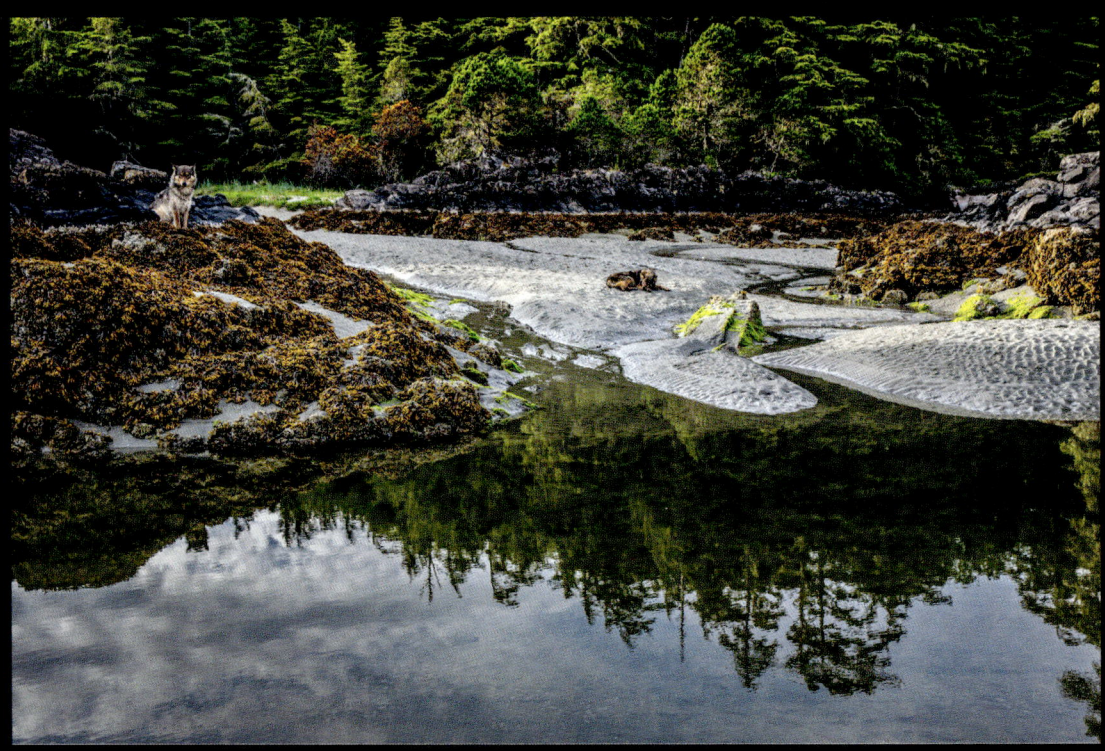

Above: Rain wolves rest in a tide pool cove, British Columbia, Canada, 2012.
Right: Rain wolves stroll through water at low tide, British Columbia, Canada, 2012.

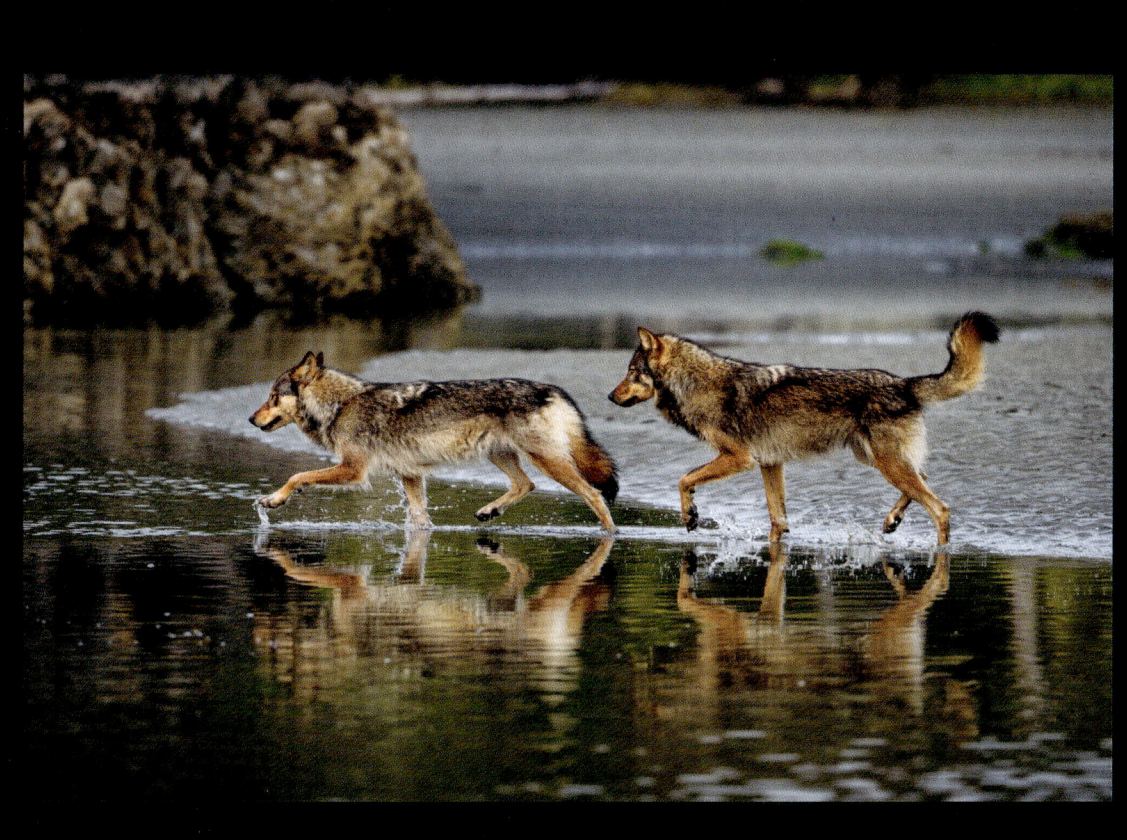

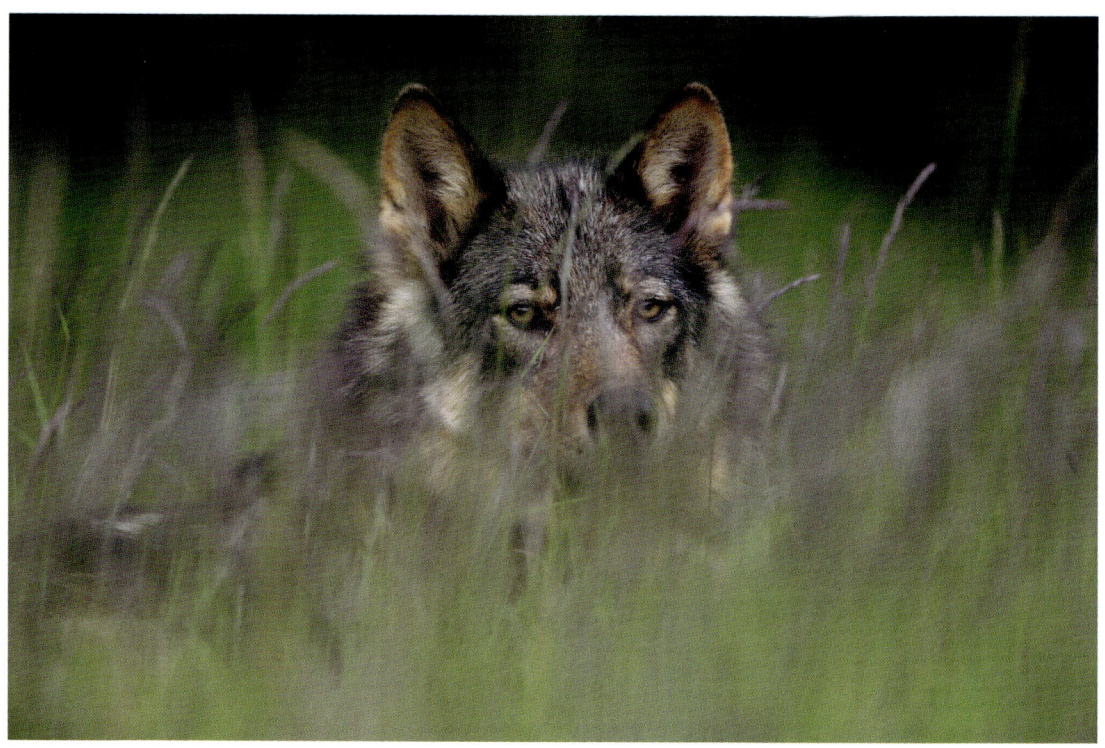

Above: *Catcher in the Rye*, British Columbia, Canada, 2014.

Cropping can strengthen individual images, compositionally speaking, which in turn strengthens a body of work. I once met a photographer who showed me his new coffee-table book. I flipped through it, and there were some great shots and good moments, but the book felt a little odd. Something was a bit off. 'None of these pictures have been cropped,' he said. And I thought to myself, 'Ah, well maybe they should have been.'

Thanks to the quality of digital cameras nowadays, with such crisp, high-resolution image files, you can factor cropping into your work.

When I'm out in the field, I'll sometimes back off a bit. Maybe I don't want to startle or disturb the animal. Perhaps I'd rather shoot on a 600mm lens, for example, and have the highest quality image knowing that I can crop in later. One of my best gatefolds (a folded page that opens out into two) in *National Geographic* was a vertical image that was cropped and made into a double-page spread. That is a testament to the quality of image files nowadays.

I think you can use cropping as an ally. There are purists who say, 'Never crop,' but my guiding light has always been *National Geographic*, and they allow it. It's what I can live with and stand by publicly. If I crop, I tell the world I have cropped. So, cropping can be a useful tool, and as long as you don't overuse it, you won't go wrong.

A final word on creating a compelling photo essay: make sure your work has weight. Produce work that matters – make what you're doing count. As an image-maker, you have a responsibility. If you are photographing an animal that is under threat and you don't turn your camera round and look at the destruction that is happening, then you're doing the subject and the subject a disservice. It's your obligation, it's my obligation as a journalist, as a photographer, as a storyteller, to tell the whole story. There's no point in photographing and celebrating bears, for example, if we're not going to look at the destruction of their habitat.

When you are fighting for the last 4 per cent of old-growth trees on Vancouver Island, for example, you've got to get in the fight. You need to turn your camera towards those issues and those stories.

Vancouver Island once had vast old-growth forests. Intense deforestation occurred in the 1970s and '80s, and the most beautiful timber was removed, causing massive destruction. Now, there is logging of second-growth trees that were replanted several decades ago. What is happening is an ecological time bomb. The trees on Vancouver Island are critical to maintaining biodiversity and play a role in combating climate change. We're potentially facing the next mass extinction of our planet because of climate change, and yet we're cutting down trees that sequester carbon. It doesn't make sense.

But I believe that the power of the people is greater than the people in power, and that's why we must use our cameras to galvanize a movement. Storytelling can affect change; images can make a difference.

" There are purists who say, 'Never crop,' but my guiding light has always been *National Geographic*, and they allow it."

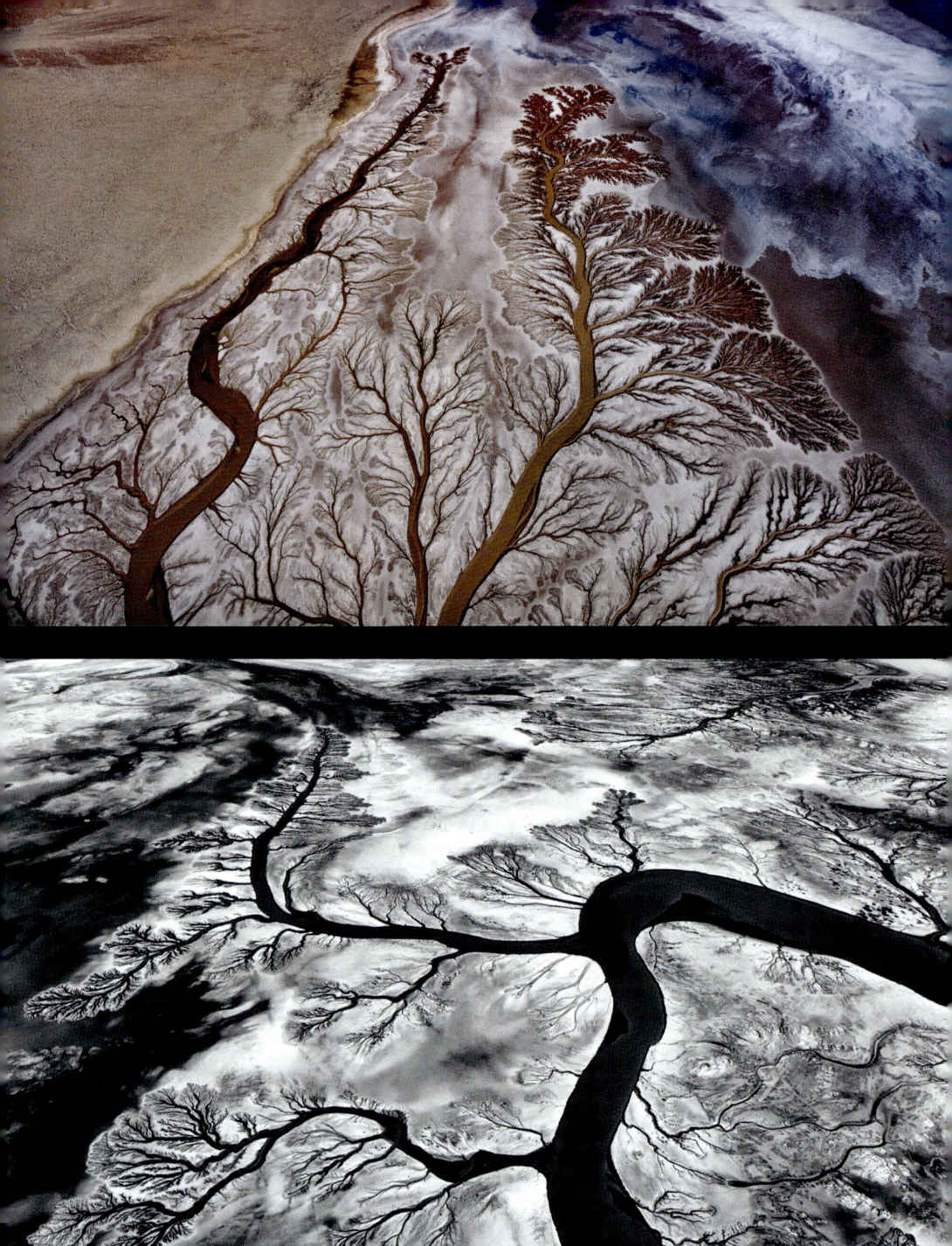

Colour versus black and white

Which approach is best?

When I was shooting journalistically, the thought of converting my images to black and white never entered my mind. I was there to photograph the world as it is. My job was to shoot journalistic coverage. But in the last four or five years, I've been thinking more about what it means to be a fine art photographer. What does it mean to make your images 'timeless' or to create images that will hang on people's walls and potentially live on forever?

I'm on a personal journey where I'm enjoying seeing my work in black and white, but not everything deserves to be converted from colour. Deciding which images will work in black and white is, for me at least, an intuitive process.

As a photographer, I believe it's crucial not to limit yourself in the way that you work. When I come across photographers who say, 'I only do that' or 'I only treat my images like this', I slightly despair. Photography is hard enough without putting rules and restrictions on yourself. That is especially true if you're shooting fine art images. I will set myself free and try lots of things until I achieve the result I'm looking for.

I thought I was going to love the top left image in black and white. It shows the Colorado River Delta in Baja California, Mexico. It seemed like a no-brainer to me, so I converted it to black and white. But in fact, it didn't do that much for me. I found it more pleasing in colour. I love the colours and the way the river contrasts with the salt.

Top: *Gaia's Lungs*, Baja Peninsula, Mexico, 2023.
Bottom: *Arterial Poetry*, Baja Peninsula, Mexico, 2023.

Interestingly in the bottom picture on the previous spread, when I go in closer on some of the details, I prefer it in black and white. It becomes a study of texture, patterns, and the black river against the white salt. I want people to focus on the details of the river, and in black and white, that is possible.

Let's take another image of the Colorado River Delta. I love this one on the right in colour – I really like the colours of the river. To me, it looks a little flat in black and white.

I can tinker with the colour version and exaggerate the colours by adding a little saturation, and I can use the Dehaze tool to reduce the haze. By lifting the whites, I can create a little more contrast, and suddenly it becomes quite a pleasing image. There are beautiful yellows leading off into the distance, and my eyes are drawn into the image; I am taken on a journey.

I thought I was going to prefer the image in black and white, but in fact, I like it in colour. So, you often don't know whether an image will work better in black and white or colour until you have played around with it in post.

When I was shooting at the Colorado River Delta, I thought I was making a body of work where all the images were going to be black and white. It turns out that 80 per cent of them work better in colour. I just prefer them that way, and my editors prefer the colour versions. Sometimes I'll ask my friends who are professional photographers what they think. If 70 per cent come back and say they like an image in colour and I prefer it in colour, then I know I'm on the right path.

It's about not being too strict or too hard on yourself, especially in the initial phases of editing. When it comes to shooting and editing, my motto is 'feel more, think less'. The image needs to be powerful – that's how I make my decisions.

Once, when I was photographing black bears on the coast of British Columbia, a bear who looked to be just a baby, perhaps only a few years old, kept coming in and out of the shadows. The shooting conditions were challenging – it was a little

"I thought I was making a body of work where all the images were going to be black and white. It turns out that 80 per cent of them work better in colour."

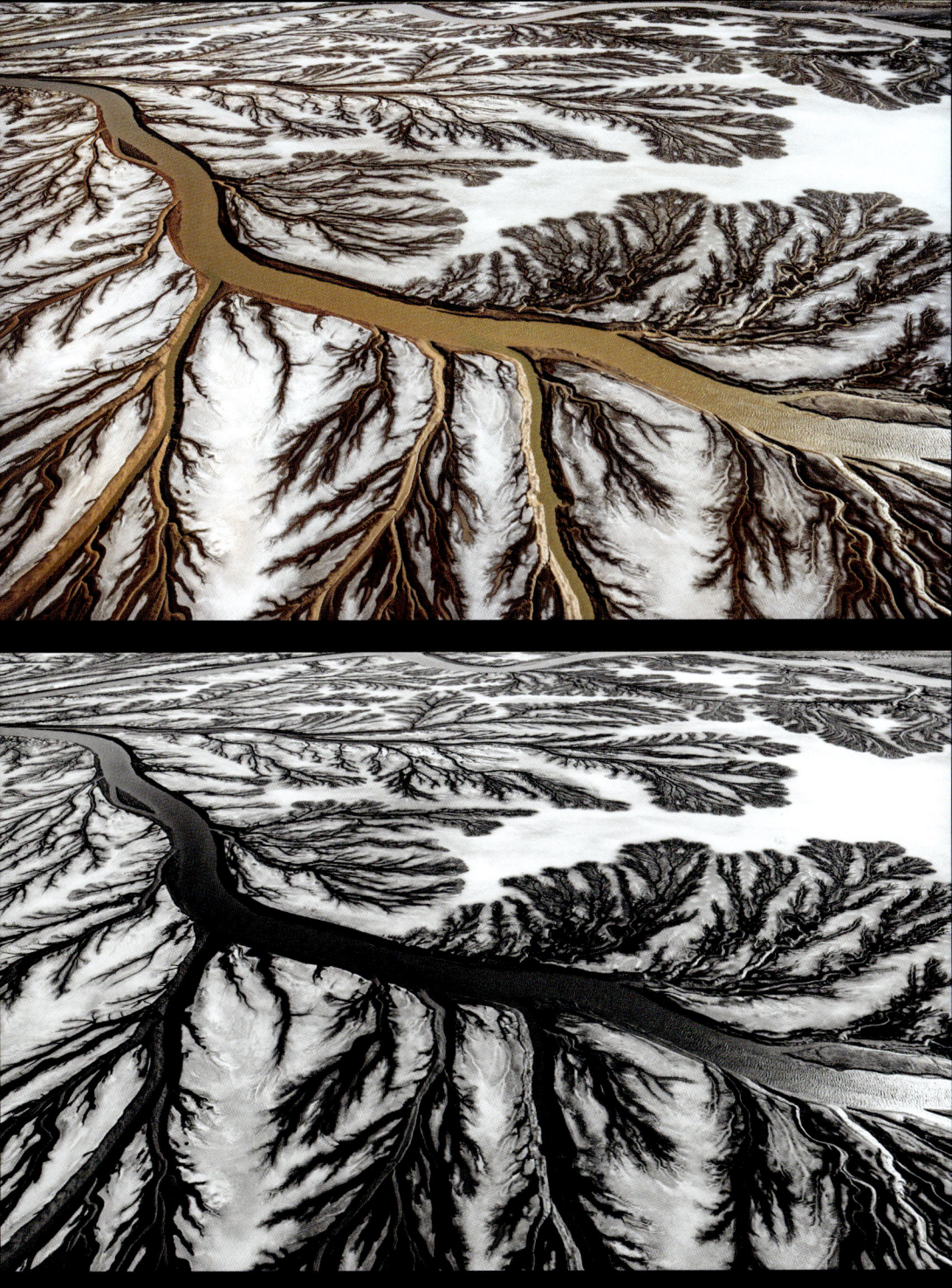

Top and bottom: *Amber Crossroads*, Baja Peninsula, Mexico, 2023.

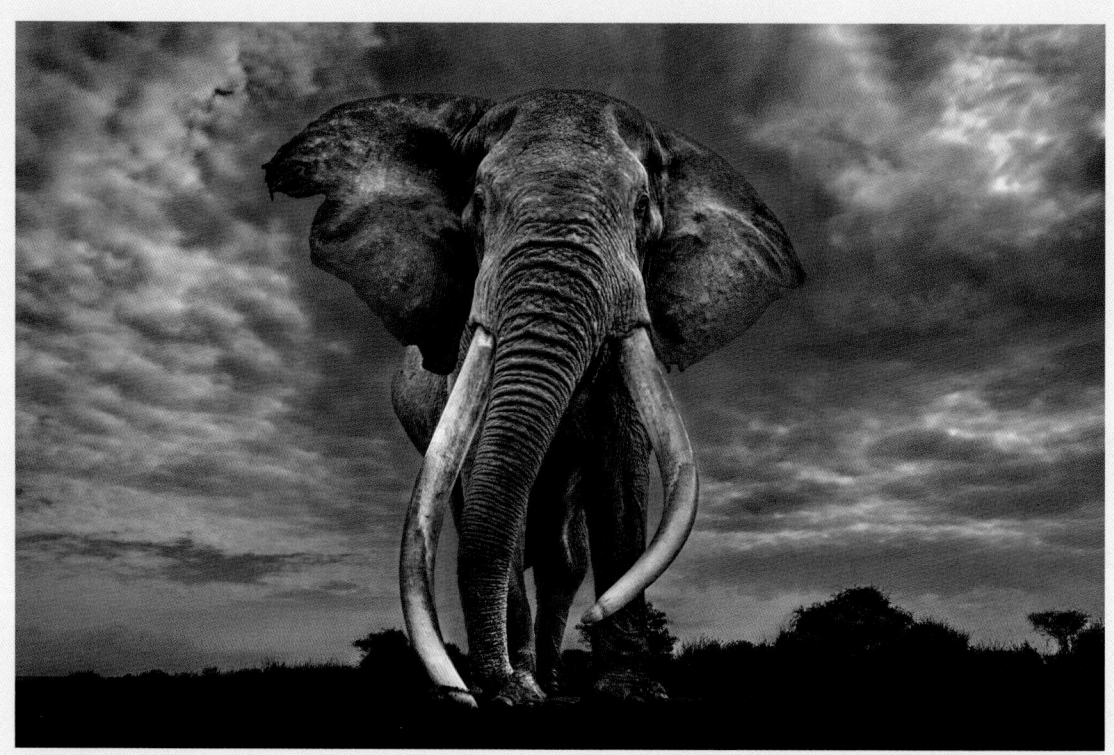

Above and right: *Legend*, Kenya, 2025.

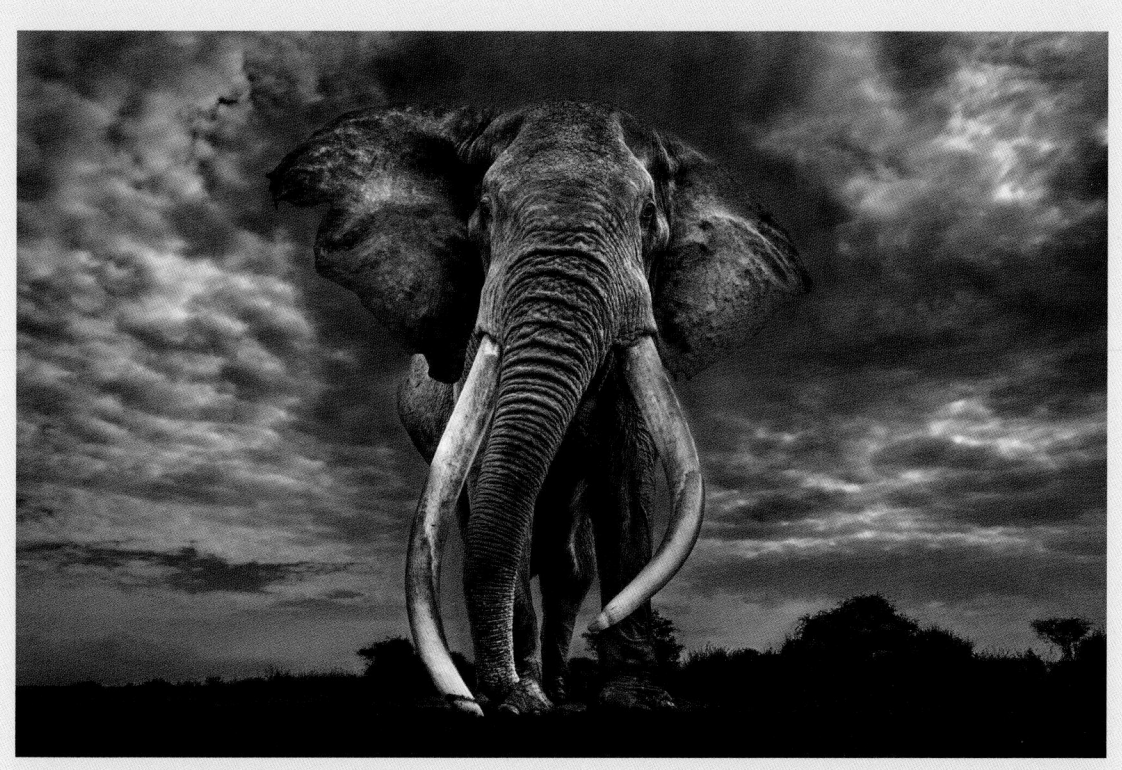

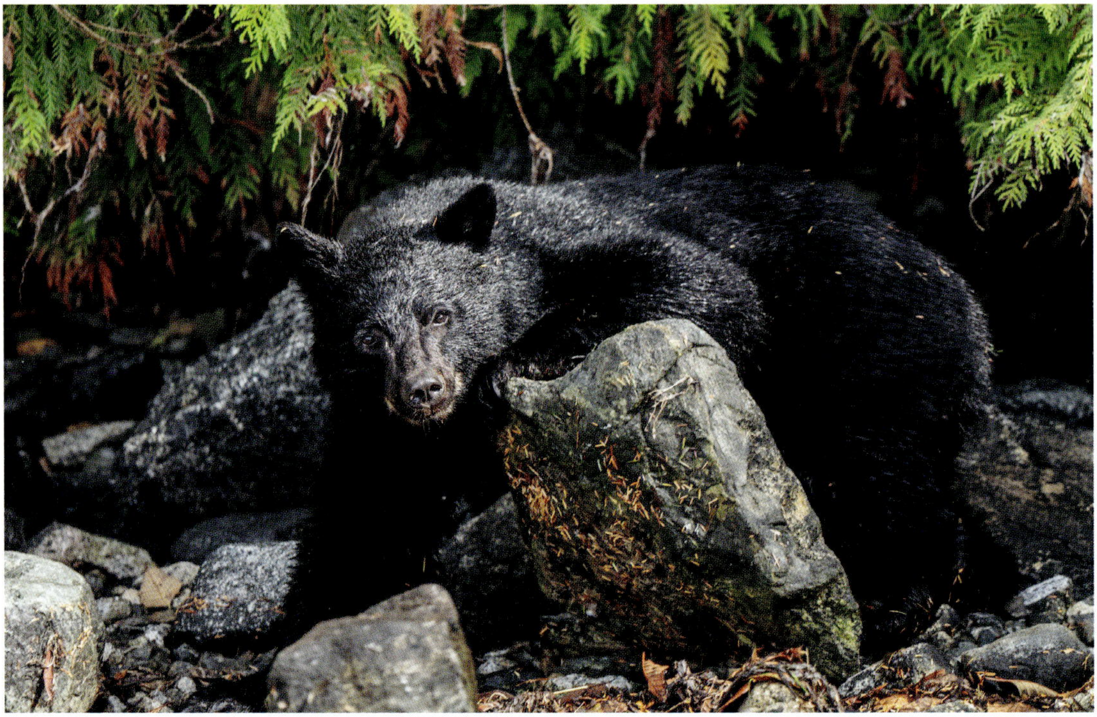

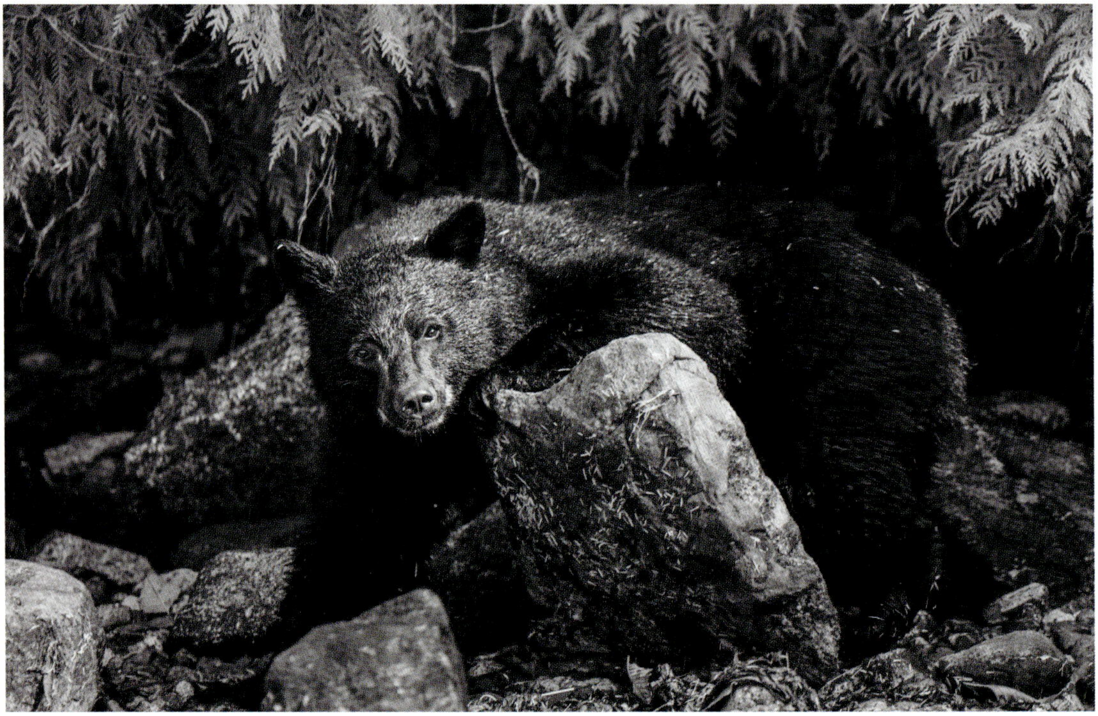

Top and bottom: A black bear turns over rocks in search of food, British Columbia, Canada, 2023.

bright, and the rocks in the foreground were completely blown out, while the black bear in the shade was, of course, dark. There were some good moments, though: one was when the bear came forward, lifted a rock and looked out around him. The image works in colour, but it also potentially works in black and white too.

When you're working in challenging conditions, when the light is harsh, it might be better to convert to black and white later. If you try and make a colour image in those conditions, it just doesn't work, as it will not be very interesting or impactful. But if you turn that portrait image of a black bear, taken at high noon – when the sun is at its highest point in the sky – into black and white, you can lift the shadows and see every detail of the bear. You are no longer looking at light or colour; you're looking at the bear's eyes, getting lost in its face. In a way, you're almost feeling its energy.

Whenever I think, 'I'm done for the day, I've shot all the images I'm going to take today,' I remember the 20-60-20 philosophy (Chapter 2). Just to recap: this is where I spend 20 per cent of the shoot getting something sharp and in focus before very quickly getting into the next 60 per cent of my time, which is when I do most of my creative work – I use my toolbox of techniques to make creative compositions or images that have a beautiful mood. Perhaps I'll try a technique that gives the image something extra, maybe I'll create a little motion blur. I spend the last 20 per cent of my time shooting 'Hail Mary' shots, which have a lower chance of success.

One of those 'Hail Mary' moments was 'Orca Ballet'. The day was done. It was almost pitch-black underwater – it wasn't worth being in the water anymore. I was already shooting at ISO 8000. (This was back in the day when ISO 8000 was unheard of; indeed, ISO 4000 was unheard of.) But it was all I had – ISO 8000 and f/2.8 underwater. I could see a massive ball of herring about the size of a football pitch and maybe a hundred feet deep. Suddenly, a single orca whale came into the scene. The way it rose up and started to twist and corkscrew around the herring, bending its body, was remarkable. As it did that, the herring split.

When I converted the image to black and white, it was, in one sense, a very imperfect photograph,

> " When you're working in challenging conditions, when the light is harsh, it might be better to convert to black and white later."

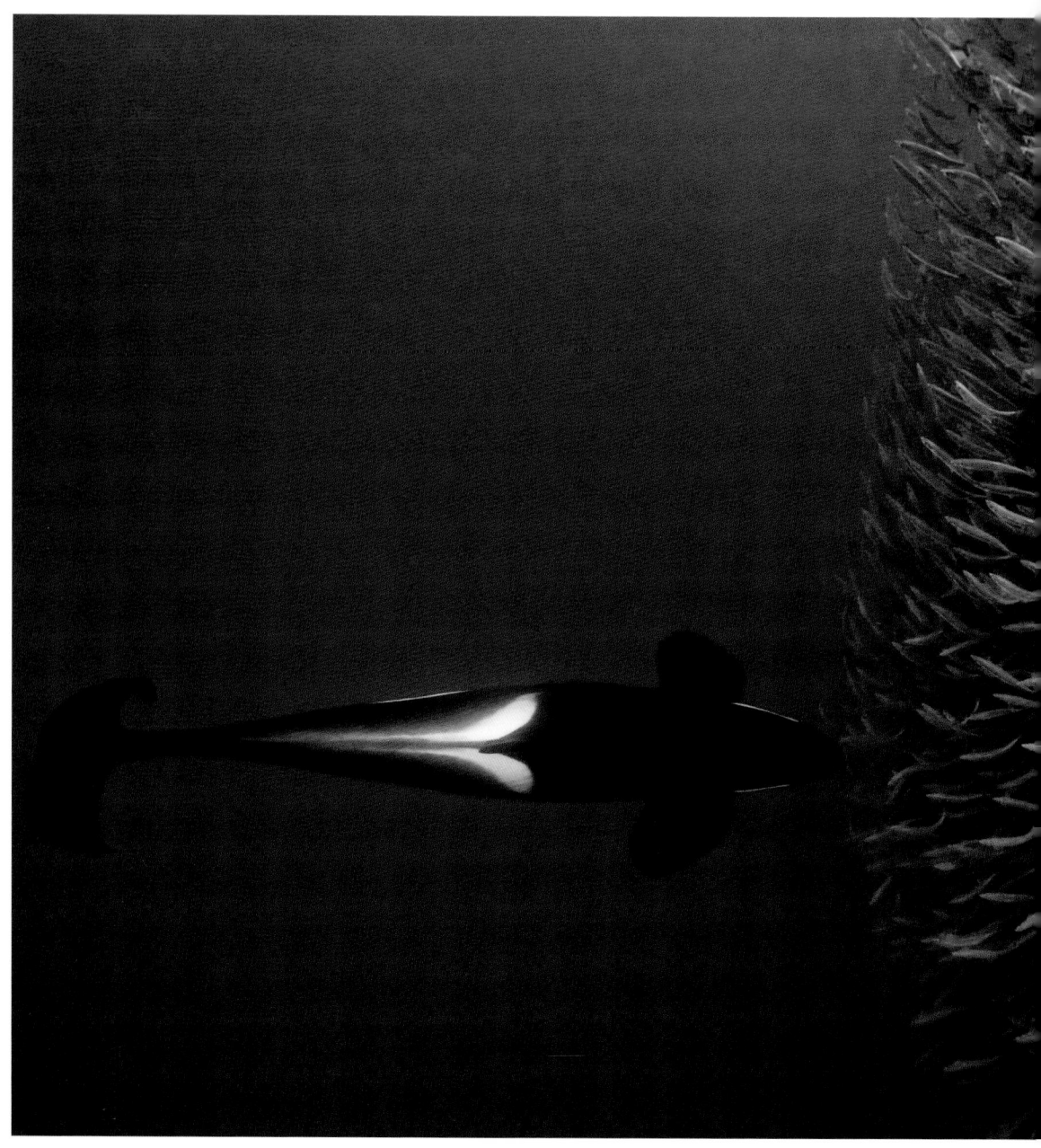

" When you think you're done, that's when
you should push your boundaries as
an artist, because it's often when you
make your most powerful images."

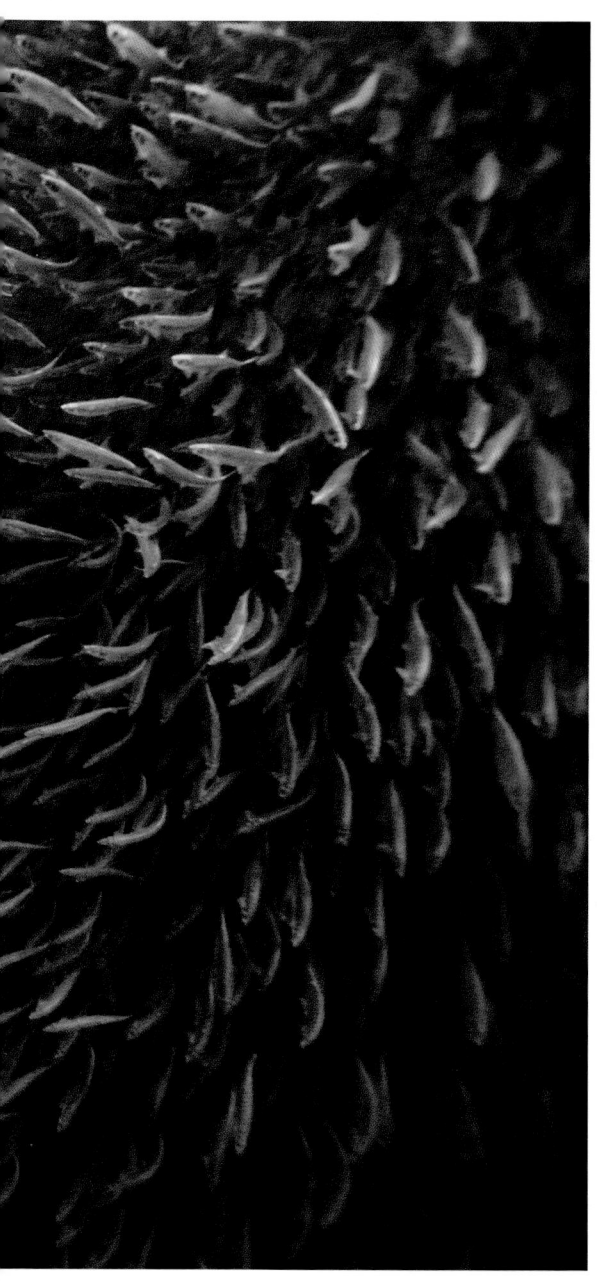

but in another, almost the perfect painting – a study of texture, grain, motion and lines. The graceful, balletic movements of the orca gave the image a beautiful feel.

So, when you think you're done, that's when you should push your boundaries as an artist, because it's often when you make your most powerful images.

Similarly, seeing what an image looks like in black and white can be surprising – in a good way. You never know, you might have an image that pops, even if you didn't think much of it at first. The bottom line is that being playful and experimenting can sometimes pay off, and that element of surprise is one of the best parts of photography.

Above: *The Hunt*, Northern fjords, Norway, 2014.
Overleaf: *Orca Ballet*, Lofoten, Norway, 2014.

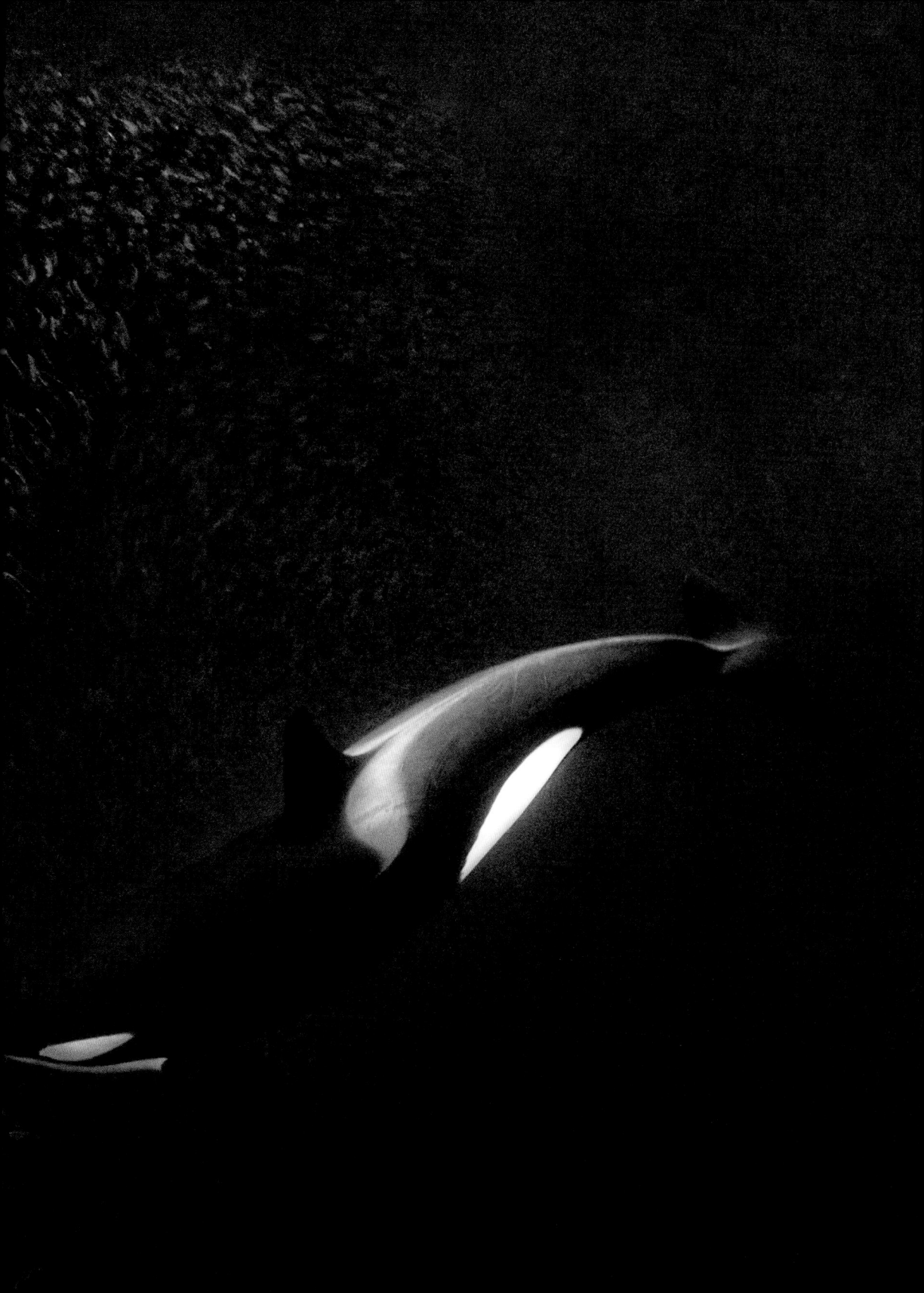

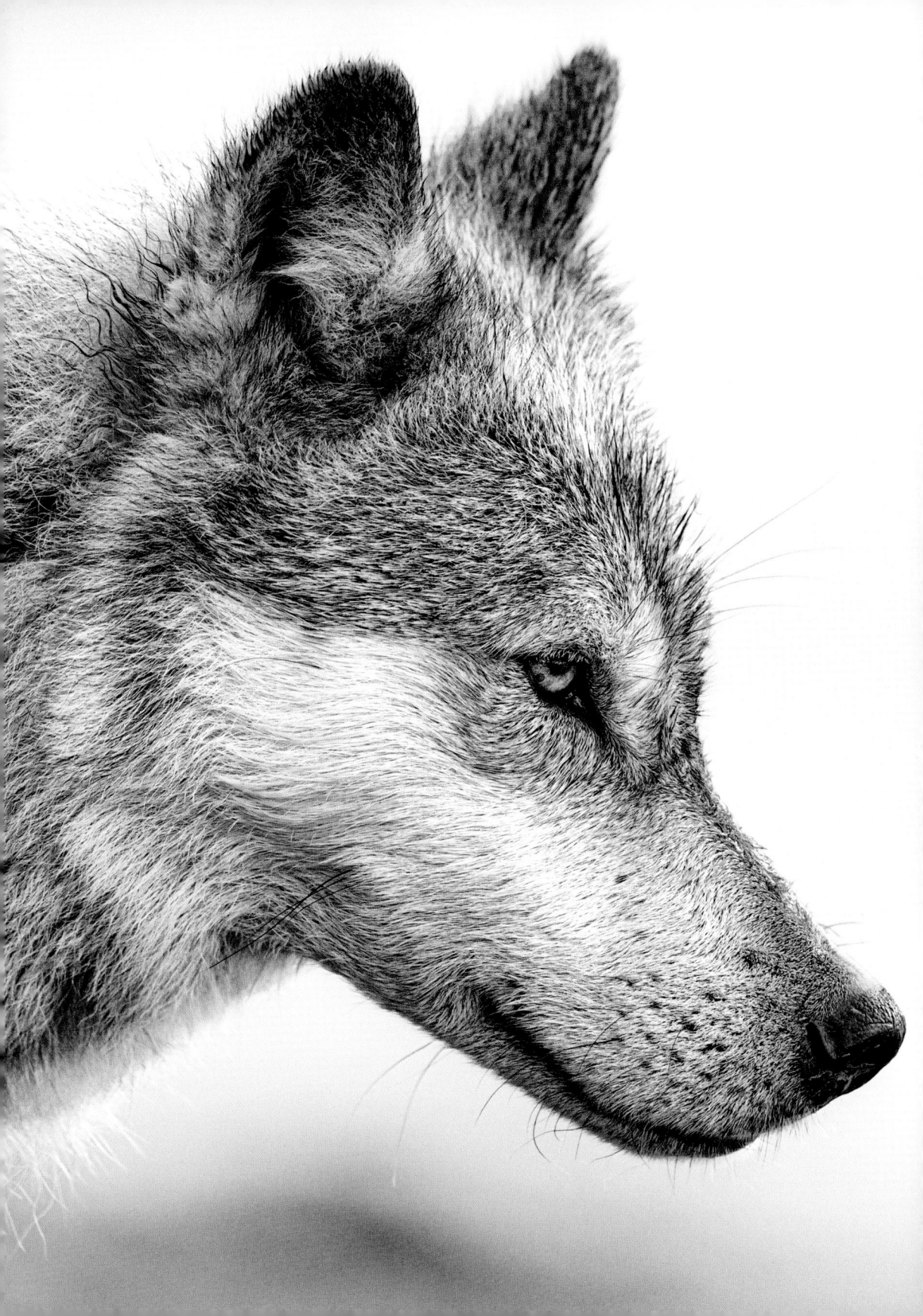

Ethical considerations

Have humility and respect nature

W hen I think of values, I think, 'What do I want my headstone to say?' I want it to say I was a good person who helped to change the world for the better, and that my photography helped advance conservation. Those are the things that matter to me.

To achieve your goals in life, you need to live by your own set of values, your own ethos, your own code of ethics, whatever it is that is your guiding light. If you go through life being unkind, not only is that not a great way to be, but it will also be difficult to reach your goals.

By being nice to everybody, you build a network of people who become your friends, advisors, allies, cheerleaders. They are the people who lift you up and give you the strength to go out there and do what you need to do.

When I was a kid and I was frustrated with or mad at somebody, my mother would say, 'Paul, be nice to everybody on the way up because you will meet them all again on the way down.' I think there is a lot of truth in those words. You might think you're all that and you're on a rocket-ship trajectory, but the journey of life is not always up; there are lots of downs as well as ups.

Left: *Coastal Guardian*, British Columbia, Canada, 2018.

It is a matter of respect – having respect for others. When you walk into a room, look people in the eye, shake their hand, introduce yourself. Be humble and quiet. As my mentor Flip Nicklin used to say, 'Wherever you go in the world, you are the second best because everybody else is busy being the best.' And second best is a great place to be. Have humility and be curious but respectful, and you'll be amazed at how much you can grow.

Be a person who asks questions. When I mentor or meet photographers, I'll say to them, 'I am at your service. If I can help in any way, if you want to ask questions, please don't hesitate, I would love to help.' If you have an opportunity to ask questions, take it.

As a kid, I was always curious. I'd look at other people's photos and try to understand where, what, when and most of all how the photographer had shot that image. The amount of knowledge you will gain when you start studying photos is unbelievable.

When I'm around animals – when I'm in their territory – I'll move slowly, gently, respectfully, mindfully. I always say that it's a little like doing tai chi. It's the same with life: move slowly and cautiously, intentionally, and you will be amazed at the things that will open up for you. People start to come up and say, 'What can I do to help?'

One of the most challenging assignments I've ever done was an assignment for *National Geographic* on Hawaiian surf culture. My job was to photograph the Native Hawaiians who are surfers and who have a deep connection with the sea.

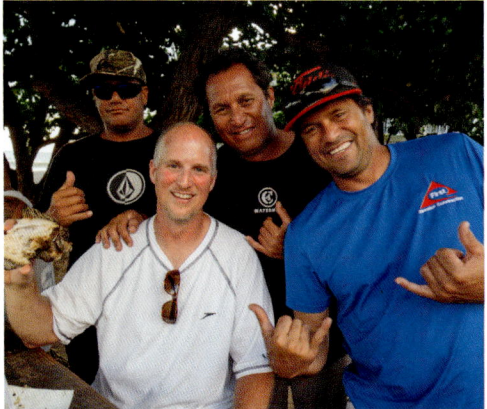

I arrived in a place called Mākaha, a place I was told I should not be. In short, if you're not Hawaiian, you are not allowed to go there; you won't be accepted. When I showed up, I went and sat on the beach. I'd brought some beer with me, and I just sat there and watched the surfers.

Over the following two weeks, I got to know the surfers and the local community, including the Keaulana family, legends of Mākaha. Brian Keaulana is a highly respected surfer and stuntman. It was the

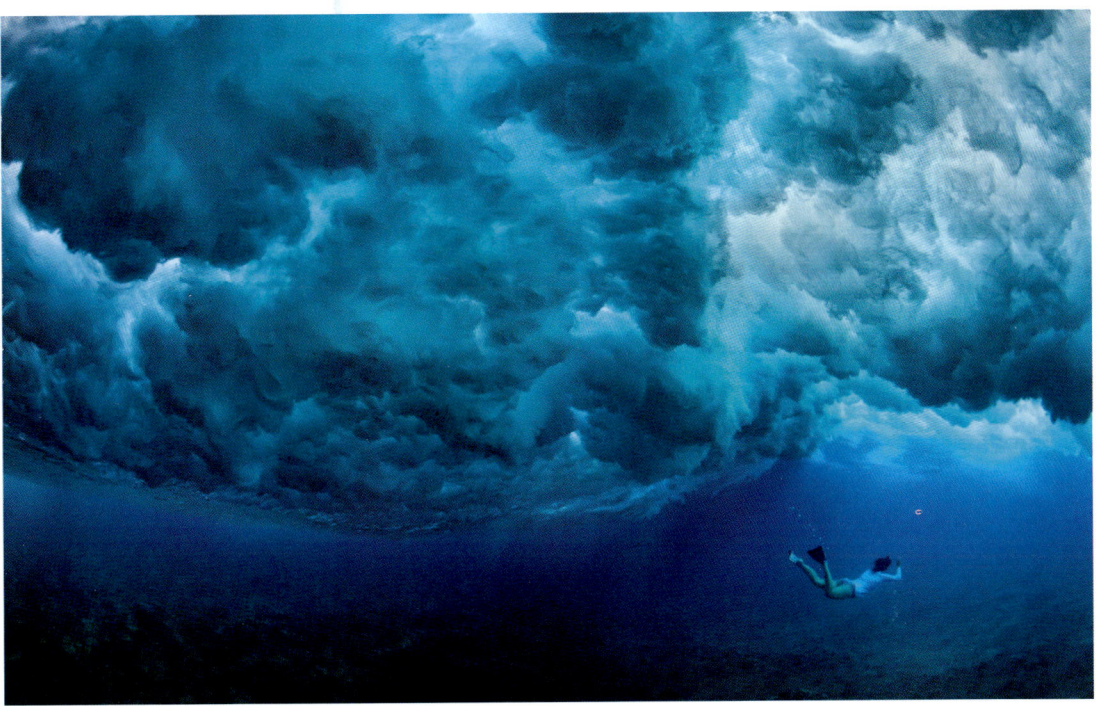

Keaulanas who eventually said to me, 'I thought you were here to take pictures of us?' To which I replied, 'I am, whenever you think it's right.'

The community became involved in the project. The amount of help, love and support I received was truly humbling. I would have failed that assignment if I had gone there thinking, 'I am a big shot photographer, I'm all that'. I was nobody. I was just a man with a camera who was there to learn and crucially learn through their eyes; to shoot images through their eyes – their experiences. They were the ones who made that assignment a success.

I go into every situation very respectful of the local First Nations people, extremely humble, with my eyes wide open. As soon as you think that because you own a camera, it makes you special, you're in trouble. That's when you put up walls.

Be willing to ask hundreds of questions, get educated, align yourself with great people who have been living in a place for thousands of years. The knowledge that has been passed down will help you succeed in telling your own stories (Chapter 12).

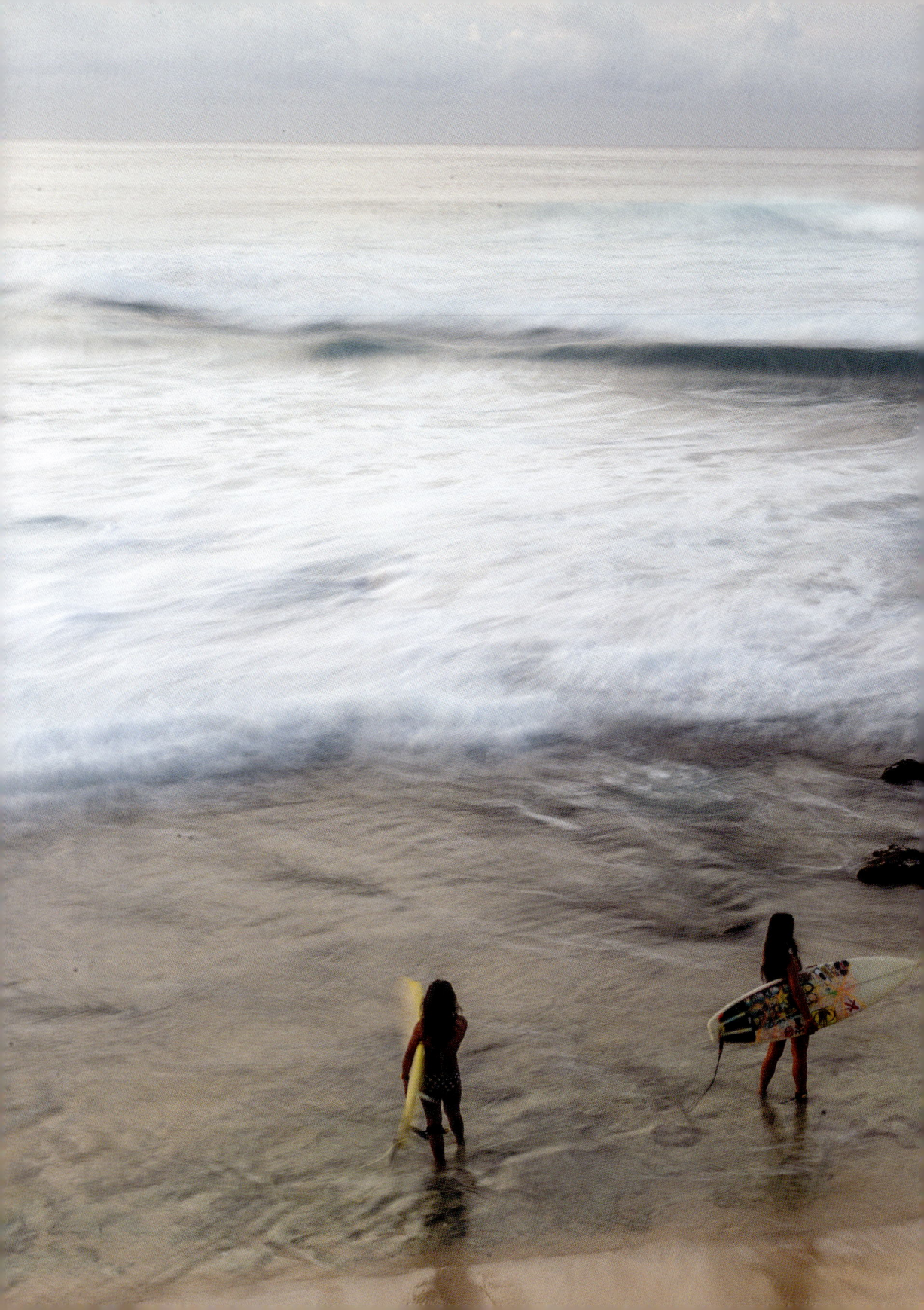

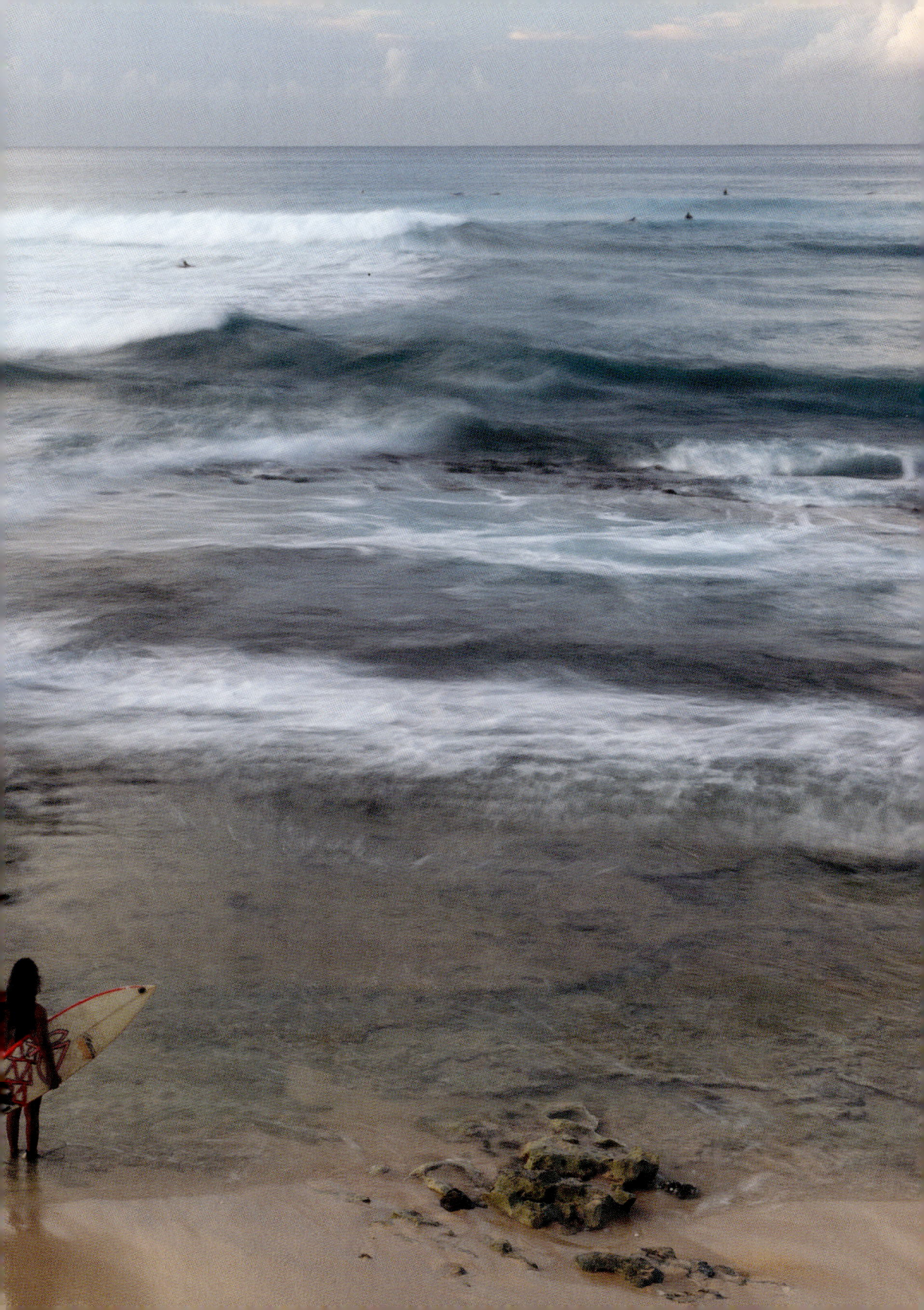

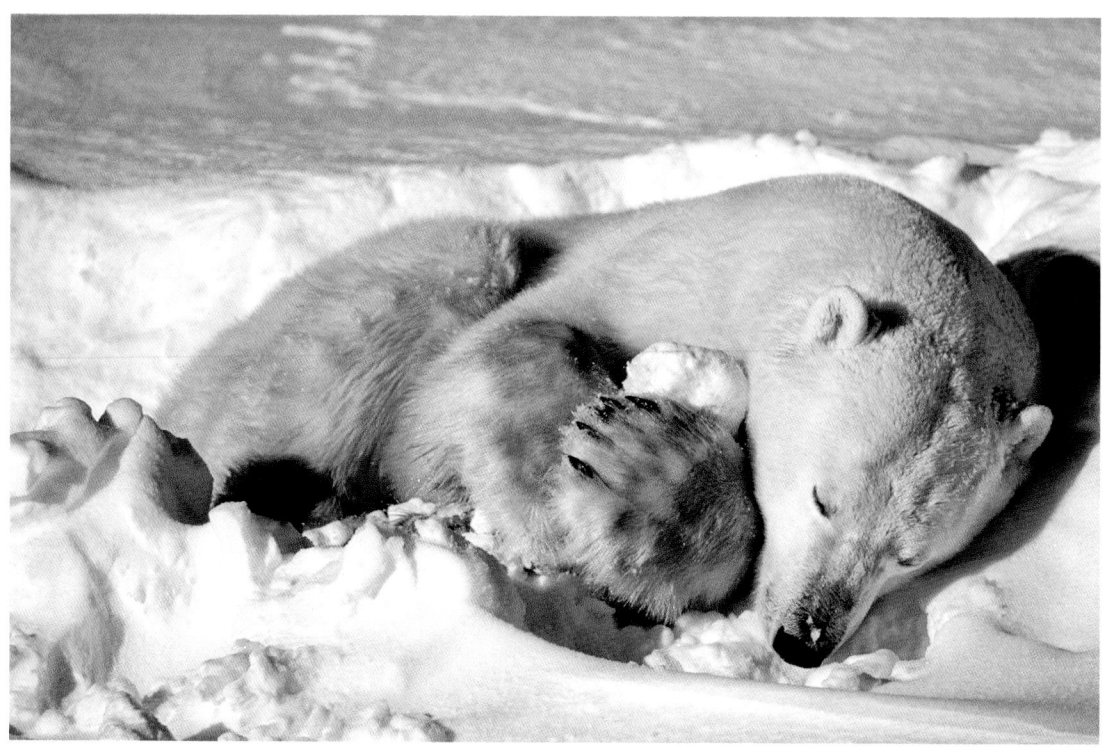

Previous spread: *Heavenly,
Virtuous, and Miracle,*
Mākaha Beach, Hawaii, 2013.
Above: *Snowball Reverie,*
Manitoba, Canada, 1997.
Overleaf: *Rock Runner,*
Mākaha, Hawaii, 2013.

Whether you are photographing Indigenous peoples or nature and animals, it is never about getting the picture at any cost. I often find it is necessary to play the long game. And you have to know when it is time to call it a day, which is not always easy to do if a shoot hasn't yielded the results you had hoped it would.

Take photographing coastal wolves in British Columbia. These fascinating foragers get their nutrition from the sea. They wait for the tide to go out and feed on limpets, barnacles, crab and even baby seals. They'll wait for salmon in the salmon runs and for the carcasses of dead whales and sealions to wash up on the beach.

On one occasion, I was watching a wolf foraging on the shoreline. What you want is for the wolf to look at you and then go back to what it is doing. It means they've accepted your presence; they've let you in. And that's really the only encounter to have with an animal.

That day, although being in the presence of the wolf was an amazing experience, I didn't get any usable images. I couldn't get close enough

> " Coming back without the images you were hoping for is disappointing, but it's not a waste; you've had the experience and will no doubt have grown as a person and an artist."

to her. It was our first meeting after all, and based on her behaviour, she seemed shy. So, rather than force a situation, it was better to leave her be, to let her see me leave and show her I'm not a threat, that I'm respectful of her and her turf, and then plan to return.

This is what I mean by the 'long game'. By reading the situation and responding appropriately, the wolf will hopefully begin to trust me, and over time, get to know me, my smell, and eventually reward us by coming for a closer look in the future.

Another time, I was working off the coast of British Columbia, photographing sea otters. They were timid. I wanted to get good images, but I also didn't want to disturb them or stress them out. It was one of those situations when the shooting is tough. Productivity was low. I was using a long lens – a 600mm – and photographing from a boat. I had depth of field issues, camera shake issues, stability issues, focus issues. Everything was fighting against me.

I wouldn't normally handhold a 600mm lens on a boat, but you always have to respect the animals you're photographing and not disturb them, which meant staying some distance away and getting what I could.

At times like that, I don't review what I'm photographing. I just keep shooting, doing what I can to get something I might be able to use if I crop later. It's one of those occasions where you really live by the David Doubilet motto: 'The better the photographer, the bigger the trashcan.' I knew I would likely be discarding almost all of what I was shooting, although I hoped there might be a couple of good shots in there.

The otters were relaxed; they were feeding, but I knew it was time to leave. Sometimes you have to cut your losses. Coming back without the images you were hoping for is disappointing, but it's not a waste; you've had the experience and will no doubt have grown as a person and an artist.

So, enter situations slowly, respectfully. Listen, ask questions, be calm, kind, generous, and you'll see a beautiful path open up before you.

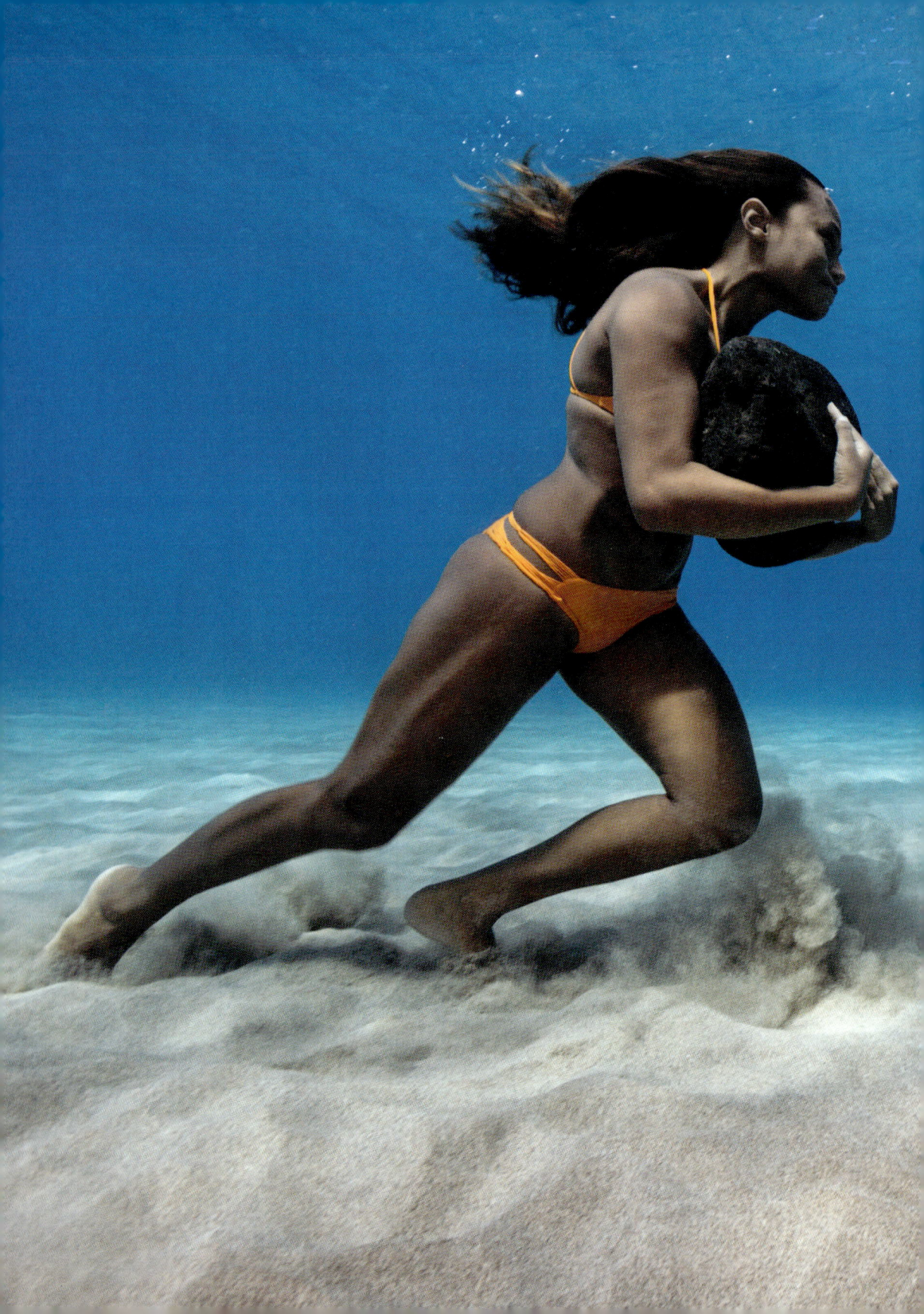

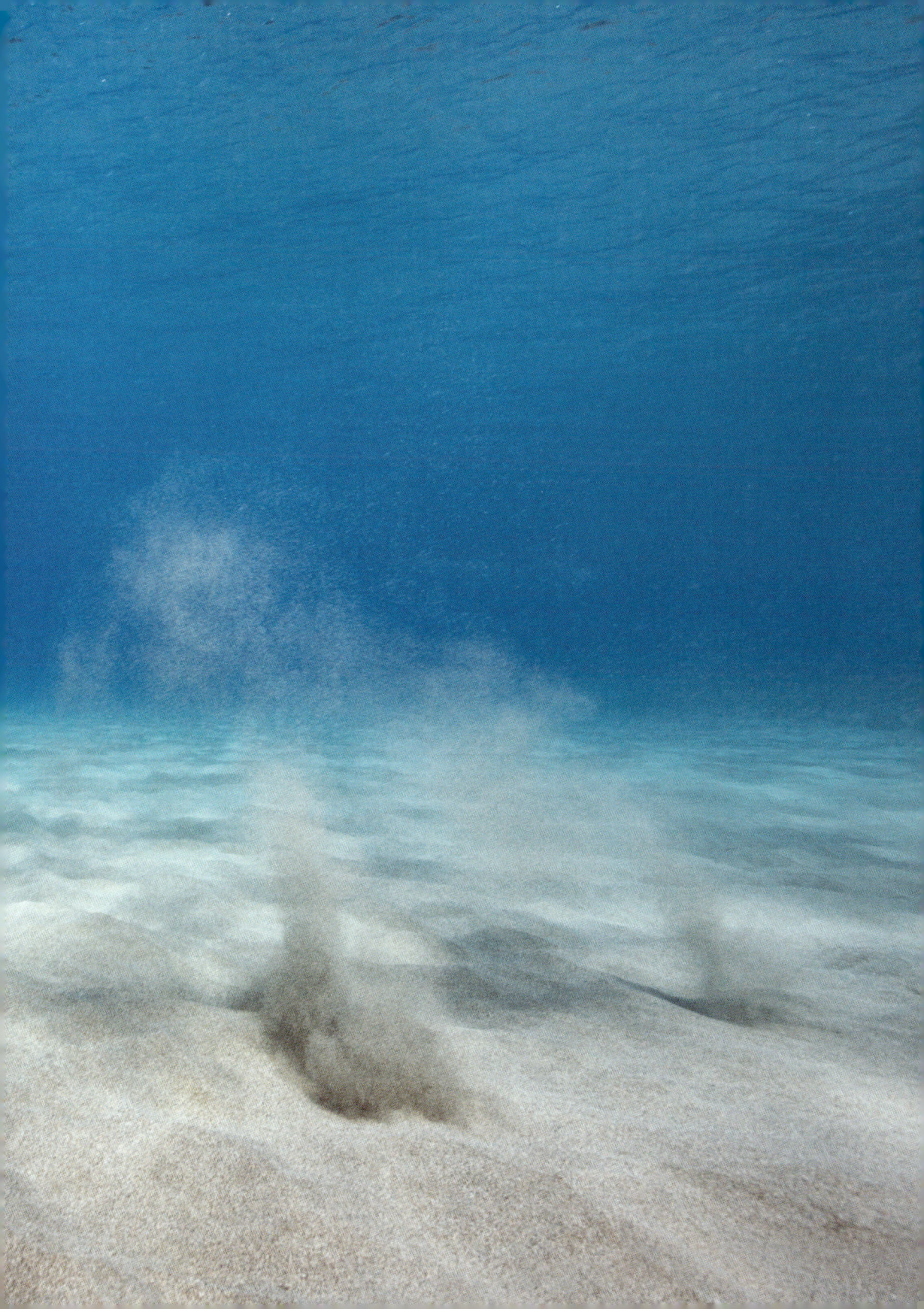

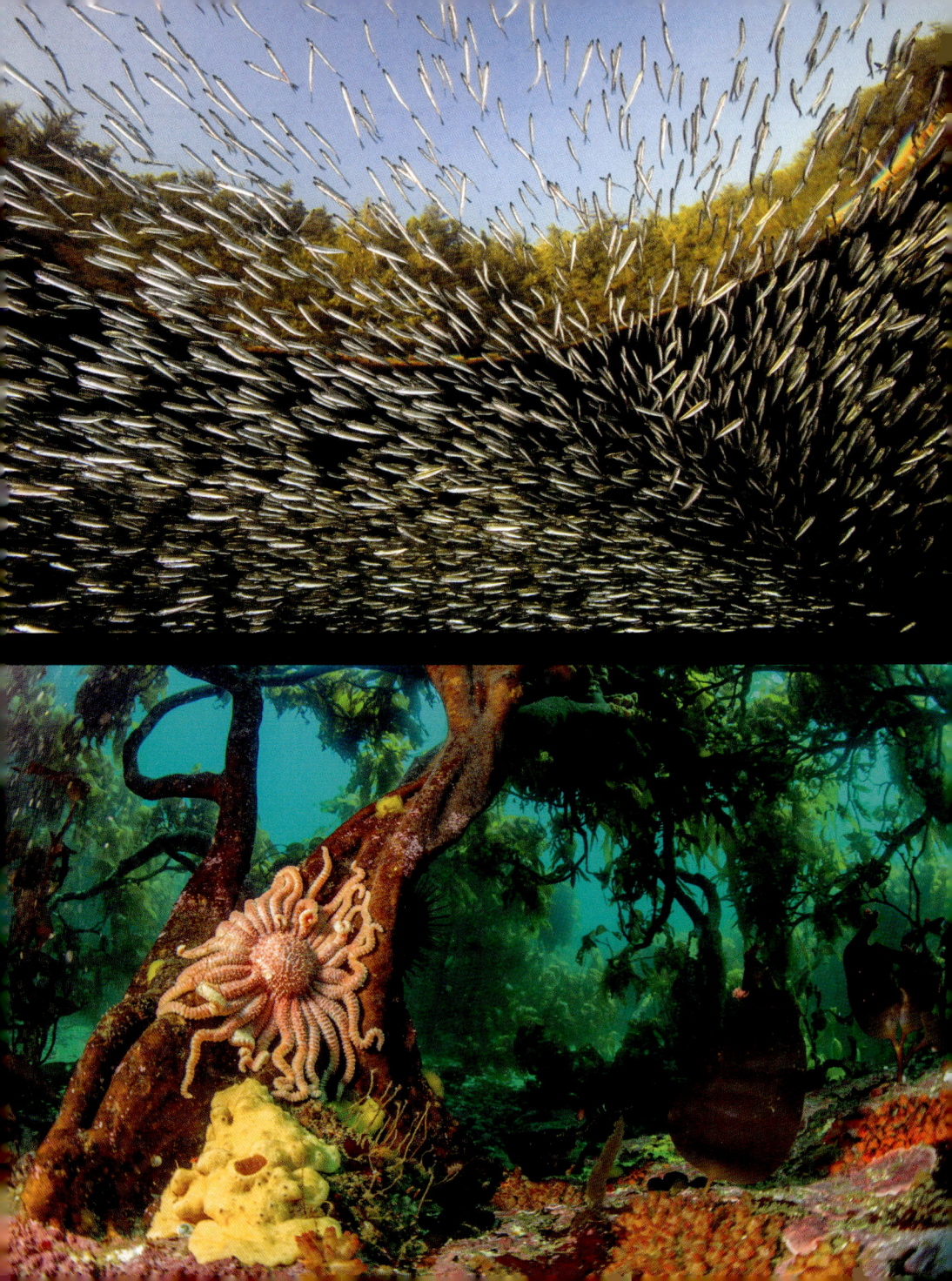

Magical, mysterious worlds

Falling in love with underwater ecosystems

How does anyone end up doing anything in life? Is it by intent or chance? Or perhaps it's a combination of decision-making and luck.

I studied marine biology at university in the hope of one day returning to the Arctic, a place I loved deeply, as a research scientist. I knew I would do something someday to do with protecting the Arctic, and the only obvious choice at the time was to go to university, study for a degree in marine biology, become a biologist, and go back and do scientific research about the animals I had grown up respecting, loving, admiring and wanting to help.

During my second year, I saw a poster outside the library advertising scuba diving training. 'Wow, really?' I thought. 'I can become a diver? I can learn to scuba dive?' I hadn't thought it was something available to me. But I enquired, and sure enough, for $120 (£90) I could take a four-month course to become a certified scuba diver. At that moment, I was bitten by the underwater bug. I knew I was on a path to explore underwater worlds.

Top: Pacific herring, Vancouver Island, Canada, 2004.
Bottom: Sun star, Falkland Islands, 2014.

I didn't know at that point I was going to be a photographer or that I would be bringing the oceans to the rest of the world through the pages of *National Geographic*. All I knew was that I was obsessed with the concept and thought of diving.

I needed an underwater camera and had only one in my sights: a Nikonos V with a 20mm lens. I also wanted to buy an SB-102 flash. The jobs I proceeded to do and the long hours I worked to earn the money to buy the camera underlines just how obsessed I was about becoming a diver and photographing underwater.

The kit cost around $10,000 (£7,500). 'How am I going to get 10 grand?' I thought. I moved to the Arctic to Yellowknife, Northwest Territories, and got a job in construction. I was part of an underground pipeline team. I had the lowest-ranking job. I also did night shifts checking and refuelling machinery.

I worked long shifts of 12 to 14 hours. That summer, I ended up doing 70 days straight. It was a company record. That's how badly I wanted the camera. Part of my job involved crawling around in a muddy ditch, connecting pipes, and on at least one occasion, I had to deal with raw sewage. But I stuck it out, and at the end of those long weeks, I went back to university and bought a Nikonos V, a strobe and a couple of lenses. I was nervous about taking the camera on its first dive. It sat on my shelf for weeks until finally, one night, I resolved to take the plunge.

My friends watched me get the kit ready. They knew how excited and obsessed I was about diving with the camera. I prepared the O-rings (the seals that keep the water out when the underwater housing is closed), which need to be lubricated to make the seal. What I didn't know was that one of my friends had been mucking around with the O-rings and had put the main body ring back on a different shelf so I didn't see it, and set up my kit without it. When I jumped into the ocean, I watched as my brand-new camera filled up with water.

I was back to square one. I had to begin the process of saving money all over again to get the camera repaired. But I managed to get the damaged camera fixed, and from then on, underwater photography became an obsession. The camera and I were inseparable.

" I was nervous about taking the camera on its first dive. It sat on my shelf for weeks until finally, one night, I resolved to take the plunge."

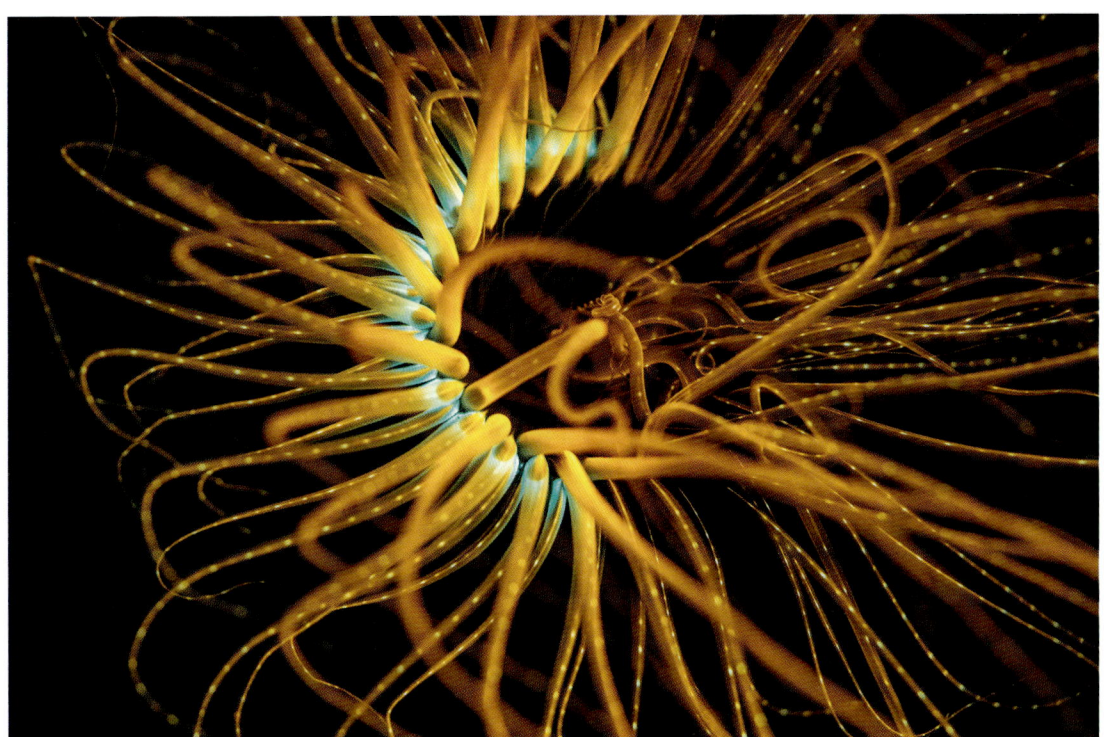

Above: An anemone under
bio-fluorescent lighting,
Indonesia, 2025.

When people remark how 'easily' things have happened for me,
I think back to moments like that. It was a setback I certainly could
have done without, but an experience from which I learned a great
deal about overcoming adversity.

When it came to my studies, I was just about maintaining a passing
average. (I was spending every possible minute diving.) At that time,
my journey in life was underwater.

One of my professors, a world authority in invertebrate biology,
would talk about various species and the ecosystem along the
British Columbia coast. He'd do drawings on the board – sketches of
barnacles, anemones and different species that make up this beautiful
marine ecosystem.

One day, I came in with a bunch of Kodachrome slides. I went over
to my professor. 'I have pictures of some of the things you've been
talking about,' I said. The photographs weren't very good – they were
poorly exposed, and some of them were out of focus – but to see my

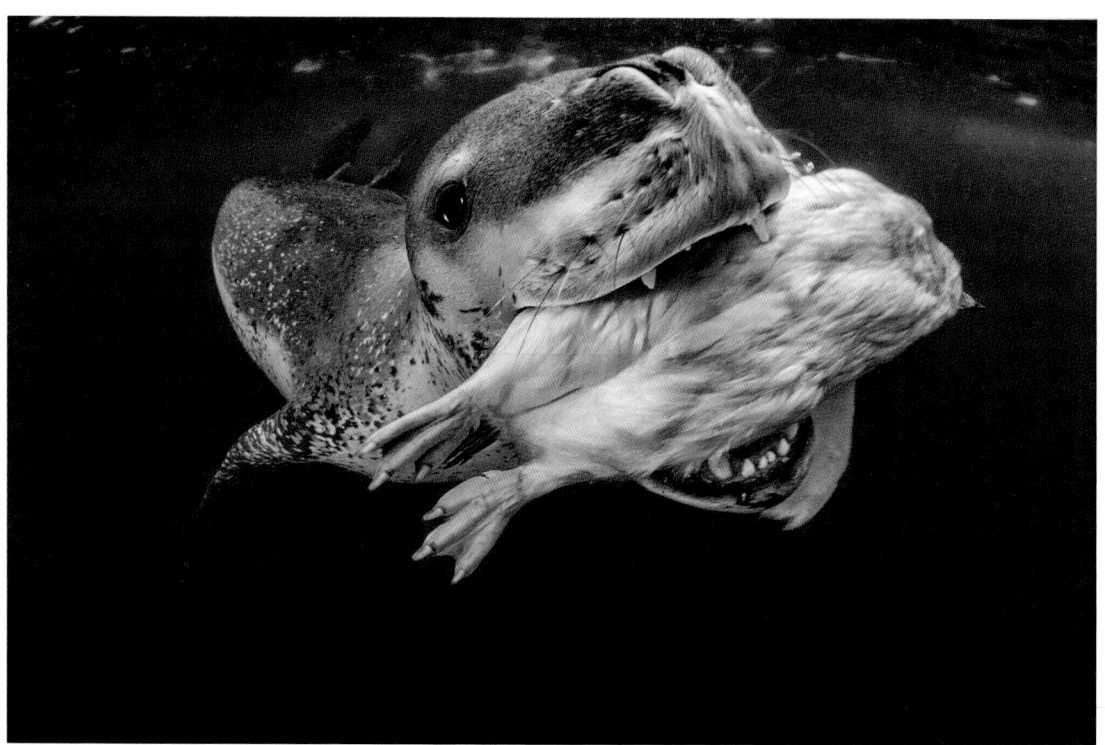

Above: A leopard seal
offering a penguin as food,
Ross Sea, Antarctica, 2006.

professor's excitement was amazing. I felt a sense of purpose. To be able to inspire a great authority on invertebrate biology through images, to show what the ecosystem we had been talking about was like using photography, was a defining moment in my journey as a photographer.

I ended up shooting a large body of work about the underwater world in British Columbia, Canada. I remember sitting my father down and showing him about 80 of my best images. I was looking for praise, for validation. At the end of the slideshow, when the lights came on, he said he had never seen a bigger waste of time and money in his life. It was a crushing moment. But that's how you find out how much you want something – when you experience a knock but refuse to let it derail you. Fast forward some two decades of me photographing with *National Geographic*, and you could hardly find any wall space in my dad's house for all the images of mine he had, he was so proud.

I still love photographing underwater to this day. I've photographed subjects including seals in the Falkland Islands, walruses in Nunavut, Canada, and comb jellies in Alaska. One of my favourite underwater subjects is the kelp off Tofino, British Columbia. Kelp, a fast-growing tissue, is one of the most important carbon sinks in the environment. Photographing kelp is a study in poetry and beauty. It is like an underwater rainforest – so many different creatures live within.

My typical underwater kit includes a Sony A1 camera, which produces 50-megapixel files and allows me to shoot 8K video. I want my images to be big, beautiful, and to endure. I want to invite people into my images and videos, so they need to be powerful. Sometimes I'll shoot 'half and half' or 'split' images to show how the world above water and the world below are connected. Half-and-half images are a great way to give the viewer a sense of multiple, dynamic, interconnected worlds in a single frame.

I'll tend to use a wide-angle lens. I'm not usually a fan of fisheye lenses because they can skew the horizon, but if you keep the lens perfectly level, they can be a great choice for split images. Another good option is a 12–24mm lens so you can zoom in and out. I'll tend to work at around 16mm on that lens, which gives a better result than shooting at 16mm on a 16–35mm lens. I might go to 14mm at a push, but that is as wide as I'll go on a 12–24mm to avoid blurry corners.

The camera sits in the underwater housing. I'll check it's locked in correctly and attach the lens, making sure it's on nice and tight, and then put on the dome part of the housing with an extender, to make sure the lens is the correct distance away from the glass. I'll check everything is lined up and then give it a shake to double-check nothing is loose. I've had domes come off underwater, and if that happens, the camera is instantly unusable. It's an expensive, frustrating and sad situation to find yourself in.

I'll plug in an HDMI cable so I can use an HD monitor. It's hard to look through a little viewfinder when you're bobbing up and down, but with a screen, you can more easily see the scene come together. There are times I use it and times I don't (it creates a lot of drag). I'll take it off when

> " I want my images to be big, beautiful, and to endure. I want to invite people into my images and videos, so they need to be powerful."

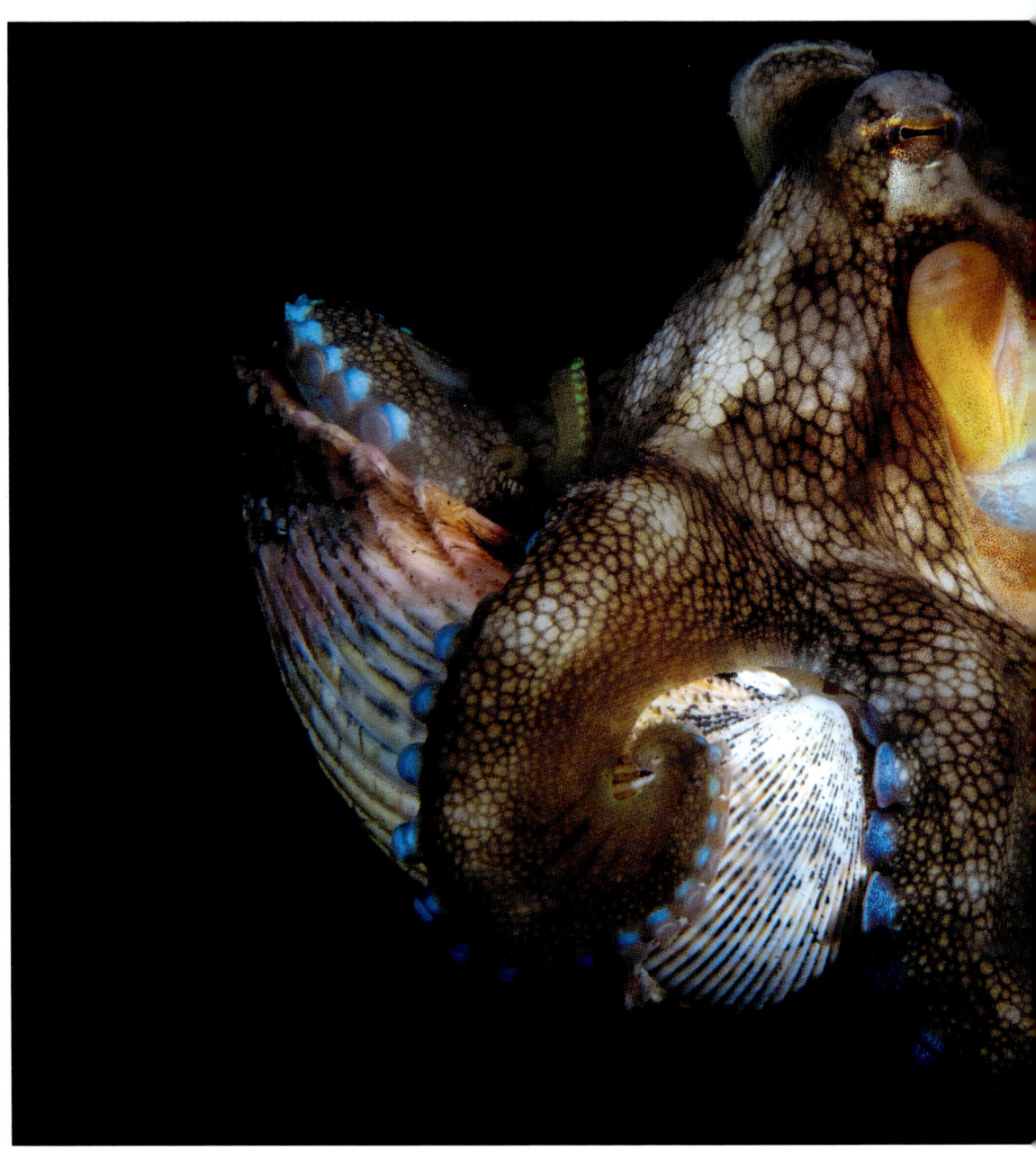

" I use flashes underwater, or sometimes
constant light sources which give
a nice quality of light and help me to see
what I'm photographing or filming."

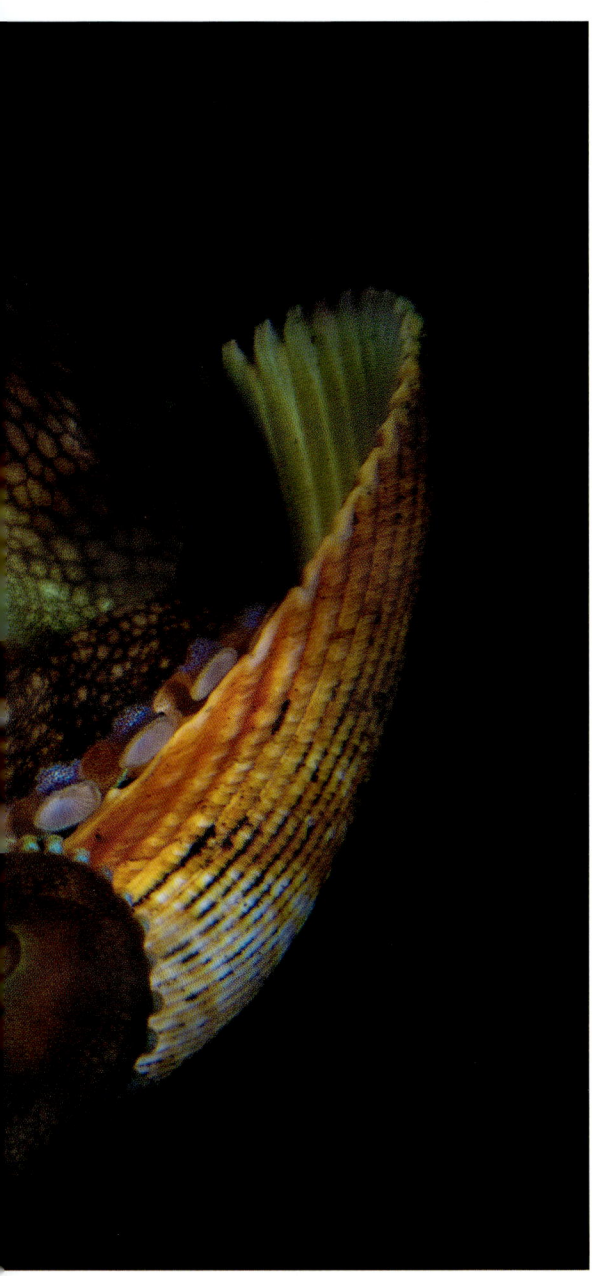

Above: A coconut octopus comes out of its shell, Indonesia, 2025.
Overleaf: Fur seals in a kelp forest, Falkland Islands, 2014.

I'm free diving, for example, but it's nice to have when you're shooting video. It's almost impossible to shoot video underwater without a monitor. You can get away without one for stills.

All of the buttons, dials and functions I need are readily accessible – for example, my ISO settings, focus mode (AF-C), preview and so on. I'll start with the camera set to ISO 400 and f/8, shooting RAW, as I would for any other scenario, and then adjust as I need to from there.

I'll make sure the O-rings are clean – they should be lubricated every other dive or so. You don't want any sand or grit or any other kind of detritus getting in because it could cause the housing to flood with water. Then I'll attach the camera back, checking it's on tight.

I use flashes underwater, or sometimes constant light sources, which give a nice quality of light and help me to see what I'm photographing or filming. I'll position the lights neatly on either side of the camera, so they are balanced – I don't want lens flare coming into my dome. I'll get everything set up before going into the water, so I don't have to make too many adjustments when I'm diving.

Photographing underwater brings me as much enjoyment as it did when I started all those years ago. I love capturing the fragility and beauty of underwater worlds, finding new ways to show these places to others, and connecting people to our oceans through stories.

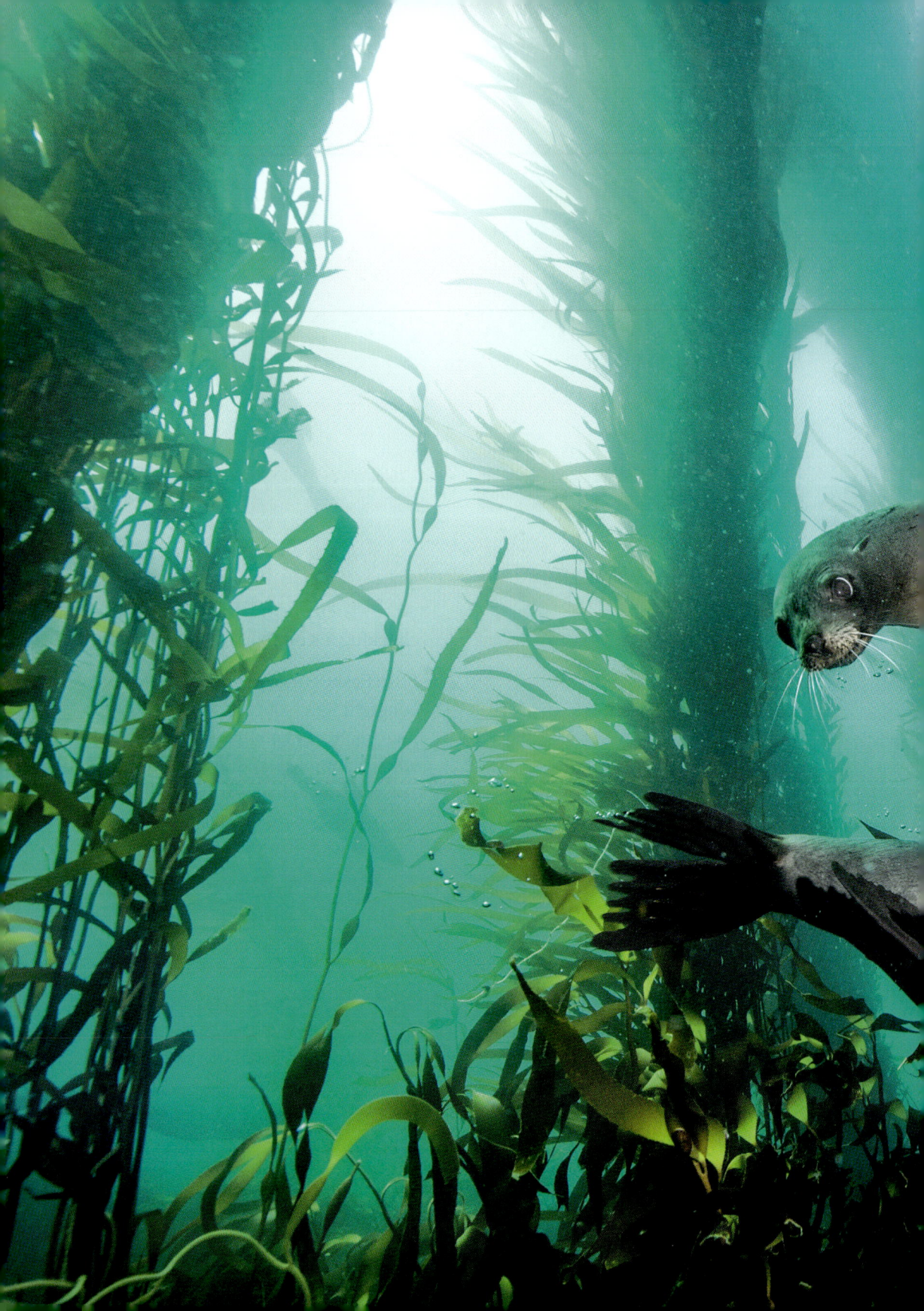

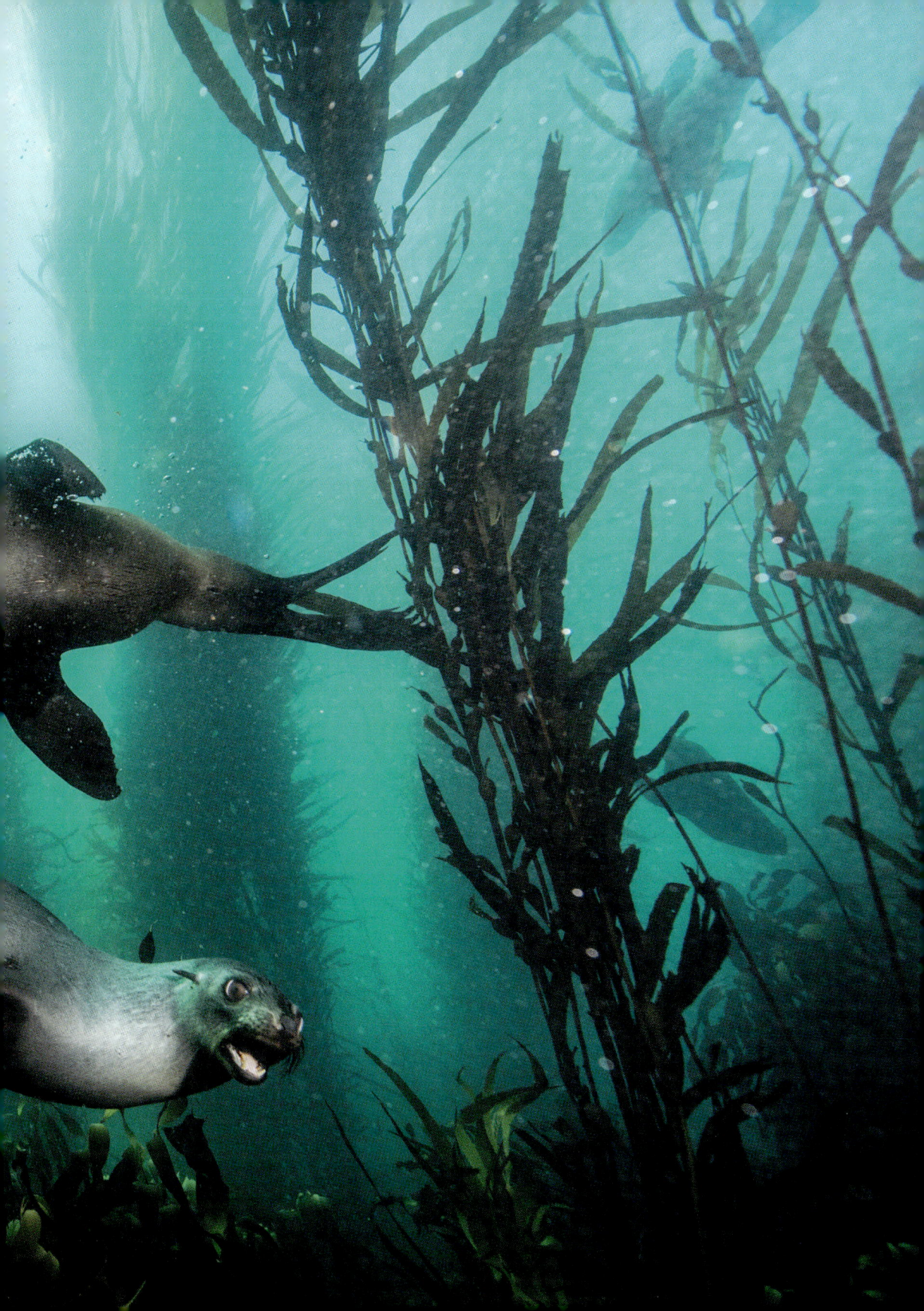

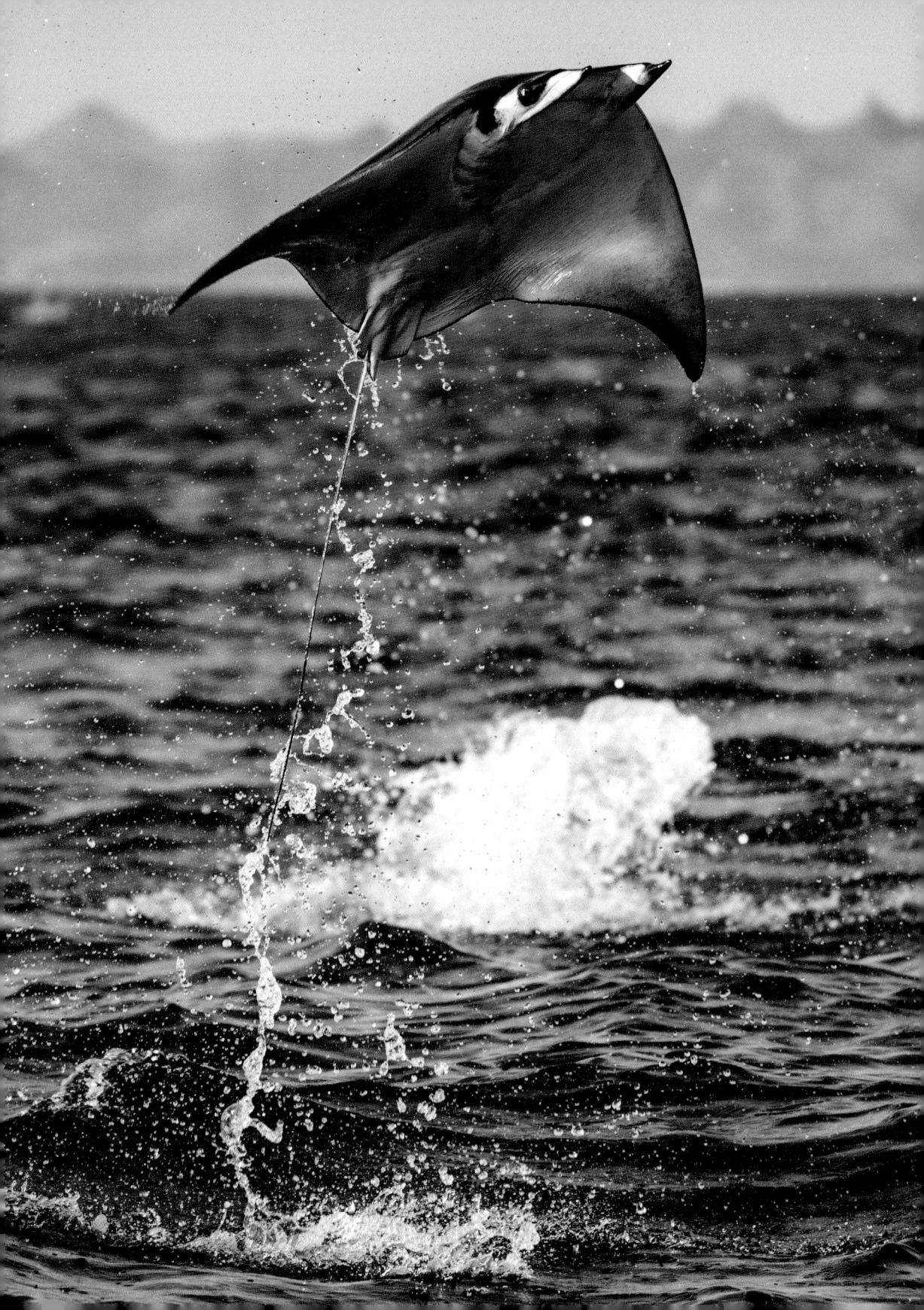

16

The art of editing

Give your work shape and meaning

O ne of the most important aspects of photography, at least for me, is the editing process. It's an opportunity to review my work and select images that will work in a series and as standalone images.

When I was on assignment for *National Geographic*, the editor would go through everything I'd shot and narrow the images down to 5,000, 2,000, 1,000. At that point, I would go to the magazine's headquarters, and we would edit together.

I would also always do my own edit of every shoot, every story. *National Geographic* editors are among the most skilled in the world; they're good at knowing what the best pictures are for their magazine. However, I am the artist, the journalist, the person who is out shooting my vision, chasing something, so I need to take time to review and select my best images for myself.

Going through your work is not something everybody enjoys doing. Most photographers, I'll wager, would rather be out making pictures than looking at tens of thousands of files on a screen. I'm no different – I don't want to be stuck at my computer any more than the next photographer. But editing is part of the job of being a photographer. And it can be fun.

Left: A mobula ray leaps into the air, Baja California, Mexico, 2024.

The best part about it is that every time you edit, you learn about yourself, about the craft of photography, your photographic equipment, the subject matter, the location, and so on. As you're looking at your imagery, you're not just looking for the perfect image; you're gaining information. You're figuring out what worked and what didn't, what you can improve next time. It's a chance to be self-reflective, another important part of being a photographer.

Editing is also a useful process if you're planning on going back to a place to try to nail a certain shot you didn't get first time around; it's a chance to spot the gaps in a story and plan how you will do things differently on the next trip (Chapter 7).

After a shoot, I'll pull all the images into Photo Mechanic. For the initial cull, I'll do a first pass of the 10,000 images, for example. At this stage, I don't think too much. I'll go through everything extremely quickly and give each image a star rating. I'll err on the side of keeping the image. If it's remotely in focus, remotely sharp, reasonably acceptable, I'll keep it. It gets one star. Consequently, I have a very fat first edit. After the first cut, I end up with around 7,000 images – so, I have around a 70-per cent keeper rate.

I want to see the entire shoot once. I am not sitting there looking for perfect moments. In fact, I never go to my five-star images first. It's risky. You might miss incredible moments, moments that only reveal themselves if you sit there and look for long enough. The best part about doing the one-to-five-star process is that you get to look at all the best images up to five times, and each time, there is a chance you'll see an image in a new way. Images can – and do – grow on you.

I've had images I shot for *National Geographic* that I thought were rejects end up running in the magazine. In fact, one image, which I'd initially thought was mediocre, became a cover shot. If I had been only looking for the best images, I would have passed it by and never looked at it again. But through the process of repeated looking, spending time with the images that weren't immediate standouts, the image grew on me. It's also helpful to have breaks between looking at images to refresh your eye.

I use Photo Mechanic because it allows me to quickly go through everything I've shot once. I'll then take my two-star images into Adobe Lightroom. At this point, I'll start

"I'll go through everything quickly and give a star rating."

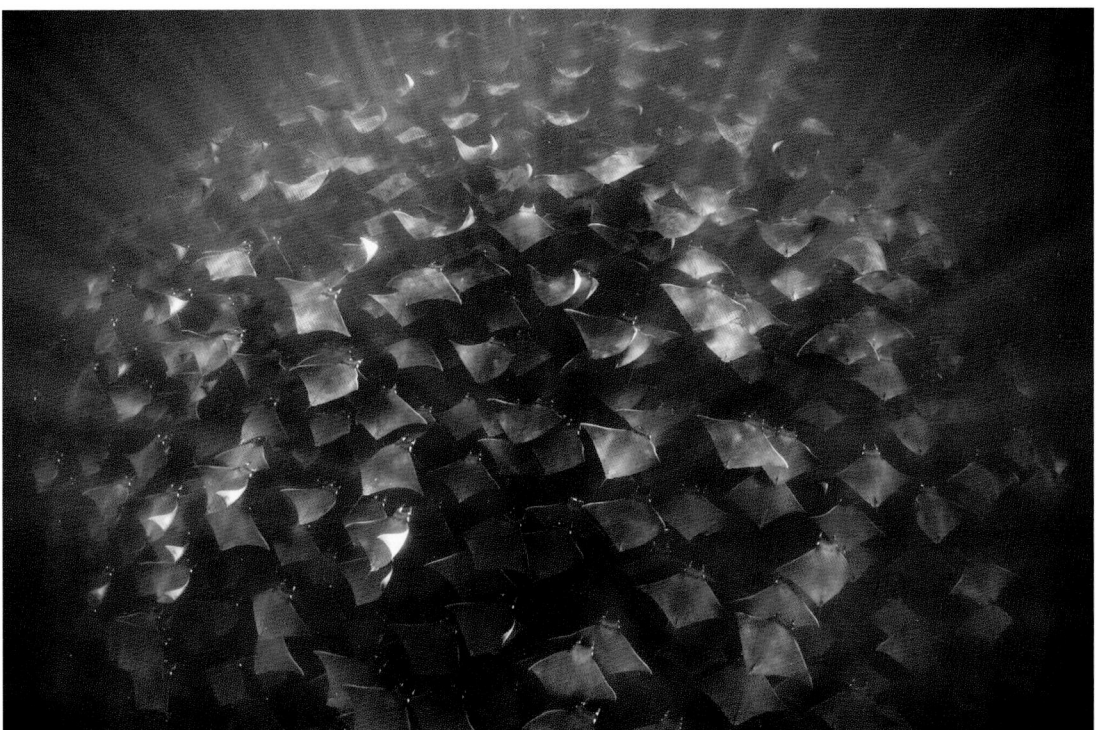

Above: A fever of mobula rays,
Baja California, Mexico, 2024.
Overleaf: A mobula ray jumping
out amongst a fever, Baja
California, Mexico, 2024.

trying things out, sketching, dabbling, playing. For example, if the image is sharp, and it's interesting, I might want to see how it looks in black and white (Chapter 13). I might use the Dehaze feature or the Clarity feature to adjust the contrast in the midtones. I might play with the blacks, up the whites a little, play around with the exposure and contrast, before deciding whether to make the image three stars or not.

Let's take a shoot I did of mobula rays in the Sea of Cortez in Mexico's Baja California peninsula. When I was going through the images, I was looking for shots that had something about them. I tried different things when I was in the water – for example, swimming behind the rays, and shooting down on them. There were also beautiful light rays in the water that day. Turning the images into black and white made the rays (both kinds) pop.

The next spread is a standout image for me, where one ray stands out among thousands of others. The ray is in the air just off to the side, and so compositionally, the image works. There is a nice mood too.

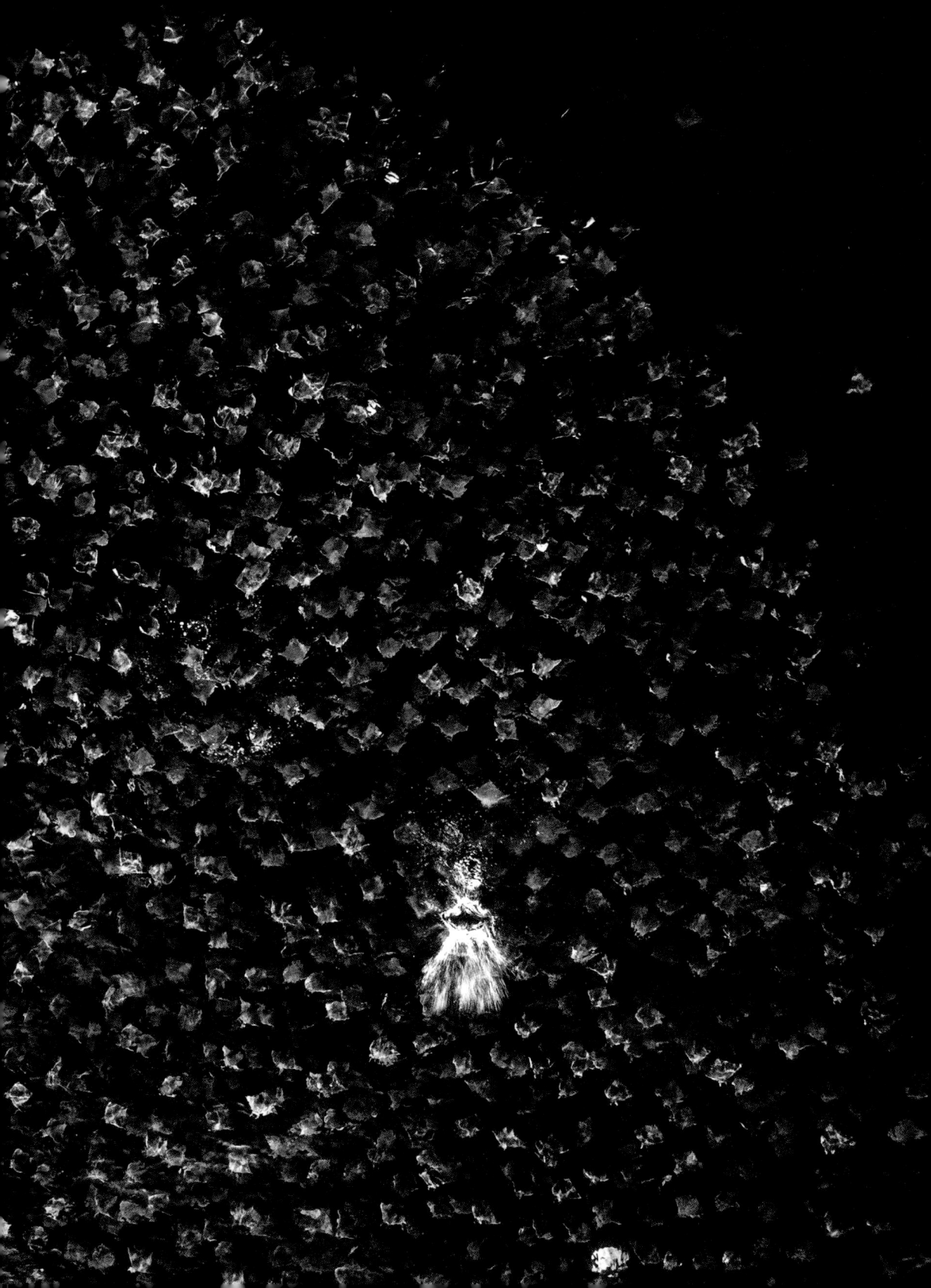

I can use these kinds of images for conservation purposes because they are eye-catching, but they also tell you something about the animal behaviour.

Sometimes photography is about simplicity – stripping things back compositionally. When there is a lot going on, it can be good to back off a bit. This top image was taken with a drone on a calm day. Several mobula rays are chasing a female just under the glassy surface of the Sea of Cortez. This is what's called a 'courtship vortex', where the rays are in a mating ritual. They are engaging in a beautiful circle dance. Shots like that, which get into the behavioural aspect of the animal, are really special to me.

So, as you can hopefully tell, as I'm carefully reviewing my images, I'll look for standout features, think about which images might work for the different areas of my business (Chapter 19), and weigh up whether any will work in black and white (Chapter 13).

I'll sit on my five-star images for weeks or even months before going back to them. Then, when reviewing them again, I'll wait to have an emotional reaction, for an image to excite me.

One of the 10,000 might become a fine art piece, but that will take time. I'll share any I think could work as fine art prints with my friend and former colleague Ken Geiger, a Pulitzer Prize-winning photographer and former deputy director of photography at *National Geographic*, who'll work on the images, preparing the files for print.

Editing isn't an exact science, and there is no right or wrong way to approach it. When you first look at your work, trust your heart, trust your gut. Don't overthink things. When you're reviewing what you've shot, turn off your 'analytical' brain, dial down those critical voices, the doubt, and lose yourself in the artistic process.

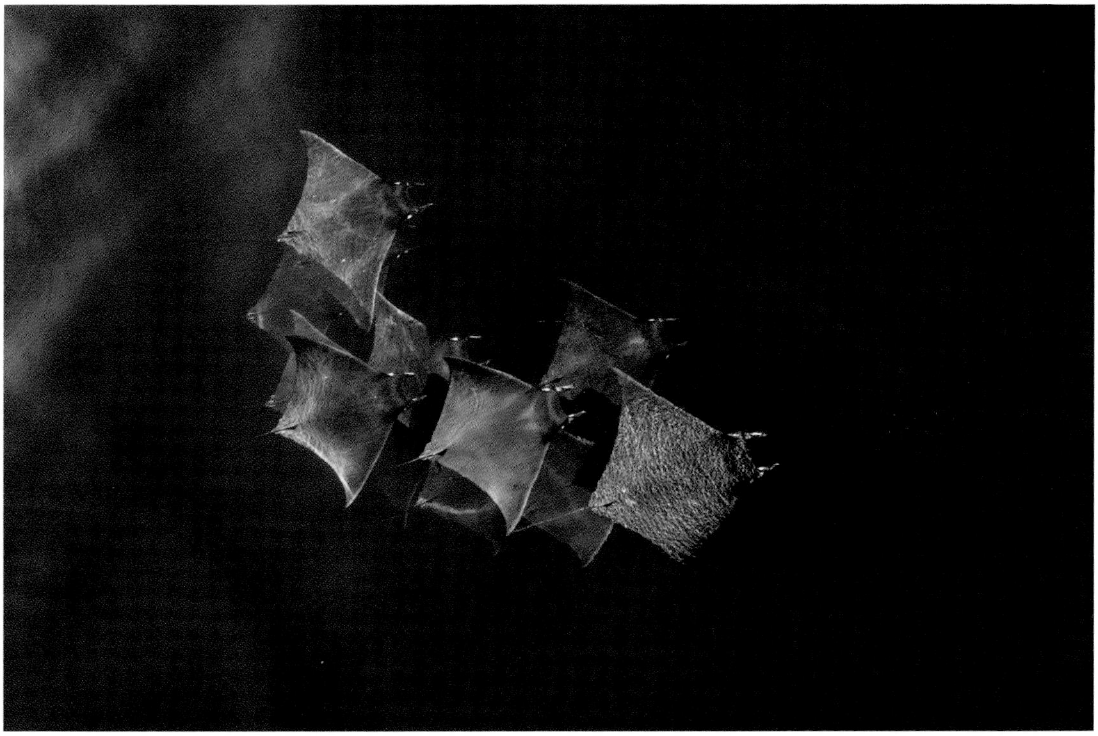

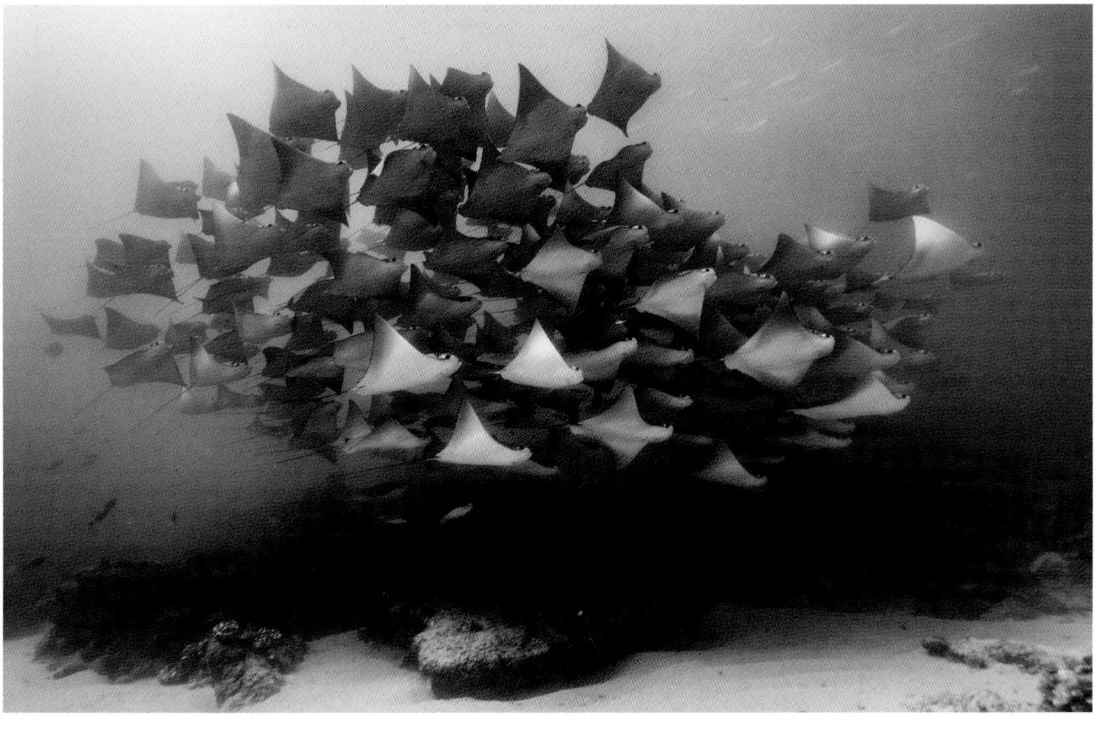

Top: Mobula rays move through the water, Baja California, Mexico, 2024.
Bottom: A fever of mobula rays, Baja California, Mexico, 2024.

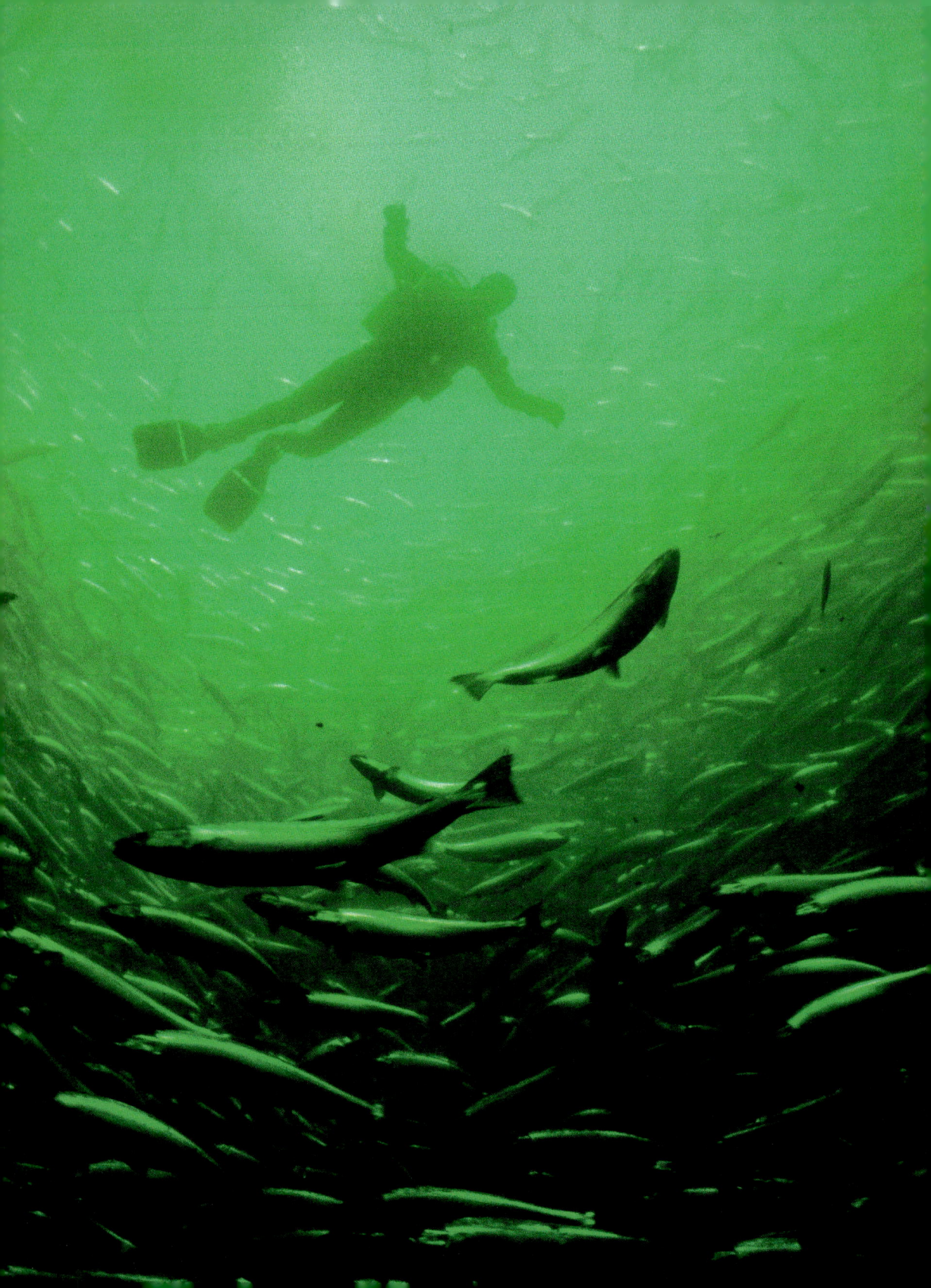

17

If at first you don't succeed . . .

Use experiences to develop your image-making

I would love to tell you about all the mistakes I've made as a photographer, but we only have a finite number of pages, and I would fill them all. That said, I hope that by sharing a few of my slip-ups, you'll be in a stronger position than I was when I started out, as you embark on your own journey in and through photography.

When I started photographing underwater, I was using an analogue camera – a Nikonos V. I was working manually, including focusing, controlling my flash and setting the exposure. There was a lot that could go wrong, and quite often, it did. I made a lot of mistakes, I failed a lot, but all of that helped me to better understand the nuts and bolts of photography – f-stops, shutter speeds, ISOs, flash power settings and so on.

I learned to use 'mistakes' as opportunities to develop my knowledge. I would obsess over camera settings. I remember doing tests at home – I'd practise adjusting my flash power and taking shots at different settings before sending the film away to be processed. After three weeks, I'd get it back and cross-reference the results with my notes. Practising various techniques in this way, on dry land, helped me to hone my photography skills for when I was in the water.

Left: A diver descends into a vortex of 50,000 farmed salmon to check nets, Vancouver Island, British Columbia, Canada, 2001.

I was learning something new every time I got a roll of film back. It was a gift to receive those boxes in the mail. I learned to envisage how I wanted my images to be before drawing them on paper and going after them single-mindedly. I would spend hours, and sometimes dozens of dives, trying to perfect a certain image.

A risk when working digitally is the instant gratification; seeing images as you go can make you think you've got the shot – it makes you settle for less. The danger is you will think, 'It's in focus, it's exposed, that's good enough.' Taking time to reflect on your work – what worked, what didn't – along with rigorous self-critique, can be helpful to keep progressing, to keep pushing yourself creatively.

My friends at *National Geographic* joke that I've taken a hard path to get to where I am because I did everything wrong. The first big assignment I did for the magazine didn't go to plan; at least, not straight away. I was doing a story on Atlantic salmon. My first question was, 'how many species are there?' The people in the room looked at me and smiled. There is only one. My heart sank. I realized how clueless I was, how little I knew about Atlantic salmon. I was young and inexperienced but determined to succeed. I'd been given my first opportunity, and I was not going to mess it up.

National Geographic is a terrifying magazine to work for. The bar is so high, and there is no room for excuses. The editors reminded us of this all the time – we publish images, they said, not excuses. And it was true: it didn't matter what happened on an assignment, you had to come back with the goods; you had to deliver.

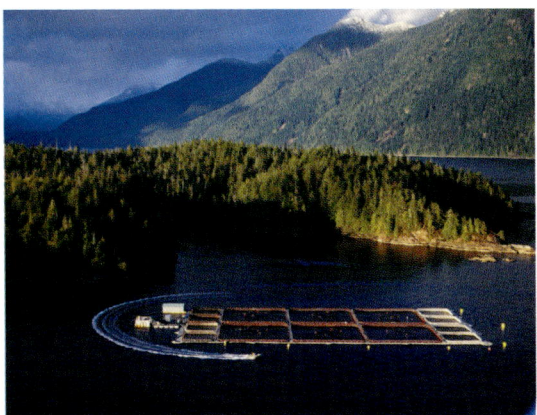

I had 12 weeks to shoot the assignment over a two-year period. *National Geographic* had given me enough money for two weeks of research. That might seem like a lot of time, but for that story, I researched for four months. I called every scientist, every fisherman, everyone I could. I ended up with 600 contacts in nine countries before I'd even started thinking about the pictures I wanted to make. I left no stone unturned.

> " I made a lot of mistakes, I failed a lot, but all of that helped me to better understand the nuts and bolts of photography."

I made sure I was in good physical shape and got to work. There were many directions I could take the story in. I could have done a story with a heavy focus on how Atlantic salmon fish farming was taking over in places, including off the coast of Norway, Ireland, Scotland, British Columbia and New Brunswick. The story could have been about Atlantic salmon escaping from fish farms and the impact on wild salmon populations. It was a diverse and complex topic.

Being the type of person I am, I decided to do all of it. I tried to find ways I could stretch my budget so I could get more done. For example, I didn't hire any assistants; I tried to do it all myself. I've always worked alone and stretched my money as far as possible.

I had been photographing in British Columbia – I was given permission to dive in the Atlantic salmon fish farm pens, which nobody else was given access to – and the next phase of my journey was to go to Ireland to photograph fishermen as they went out in the morning, to compare what they were doing with the commercial fishing industry.

I remember landing at Shannon Airport. I had 20 cases of equipment, each weighing 70 pounds (32kg). I loaded my gear into a van, pulled away and went the wrong way round the roundabout, blocking traffic in the process. Luckily for me, a kind gentleman got out of his car and helped me to get back on track.

Several months went by, and I was steamrolling through film. Half my budget was gone. I sent what I'd shot so far to my editor at the time – Bert Fox, an award-winning photo editor. I couldn't wait for his report. I was on a river in Quebec trying to photograph salmon underwater when the phone rang. It was Bert. He said, 'Paul, I've looked through your film and I want you to know how disappointed I am.' I sat at the side of the road and started to cry. I called my mentor, Joel Sartore, who called Bert. 'Yeah, it's not good, you're failing at this assignment,' Joel said. I asked Bert what would happen. 'Well, you're under contract, but you'll likely never work for the magazine again. We may pull you off the assignment, I'm not sure, but keep shooting what you're shooting for now.' So I kept going.

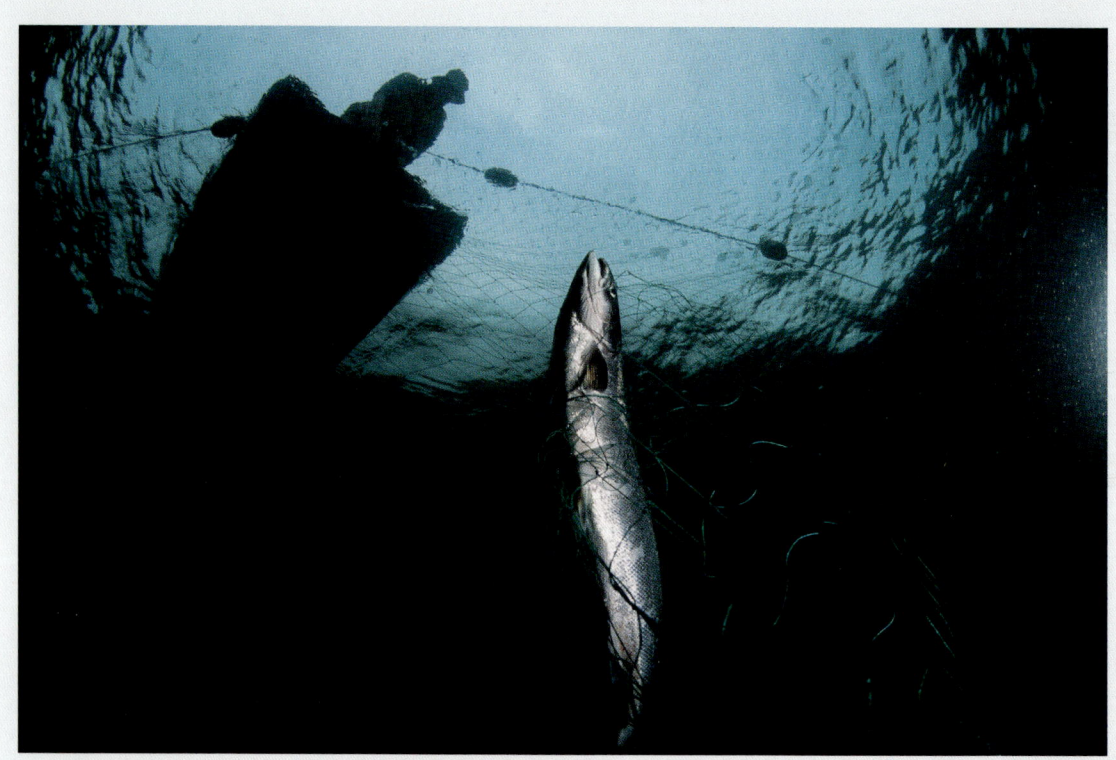

Above: A fisherman in a currach retrieves an Atlantic salmon, Achill Island, Ireland, 2001.
Right: A determined 2–6 pound grilse makes his way through the water, Quebec, Canada, 2001.

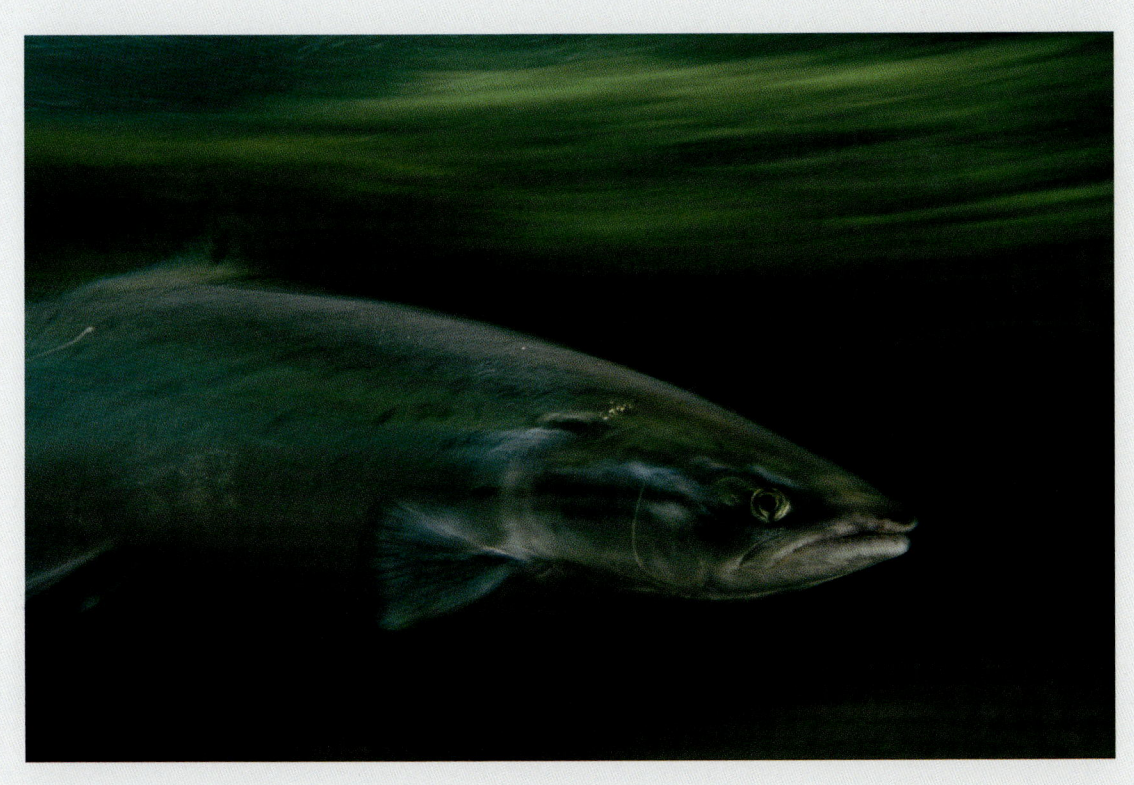

Fast forward a year and a half, and I was sitting down with editor-in-chief Bill Allen and other editors at *National Geographic*. I knew it was probably the last time I'd be in their company. I was nervous, trembling, and got a little wordy. Bill Allen is famous for cutting people off if they're talking too much. 'This is a unique moment of . . .' *Click*, I was cut off. (Bill had the remote control and was controlling the slideshow.) It kept happening. I was sweating, and the room started to spin; I thought I was going to black out.

The lights came up. Well, this has been fun, I thought. At least I tried. 'My take,' said Bill, 'is that this coverage is strong, so we can publish it now. It's good enough to publish the 14-page story it's slotted for.' I started to beg. 'I have so much more to do,' I pleaded. 'There are so many things I haven't covered yet, please let me finish this assignment.'

Luckily for me, they did. From there, I got smart. I hired assistants and whatever else I needed to get the story done. I went and finished it in full, came back, and presented the final tray of images.

Instead of a 14-page story, it became a 24-page story and ended up winning first prize in the Nature category at the 2004 World Press Photo Contest for journalistic coverage in wildlife and nature. A bunch of the images went on to win awards at other photo contests.

Bert Fox, who had been as good as telling me that my career was over, patted me on the back and said, 'I knew you had it all along, good job.' That's how the editors at *National Geographic* worked. They wanted you to be terrified, to think that each job was your last, because then you would go out there striving to shoot the best work possible.

As you start making images and putting them out to the world – you might be taking images to a magazine, or a newspaper, or sharing them on social media – you're going to feel vulnerable, exposed. Another lesson I've learned is to use rejection as fuel.

" When you taste rejection, use it as fuel to drive you to the next level."

I was twenty-five years old and working as a biologist, but I was falling in love with photography. As I was going out to my research site one day, I saw a porcupine and a tree. It was a beautiful sight – the most amazing situation I have ever shot. Beautiful white snow had lit up the porcupine in the tree. When I got the slides back, I went to a local magazine in Yellowknife, Northwest Territories.

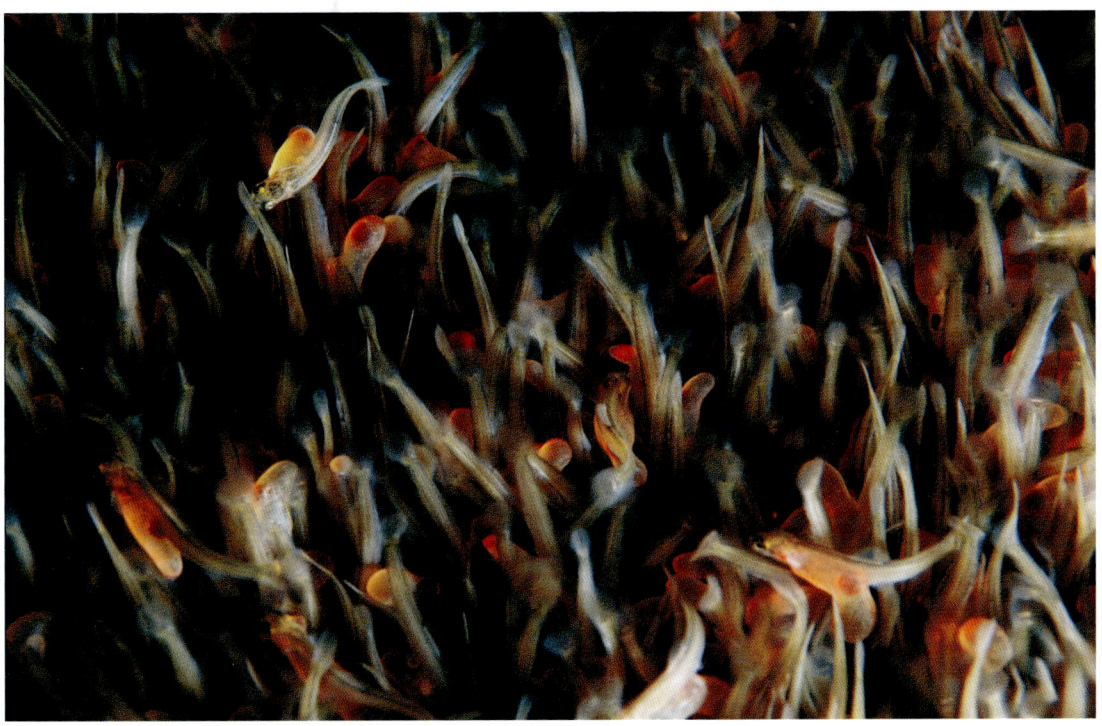

Above: A close view of a group of alevins – recently hatched Atlantic salmon, Vancouver Island, British Columbia, Canada, 2001.

I told them rather presumptuously that I'd shot their next cover. The editor looked at my slides. 'What am I looking at? I can't tell what it is. Why is it overexposed? We can't publish anything that is overexposed. And the eye is completely soft.' I was upset I'd had such a misfire. But rather than letting the rejection take me out, I used it to my advantage – fired up, I vowed to do better next time.

So, when you taste rejection, use it as fuel to drive you to the next level. I've been rejected hundreds of times – whether it's book project proposals or magazine pitches. The editor who dismissed my porcupine images very soon after published images of mine for an article on narwhals, and then for one on polar bears.

You may not get it right the first time; it's likely you will fail over and over, but you're also going to succeed. So don't worry about making mistakes. Think of it as embracing learning curves, because if you learn from a situation that hasn't quite gone to plan, it's been worthwhile; you've no doubt grown as a photographer.

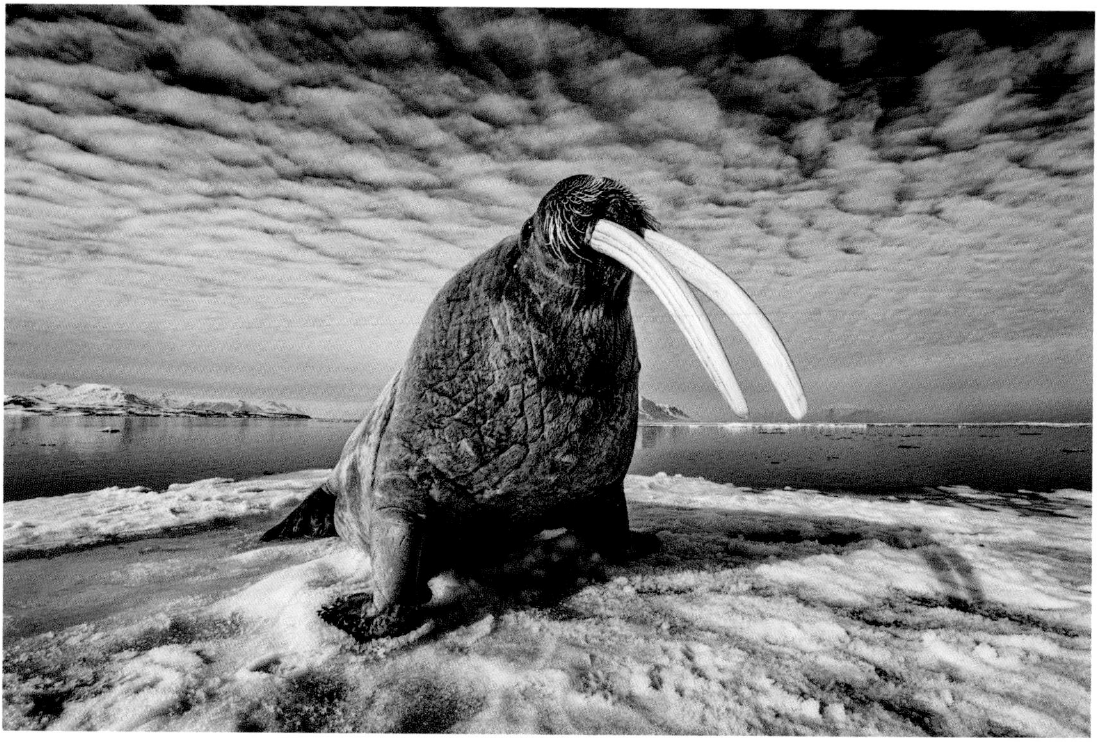

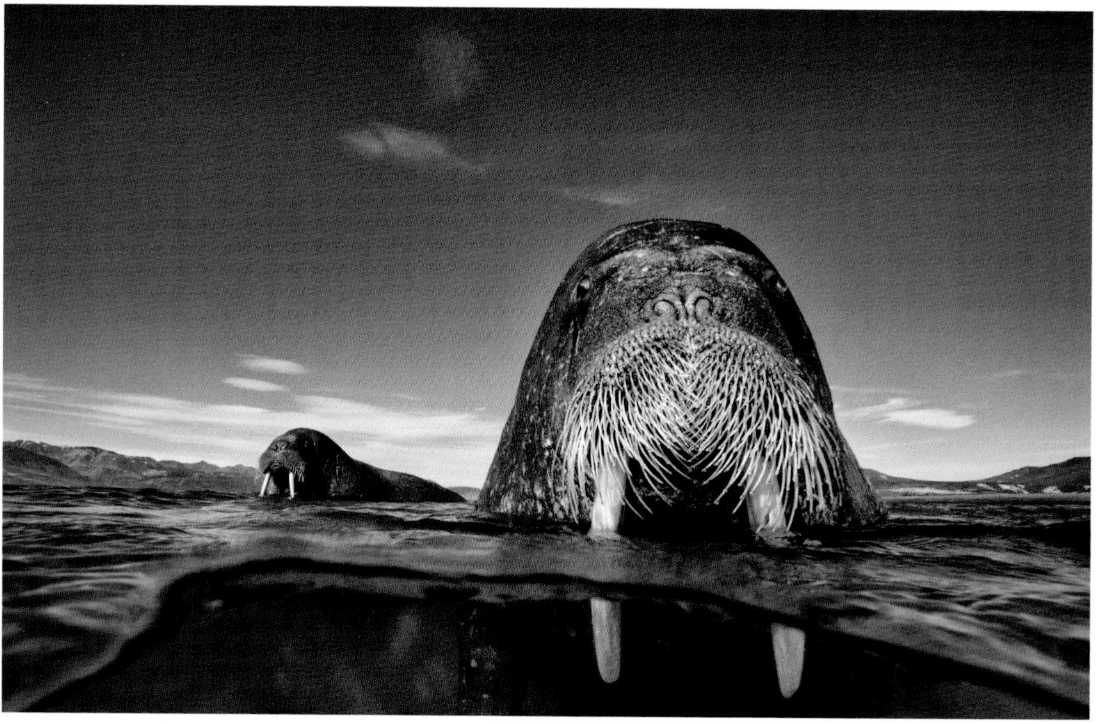

Getting noticed

How I got my break

One of the questions I get asked the most is, 'How do I get a job at *National Geographic*?' I remember asking a similar question thirty-five years ago when I approached *National Geographic* director of photography Kent Kobersteen. How could I shoot for the most famous, most revered magazine in the world, an institution that's been in existence since 1888 and reaches millions of people? It's every photographer's dream, and it was my dream too.

Kent Kobersteen told me he had a team that was like an NFL squad, but unlike in the NFL, there was only one line-up, and it was made up of the best players in the world. The best photographers, underwater photographers, aerial photographers, journalists and explorers all worked for the magazine. Who was I going to replace? Just because I was passionate and dreamed of shooting for *National Geographic*, that didn't mean I would or could. It didn't work like that. Everyone had to earn the right to be on the team with the best of the best in the world.

Even if you got a look in, it didn't mean you would parachute in at the top. *National Geographic* would take photographers and mould them into journalists worthy of shooting regularly for the magazine. There was a core group of photographers who would be booked often – photographers who were good enough, reliable enough and trustworthy enough to do what was required – but very few would end up doing regular work.

Top: *Ice Walker*,
Svalbard, Norway, 2006.
Bottom: *Split World*,
Svalbard, Norway, 2007.

When you shoot for *National Geographic*, you're not just a photographer; you wear multiple hats. The responsibility is massive. You could be gone for a year or two on assignment and spend hundreds of thousands of dollars. You might come back with anywhere from 200 to 700 rolls of film, which the best, most discerning editors in the world would pore over before deciding whether your work was worthy or not of being in the magazine. It was terrifying.

There's the dream and then the reality. Getting to shoot for *National Geographic* requires a huge amount of work and dedication, with a singular focus to fight every day to make it to that end point, that destination – to be able to call yourself a *National Geographic* photographer. And, once you're there, you're only as good as your last story. You are hanging on by a thread all the time. It's never a place of comfort, or a case of resting on your laurels and thinking, 'I've made it'.

The deeper you go into the journey of being a photographer, of doing something as subjective as photography, the more terrifying it becomes. It's a journey full of doubt, insecurity and fear.

You need to be tenacious, to summon the courage to do things you're scared to do. For example, approach people for advice or make yourself known to people who might be able to help you get to where you want to go.

I was around twenty-three years old and photographing in Alaska. I had heard there was a *National Geographic* photographer flying into Katmai National Park. I had to try to meet them, but I was terrified. I couldn't just go up to a *National Geographic* photographer, could I?

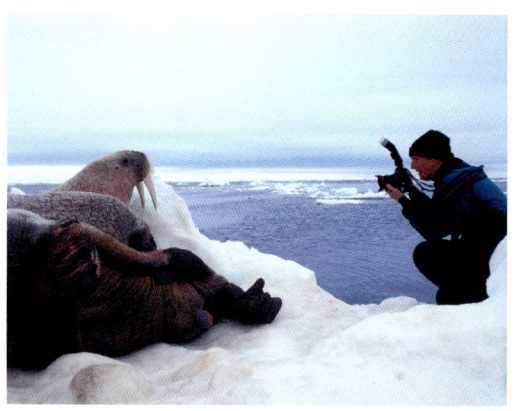

The photographer was Natalie Fobes. She was working on a big piece for *National Geographic* about Alaska, its fisheries and the Bering Sea. I remember introducing myself at the airport. 'Can I help you in any way?' I said. I ended up asking a few questions and even showed her some of my work. Looking back, the pictures I showed her were terrible. But Natalie graciously gave me her time and some honest feedback, which helped to build my confidence.

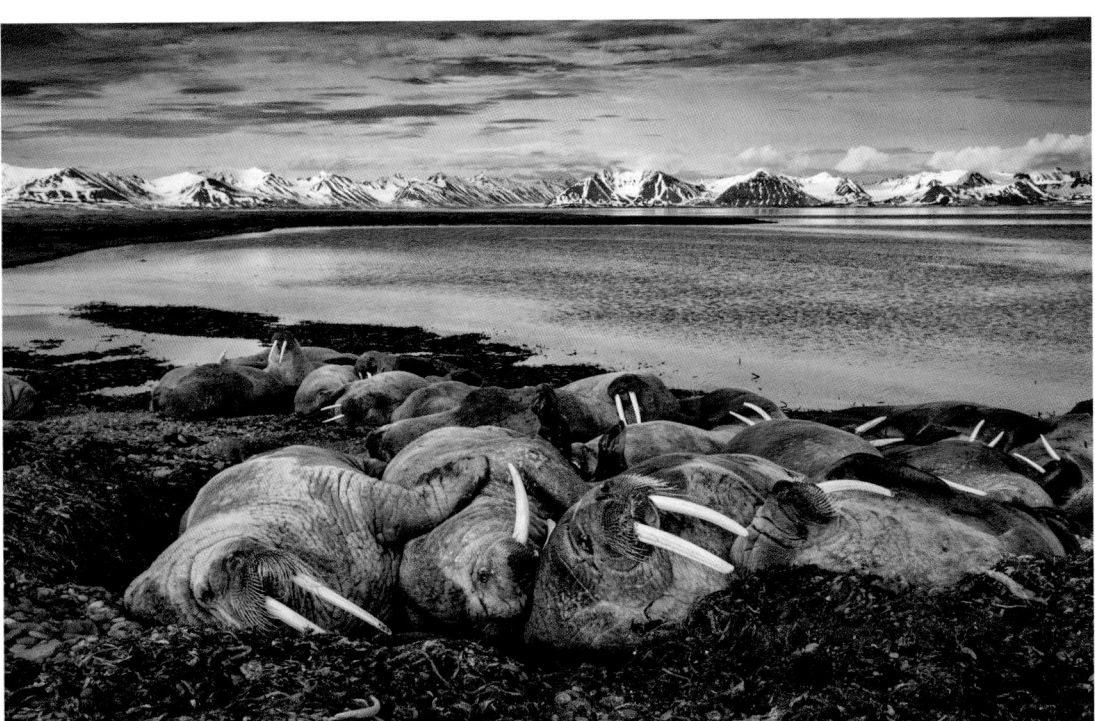

Left: Paul photographs
three Atlantic walruses,
Igloolik, Nunavut, 1997.
Above: *Slumber Party*,
Svalbard, Norway, 2007.

Fast forward another few years, and I ended up meeting my hero, Flip Nicklin, who did, in fact, become a mentor to me. He told me if I ever shot for *National Geographic*, I was likely to fail. Perhaps he was just trying to be realistic. Nonetheless, it was devastating to hear. But just when I felt I had been defeated, that I was never going to make it, I met Joel Sartore, another *National Geographic* legend. He took me under his wing, and we ended up building a beautiful friendship full of camaraderie, helping each other on shoots and so on. I asked questions, tons of questions, and soaked up everything he was telling me.

I was moving in the right direction, but getting established was taking time. I kept chipping away, creating opportunities for myself where I could.

An early chance to get a foot in the door with *National Geographic* didn't quite pan out as I'd hoped. I'd been photographing walruses in the Arctic for a personally funded project and had some images I was

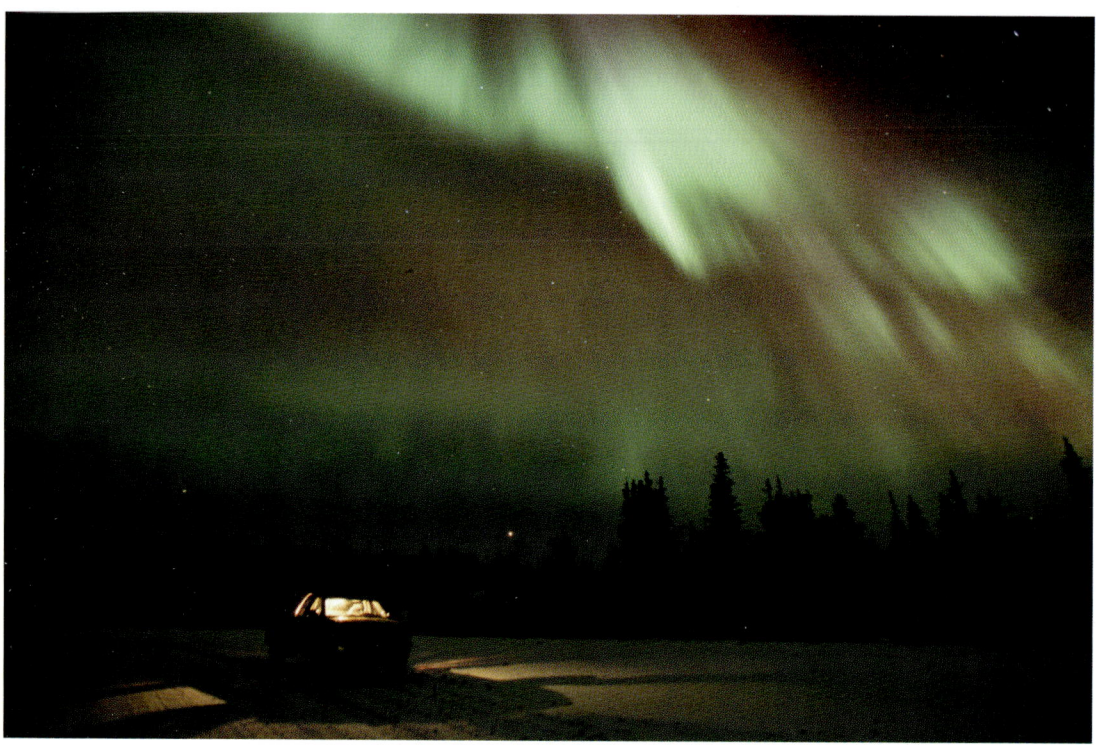

Above: Paul's truck, Yukon, Canada, 1998.

proud of. I shared them with the magazine's editors but was pipped to the post by another photographer. Flip and Joel were encouraging and suggested I try photographing closer to home – not least to keep costs down.

Off I went to photograph sockeye salmon in the Adams River in British Columbia. For three weeks I photographed the fish, including the entire salmon run. On my way home I stopped off at Vancouver Aquarium for a meeting. Devastatingly, someone broke into my van and stole my camera equipment, including 70 rolls of undeveloped film.

Local police told me I'd likely never see my belongings again, but four months later I got a call out of the blue. Park police had found my undeveloped rolls of film, and they were completely fine. No water damage, which was beyond lucky. I flew to *National Geographic*'s headquarters to meet with editors and ended up showing some of the images at a work-in-progress event. I had three minutes to demonstrate to some of the greatest photographers and editors in the world what I could do and what I was about.

It was a terrifying but incredible experience. I had lots of positive comments about the images. A couple of months later, Kent Kobersteen asked me to pick up a story on Atlantic salmon – my first paid assignment for *National Geographic*.

So, being tenacious and bold can really pay off. Create opportunities for yourself and seize them when they happen.

Long before I had a story published in *National Geographic*, as I was trying to get established in the industry, I embarked on a trip that would push my commitment to what I was doing to the limits. Luckily for me, it paid off.

I had just left my job as a biologist and was keen to photograph something I thought would be worthy of the pages of *National Geographic*. I had heard the magazine was doing a story on the aurora borealis. I had some shots of aurora in my portfolio, but none were worthy of the magazine. How could I get noticed?

Anybody can go and shoot a picture of the aurora borealis where you stand under the night sky with your camera shutter open. I needed to shoot something journalistic.

It was January, and minus 35 degrees. I got in my pickup truck and drove 750 miles (1,200km) to Fairbanks, Alaska, from my home in Whitehorse, Yukon, Northern Canada. I went to the Poker Flat Research Range, the largest land-based rocket research range in the world, where NASA was building a rocket to explore the aurora borealis.

In temperatures of minus 45 degrees, I parked my truck under a radio telescope and crawled into my sleeping bag. Every night I photographed the aurora borealis. In the daytime, I met some of the scientists who were working there. After living in my truck for three weeks, the scientists invited me to photograph them building and assembling the rocket. They agreed to pay a nominal fee for my time.

Another month passed, and the rocket was never launched. The conditions hadn't been right.

"Being tenacious and bold can really pay off. Create opportunities for yourself and seize them when they happen."

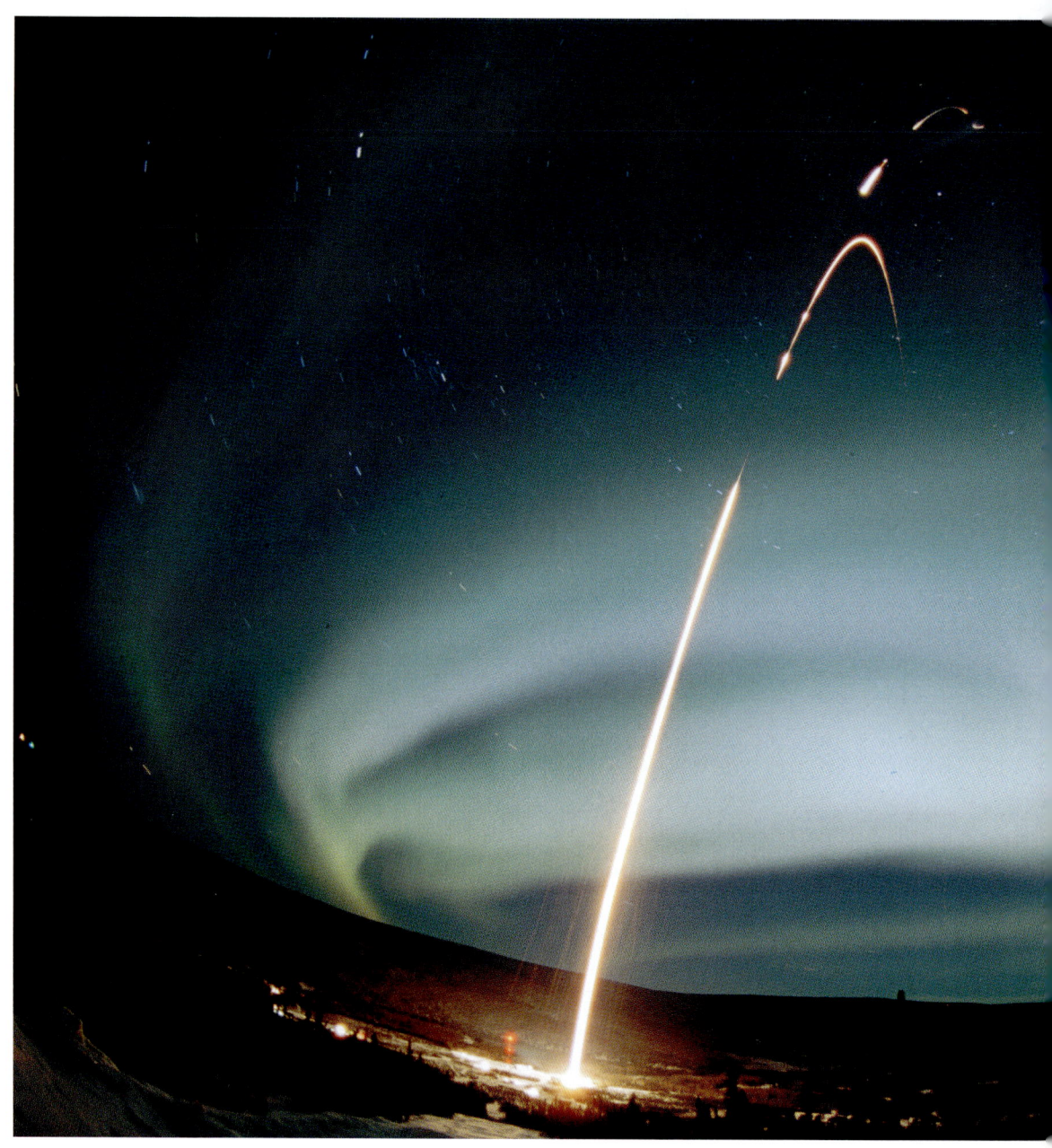

" 'The conditions to launch are perfect,
we're launching the rocket tonight,' they said.
So, without much sleep, I got back in my
truck and drove as fast as I safely could."

Above: Three-minute exposure showing the flight path of the GEODESIC rocket, Poker Flats Research Range, Alaska, USA, 1998.

I packed up my equipment and drove the long 750-mile drive back to Whitehorse, Yukon. At 7 a.m. the next morning, the phone rang. It was the head scientist. 'The conditions to launch are perfect, we're launching the rocket tonight,' they said. So, without much sleep, I got back in my truck and drove as fast as I safely could back to Fairbanks. I arrived there at around 11 p.m., about an hour before the rocket was due to launch.

I set up five cameras. The aurora borealis came dancing across the scene. I have images of the four stages of the rocket booster flying through the aurora borealis. *National Geographic* published one of my images in the magazine.

Although it would be a while before I did my first assignment for the magazine, the experience gave me the boost I desperately needed to push on and make my dreams a reality. Creating opportunities for small wins will propel you on to bigger ones.

Your start will be different to mine, of course, but with perseverance, it will hopefully be as positive.

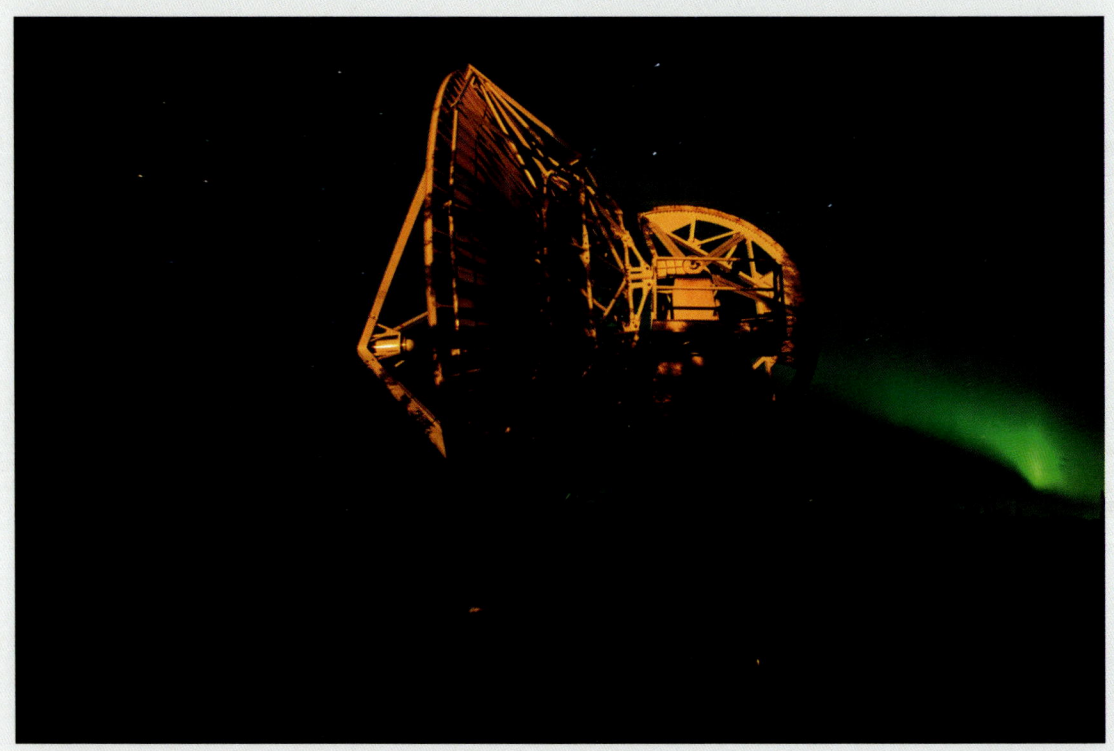

Above: Satellite dish and aurora borealis, Poker Flats Research Range, Alaska, USA, 1998.
Right: Satellite station, Poker Flats Research Range, Alaska, USA, 1998.

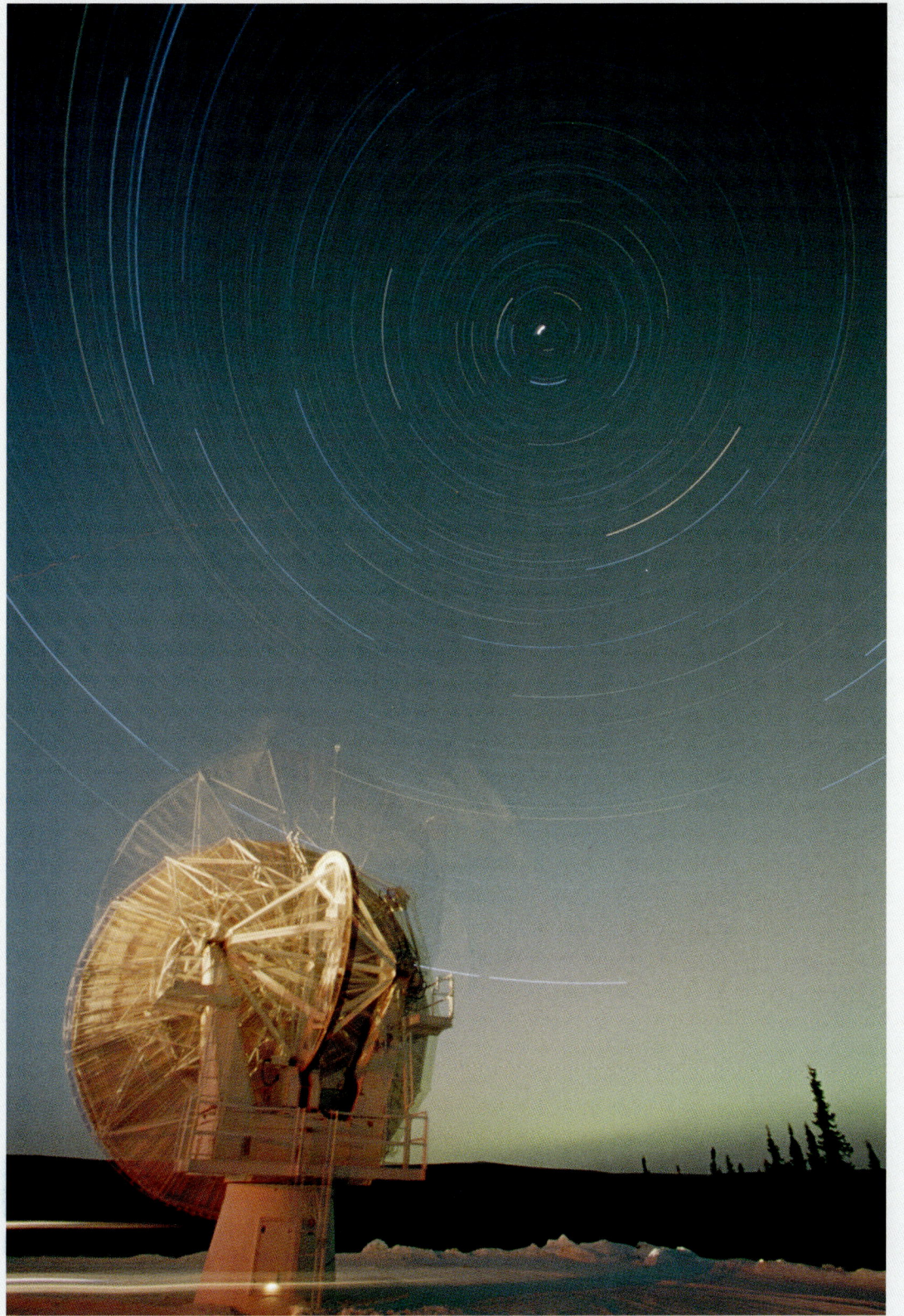

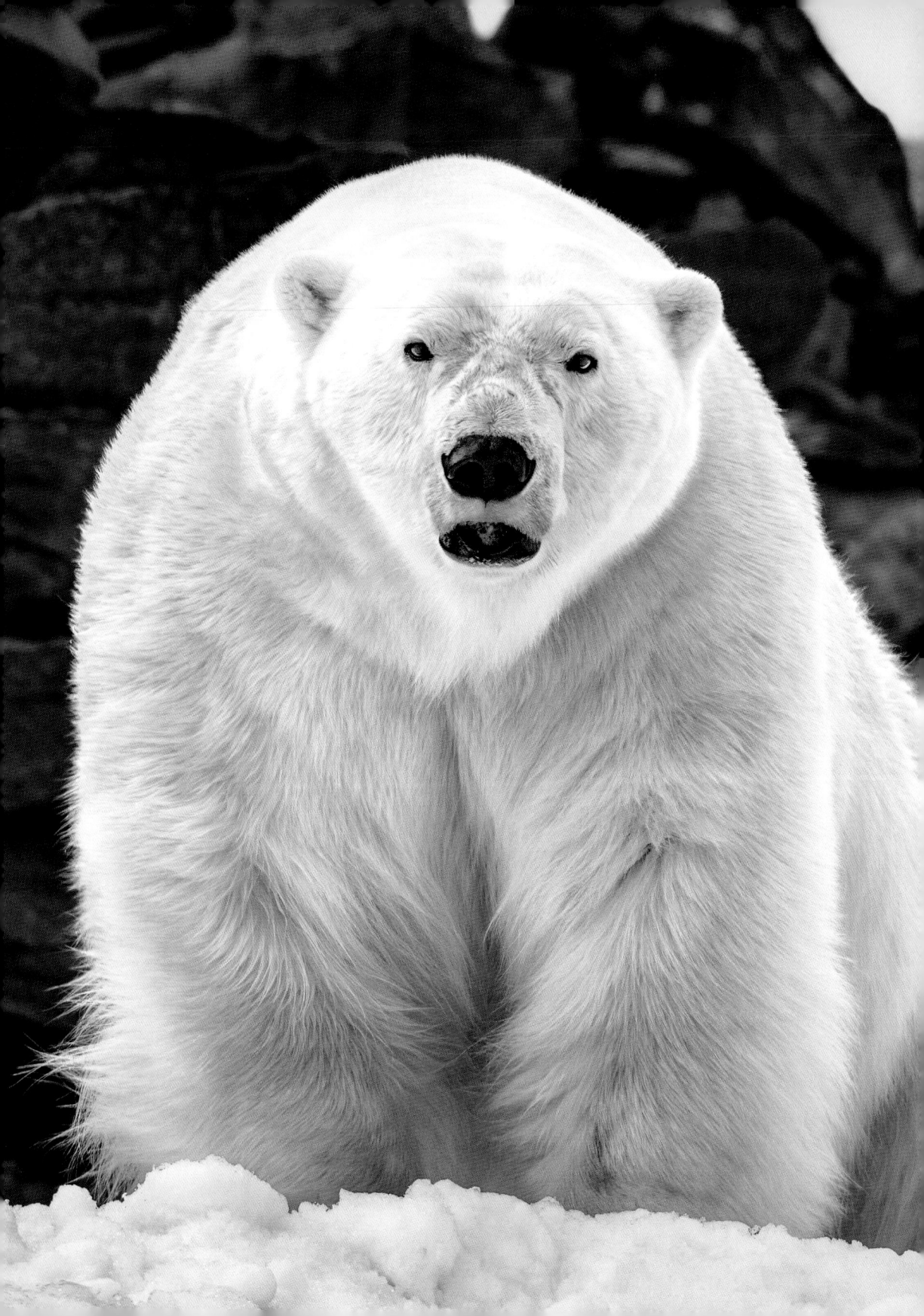

The business of photography

Build your name and reputation

I n the time I've been working in photography, the industry has changed, and it continues to evolve. As we move further into a digital world, new challenges arise, not least in terms of how work is commissioned and the money that can be made from magazine assignments. The changing state of the photography industry is not a reason to be paralyzed by fear, however. It's a chance to be smart in the way that you work and make a living.

To succeed in this industry, you need to diversify. It's probably not the smartest strategy to say, 'I only want to do X'. If you do that, you're limiting yourself. Far better to have several irons in the fire.

When I started out, everybody was shooting stock – images that can be licensed. Your strongest, most sellable images would go on the books of stock providers such as Getty Images, the National Geographic Image Collection (now defunct) or Minden Pictures, who license wildlife and nature stock photos and feature stories. That was how you made your living.

Left: *Polar Wisdom,*
Svalbard, Norway, 2007.

If you were on assignment with a magazine such as *National Geographic* or *Geo*, or any other big magazine, you might get a day rate of between $300 and $600 (£225 and £450). Most magazines kept you in the field for a week or two, or maybe twelve weeks over the course of a year if you were working with *National Geographic*. That might sound like a lot of time and income, but buying your own equipment, keeping it all up to date, paying rent or a mortgage, bills, and so on, all add up.

In those early years, I wanted to dream big, to have money to go after my goals, and to do more of the kind of photography I wanted to do. The way I could realize my ambitions was to develop multiple income streams. I could still do magazine work, but I needed to do other things too. For me, part of that involved going on a lecture tour. I worked hard to become a proficient public speaker so I could be hired to speak to large audiences of several thousand people.

I still sell some stock video footage and stills, but I tend to steer away from it because it's a huge time commitment for not much return. The stock side of the photography industry has gone the way of the music industry – everybody expects everything for free. People are almost shocked if you want to charge for an image.

I have some sponsorships – nothing too big, but it helps. And making a photography book is a great way to showcase your work. A book can be a kind of calling card, a way to put yourself out into the world. Magazine assignments, when you can get them, are also a useful way to build your identity as a photographer.

I'm really enjoying selling my work as fine art. I'm going back through my collection of millions of images and re-editing. With an agent, I'm releasing limited edition prints. It's gradually becoming a successful revenue stream, not least because I can be out shooting and creating new work while my agent is selling fine art prints for me. It is taking time to build, but it's something I'm excited to explore and invest time in.

> " It's crucial to build your name, your brand, your reputation, but be careful how you do it. Do it in a conscientious, humble way."

You could sell prints through a gallery, or directly from your website. I had a gallery in New York for a time. It was a successful endeavour, a positive experience. I met a lot of great people, but I found

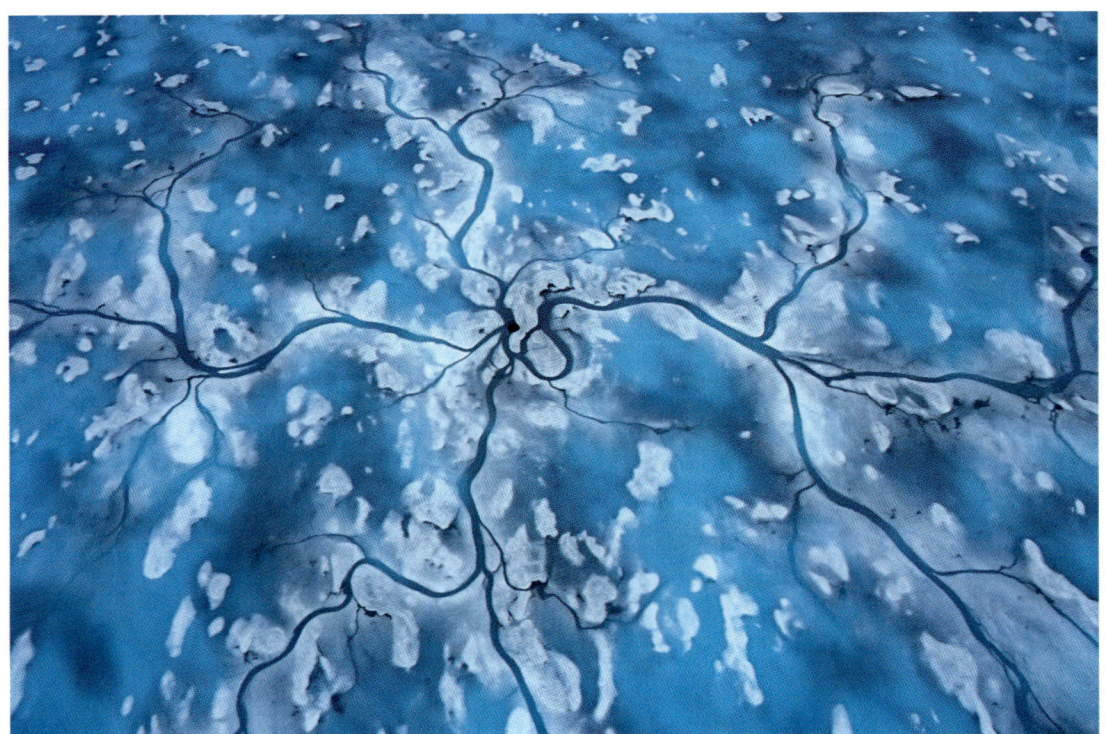

Above: *Albedo*, Coronation
Gulf, Nunavut, Canada, 2002.
Overleaf: *Morning Kings*,
South Georgia, 2008.

I had to be in New York more often than I wanted. I knew I would rather be in the field creating new work than in New York selling art.

I work with other galleries on occasion, and showcase my work in museums, but a lot of my fine art sales come from my website. By building my reputation and reach on my social media channels (Chapter 20), I've been able to drive traffic to my website.

I never would have thought that having (and growing) a social media presence on Facebook and Instagram would become such a key part of my business.

It's crucial to build your name, your brand, your reputation, but be careful how you do it. Do it in a conscientious, humble way. What you are doing needs to be sustainable as well as authentic and relatable. That way, the world will genuinely want to know what you are doing, and brands will want you to use or endorse their products and services.

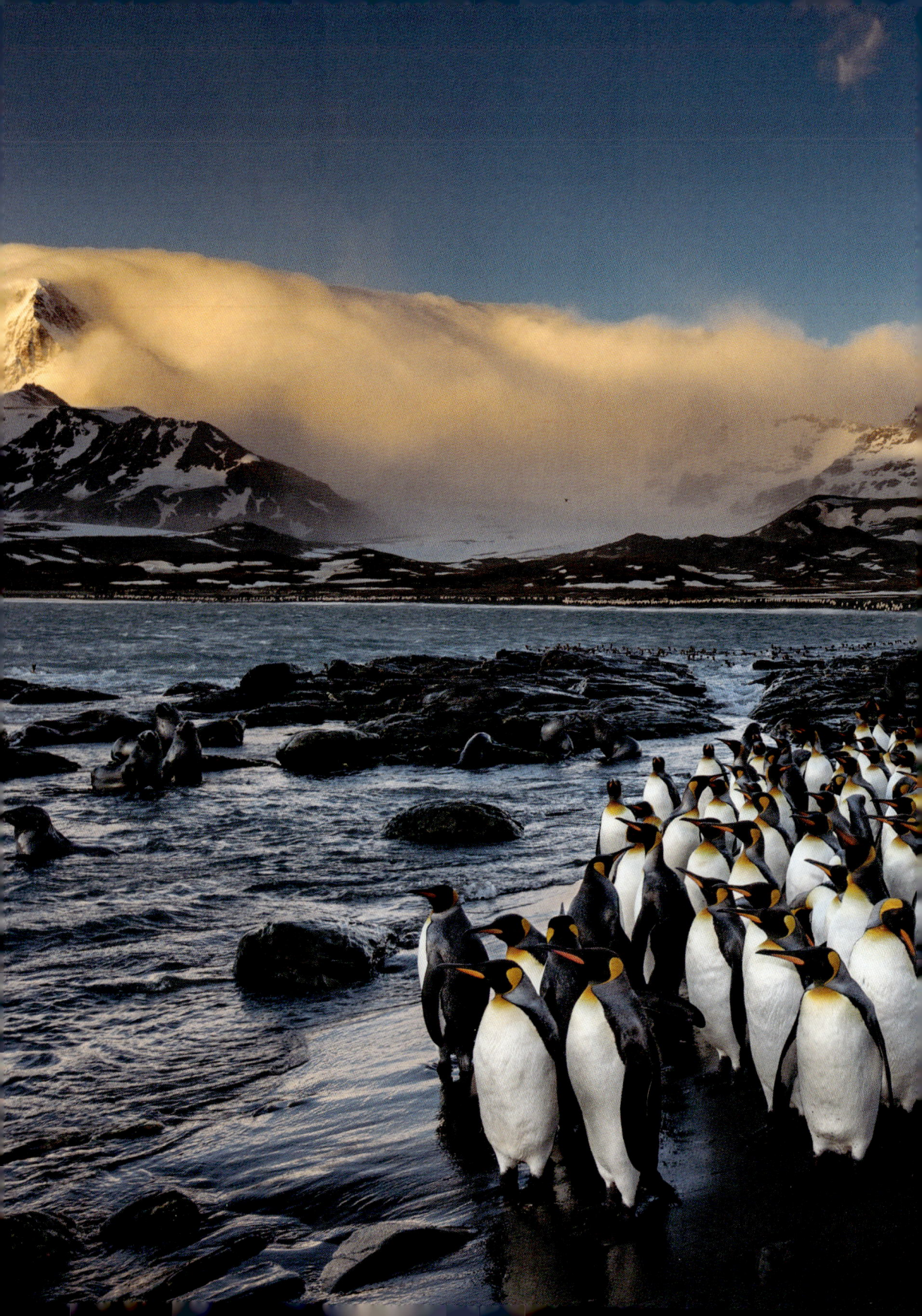

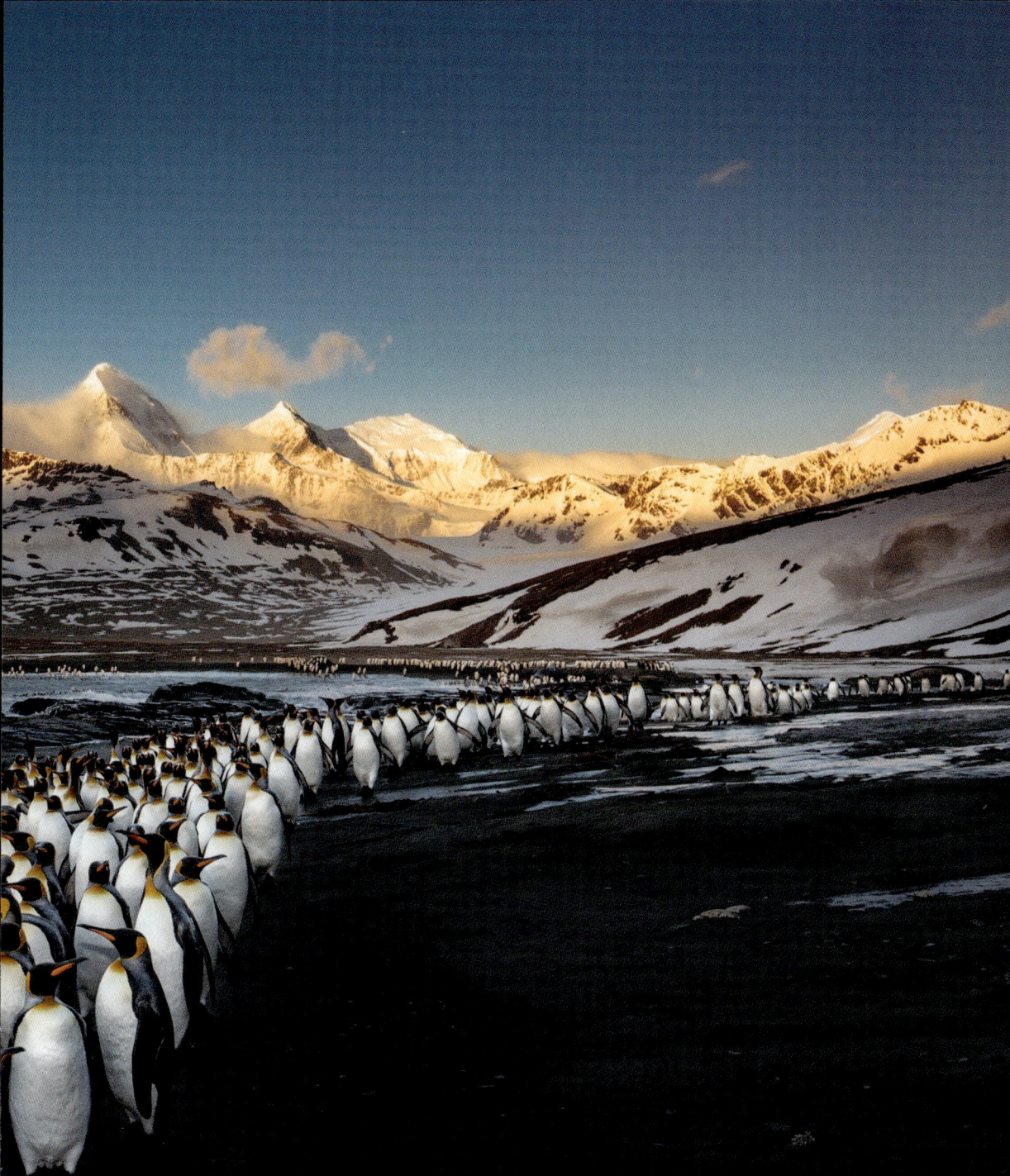

This is where my life and business partner, Cristina, has been so influential. She founded the International League of Conservation Photographers in 2005 and has long advised photographers to be characters in their own stories.

Back in the day, *National Geographic* would hire you, pay you a day rate, send you on an assignment and publish the pictures. If you wanted to elevate yourself and what you were doing, to grow your own brand, it wasn't exactly encouraged. But nowadays, it's generally accepted that building your brand is an integral part of life as a professional photographer. It is an important part of the journey we're on. This might involve regularly checking in with yourself, making sure you're on track.

Whatever I'm doing, I'll make time to review my current situation, to assess how things are going. Part of this involves sitting down every six months or so and evaluating and rewriting my goals.

When it comes to my business, I think in terms of an umbrella. If the canopy is who I am (a wildlife and nature photographer and conservationist), the spokes are all the things I could do and am doing – what I'm shooting, for whom, the type of project and so on. Examples of spokes could be a book project, a social media post, a fine art print run, footage for our non-profit, SeaLegacy, a public speaking engagement, all under the same theme. Sometimes I'll take a piece of content and use it in different ways. For example, the same images might work as both a social media post and in a lecture slideshow.

So, set your goals, have a game plan, but be open to how you generate income. Be flexible, learn to pivot, be open to trying new things.

If you have a little money to spare, the best way to invest, I believe, is to hire good people to support you in what you are doing. You can't do it all, and by acknowledging your weaknesses and filling those gaps with amazing people, you're investing in yourself, your brand, your business. It might be the best fixers, field guides, or, closer to home, a great office manager or someone to help you edit your work or sell your prints.

When I think back to the beginnings of my career, I didn't realize it at the time, but I was

"Set your goals, have a gameplan, but be open to how you generate income. Be flexible, learn to pivot, be open to trying new things."

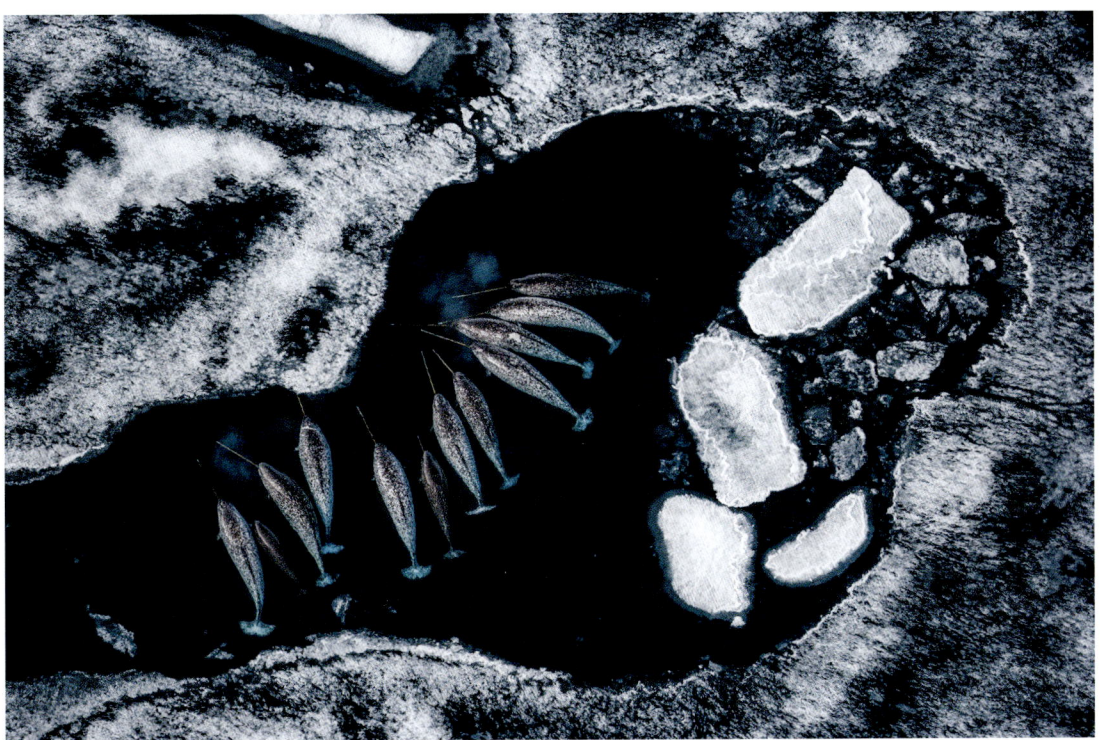

Above: *Gathering of Unicorns,*
Nunavut, Canada, 2006.

in fact doing everything I'm doing now. I was selling a few small fine art prints here and there, giving talks, getting the odd picture published in a magazine, going off on small assignments. It all added up. You have to just start – somewhere, anywhere – and build your experience bit by bit.

Essentially, my advice is to never say 'no'. Treat every opportunity as a chance to learn something new. If somebody asks you to shoot a wedding, go and shoot it. You're probably going to learn something, and being there may lead to something else.

Grow your social media presence, try being on the other side of the camera, do some Instagram stories. Try selling a few fine art prints. Go and shoot some local stories, hit up a local magazine, volunteer with a non-profit. Maybe they'll end up offering you some work. Work on your stills photography, your writing, your videography work, video editing, stills photography editing; find your voice, your style, your persona. Before you know it, everything will start growing together.

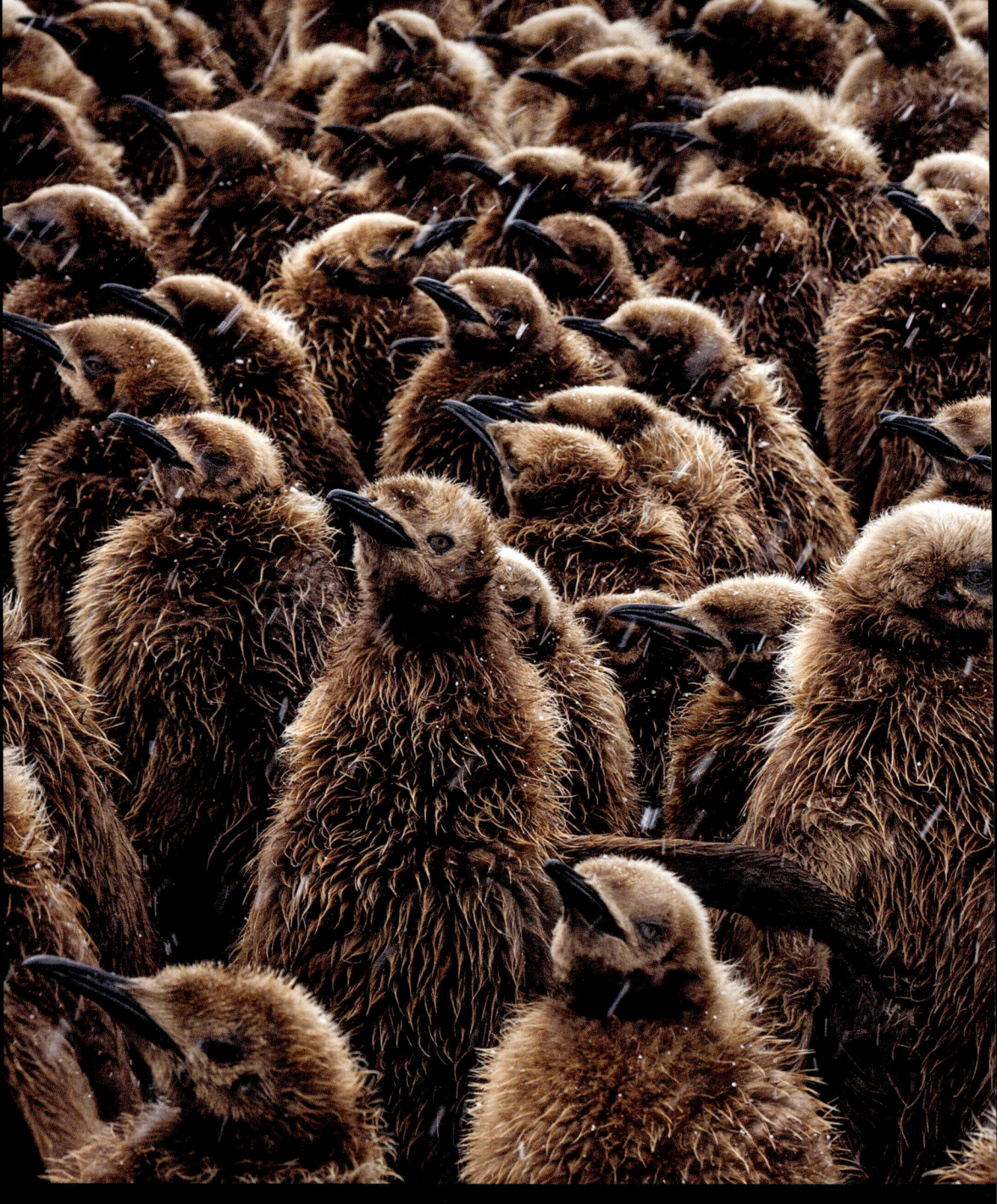

Above: *Teen Spirit*, South Georgia, 2008.

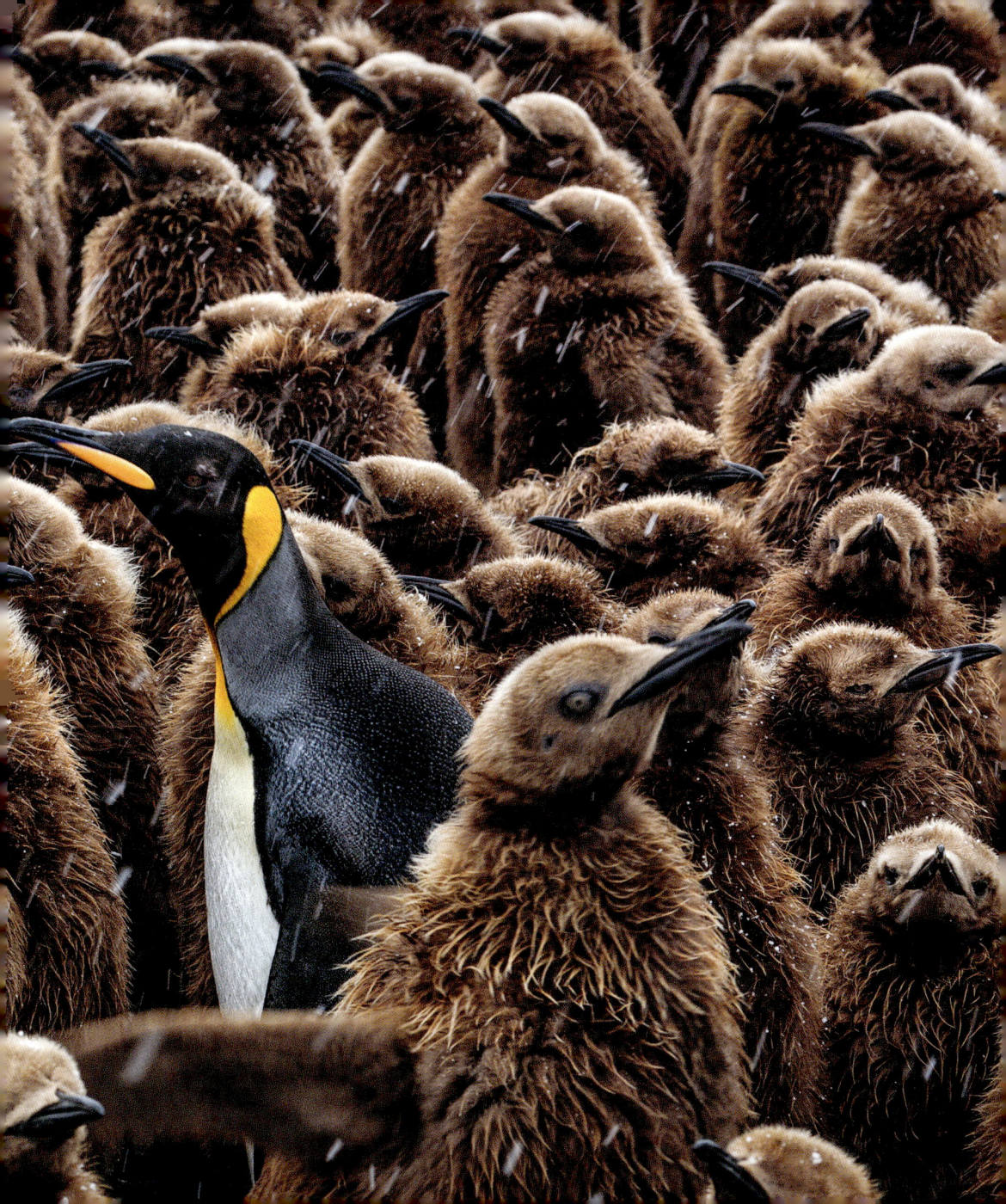

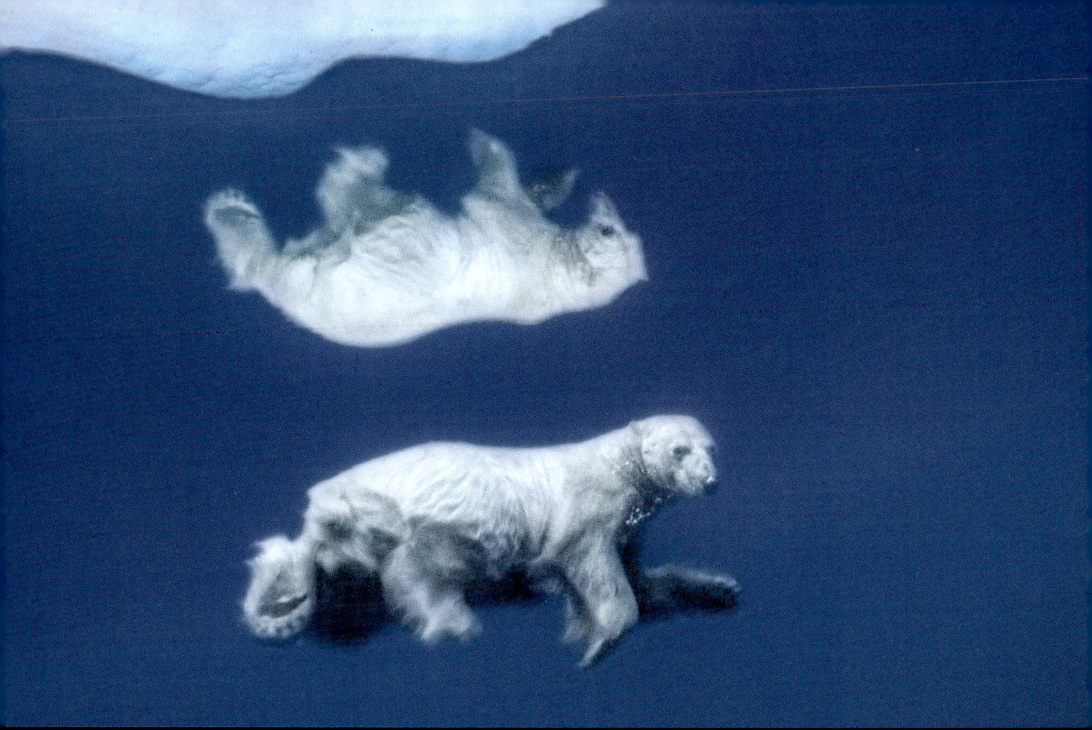

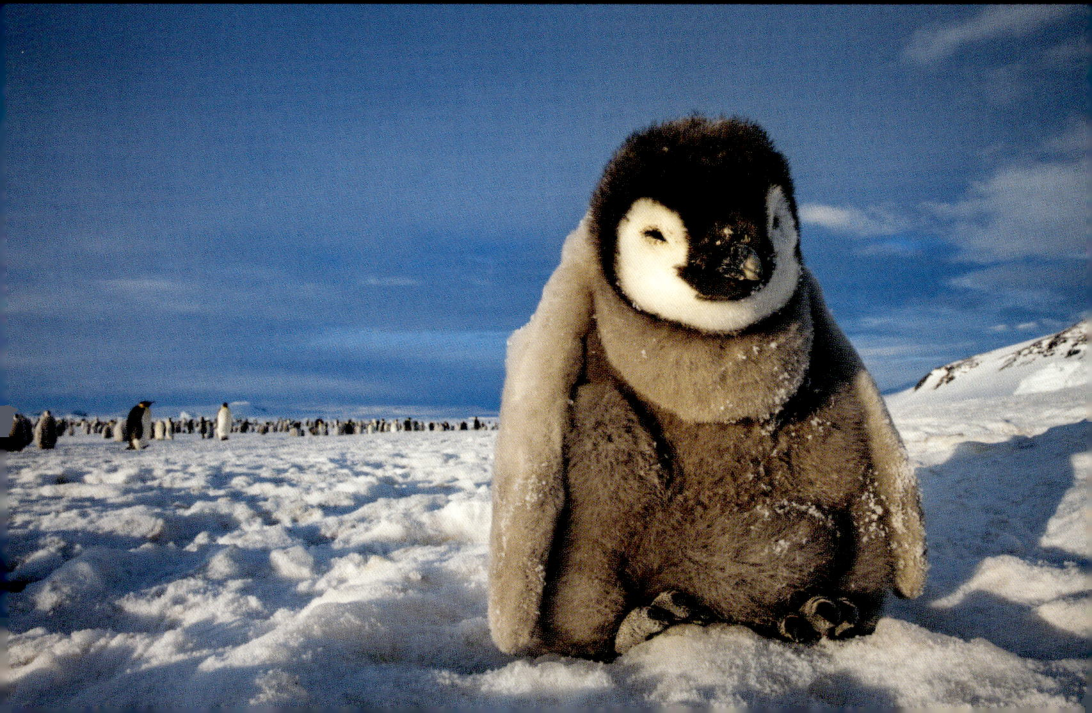

20 The role of social media

Grow your following

I n our final chapter, I'm going to talk about social media, and in particular, Instagram, the platform I use most often, as it's more visual.

I wish I could claim to be a social media guru and say I had it all figured out from the beginning, or that if you take X number of steps, you'll become a hit on social media. I can't. I've made a million mistakes, but through those mistakes I have figured out, at least for me, what works and what doesn't.

About ten years ago, a filmmaker and photographer friend of mine who was visiting me suggested I give Instagram a go. My immediate response was, 'No way'. I want to be out in nature with a camera, surrounded by wildlife. Why would I want to spend more time looking at a screen?

Top: *Polar Reflections*, Nanavut, Canada, 2006. Bottom: An emperor penguin chick waits for his parents to return with food from their long sea journey, Ross Sea, Antarctica, 2011.

But, it's important to try things in life, so I put up a couple of posts. They did okay, but it was nothing to shout home about. I enjoyed the feedback of being able to tell a story, though. I'm a journalist and a conservationist, but I'm also a storyteller. Suddenly, I had a voice. And not just once a year in the pages of *National Geographic*. I got to have a voice every day or every hour, or however often I chose to post.

At some point, I was invited to do a post on *National Geographic*'s Instagram page. I posted a picture of narwhal tusks with a caption that said if people wanted to see what narwhals looked like underwater, they could go to my Instagram page: @PaulNicklen. Over the next three or so hours, I had 55,000 new followers. It was a lightbulb moment for me. 'Wait a minute,' I thought. 'This is a new way to communicate with the world.'

My fellow photographers at *National Geographic* and I used to be on assignment for a year or two, sometimes three, and it was amazing when the issue with your story in it finally came out. But the magazine would be on newsstands for a month, and then it was gone. Social media, by comparison, allows you to have control over how and when you show your work. It also serves as a kind of living digital archive.

As *National Geographic*'s social media following grew into the tens of millions and beyond, my number of followers grew too. I hit a million, and then two million in my second year of using Instagram. Then it hit me: My team and I were building our own self-contained communication platform to reach our audience every day. It was exciting to see things grow and to imagine where it could take us.

I started to put a little more effort into what I was posting, how and when. What became apparent was it wasn't just the photographs that mattered; people wanted to hear stories. Social media (and Instagram in particular) offers an incredible opportunity to tell stories. When people reach out to me, a lot of the time they will say, 'I loved that post; I really liked what you had to say.'

> " Social media allows you to have control over how and when you show your work. It also serves as a kind of living digital archive."

For me, each social media post is like a mini magazine article. It's possible to post a carousel of images, and you can share multiple stories with chapters – you can build a narrative arc. Social media is a way to direct traffic towards issues that you care about.

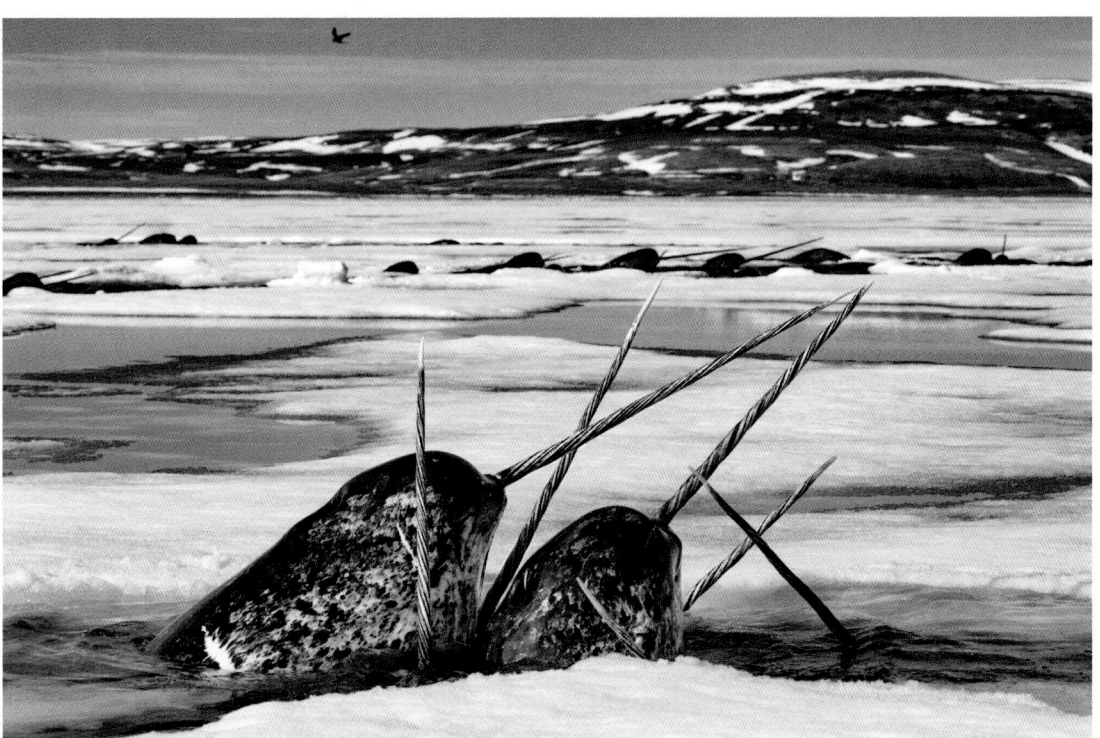

Above: *Skyward*, Lancaster Sound, Nunavut, Canada, 2006.
Overleaf: *River of Dreams*, Lençóis Maranhenses, Brazil, 2024.

I use a formula for sharing content on Instagram, which I equate to boxing – it is 'jab, jab, jab, punch'. I care about the planet and feel an enormous amount of anxiety every day about the state of our world. We're losing species. We're losing habitats. We're losing ecosystems. But if I only post about the tragedies and disasters that are happening, I'm going to lose my audience pretty quickly.

I need to find a pace, a rhythm, and that is the 'jab, jab, jab' – content that is about the beauty of nature or humanity, what is interesting, engaging, thought-provoking, educational; content that invites people into my world.

Once I have a base that trusts me, and they're following along, then I can present my audience with more heavy-hitting issues such as the slaughter of dolphins in the Faroe Islands or the starving polar bear that was viewed two billion times around the world. Those are the punches. I've earned the right to punch because I've worked to build a loyal following.

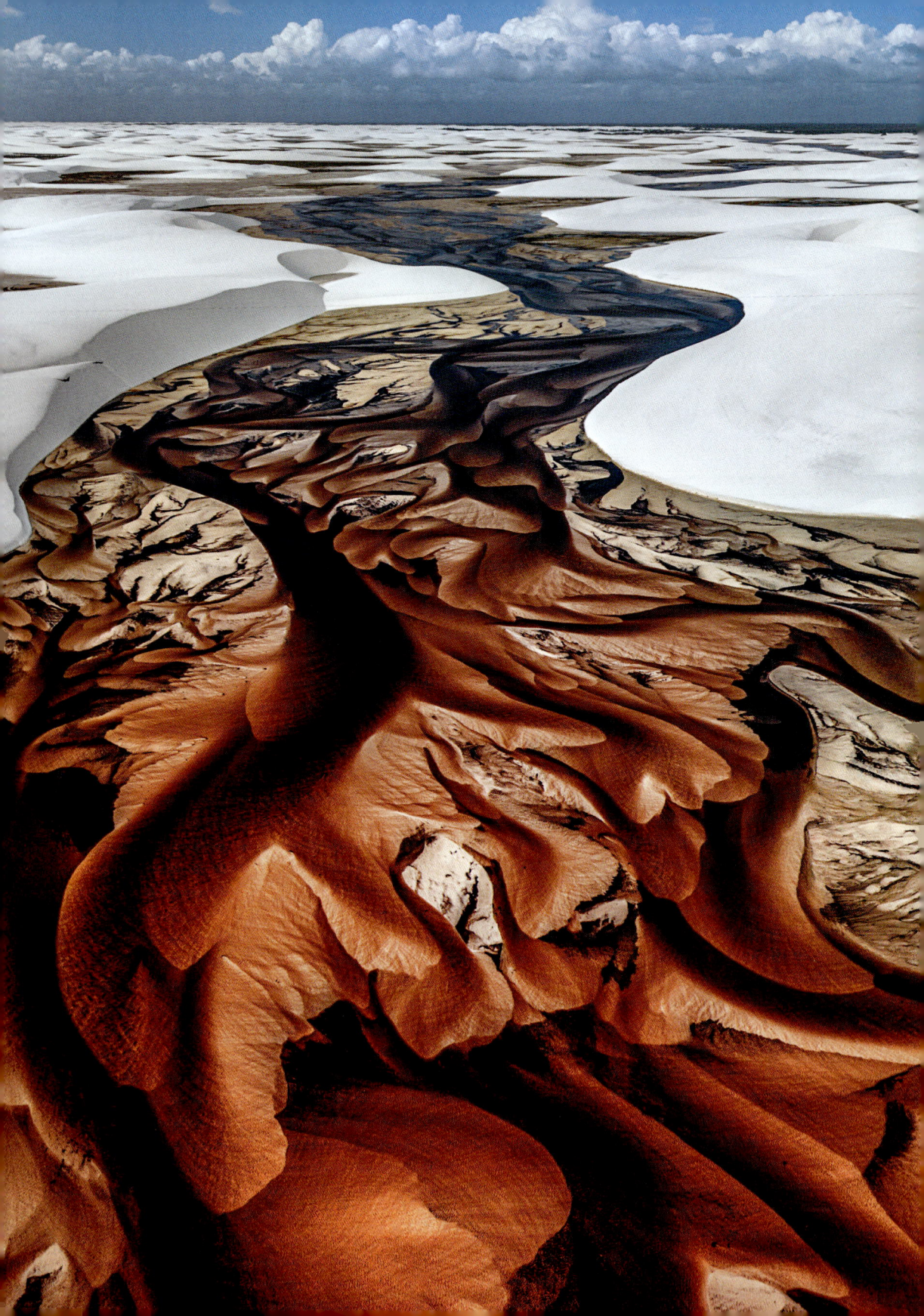

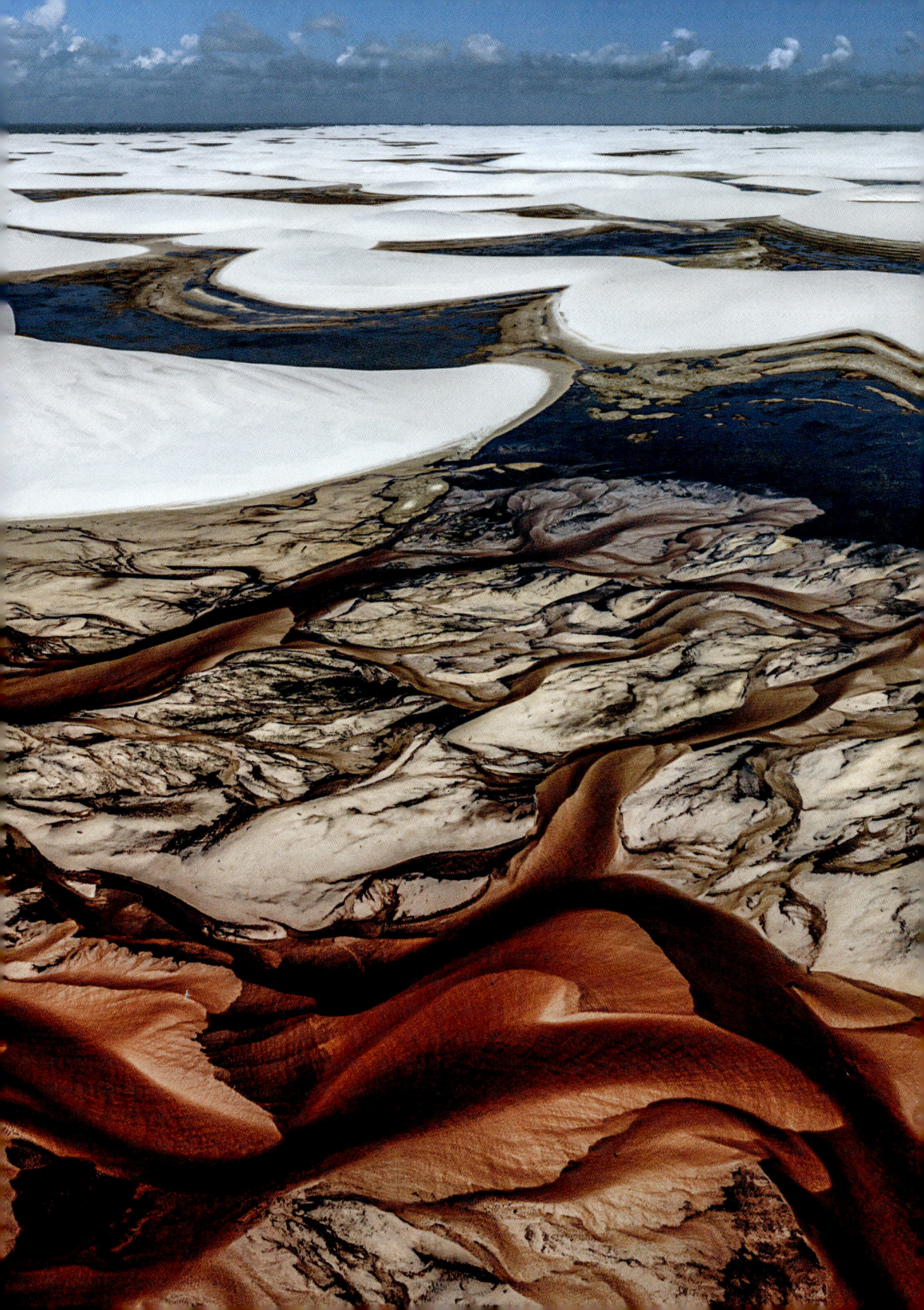

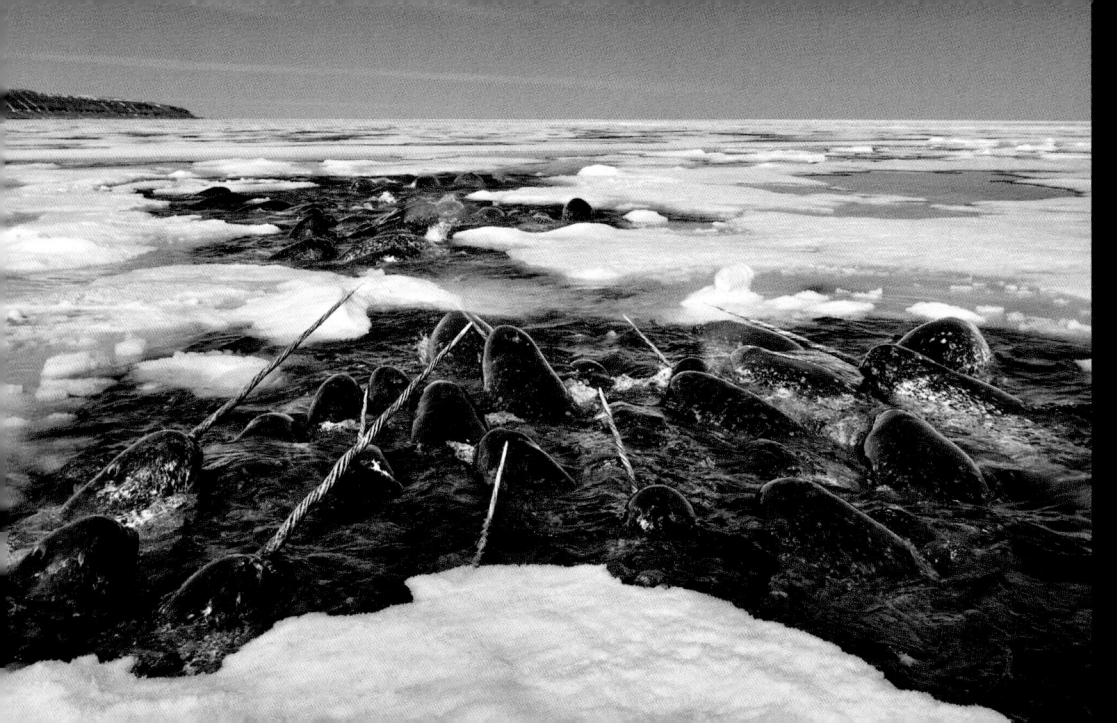

When it comes to social media, just like with everything I've been talking about, you have to have a Swiss army knife of skills. You need to be a storyteller and a photographer, but also a writer. Writing is a skill I urge you to develop. Even though this book is about photography, I encourage everyone who makes photographs to try and become a better writer, a better storyteller.

As photographers, we want to be out there with the animals, amid the scenery, experiencing moments in nature. We don't want to be on our smartphones waxing lyrical about this and that. But it is important to show your voice, your feelings, your emotions, because doing that invites people into your story, into a photograph, into your world. Magazines run images and text; social media is no different in that regard.

Like anything and everything in the world of tech, social media has been an evolution. In the early days, you might post multiple times a day or even every hour. But as we've become more adept at using this technology, my team and I started to see that posting once a day was sufficient to grow our following. Then we discovered that posting once, twice or possibly three times a week was enough.

My social media platforms have become extremely important to me because they are how I make a living. I may have a sponsor who I'll give a shoutout to, so I'll fit that into my schedule, or I will use social media to promote the fine art side of my business. Another important way I use social media is to raise awareness for conservation work and to drive traffic to our non-profit, SeaLegacy.

I want my base – and I call it my 'base', but I mean my followers – to get into a rhythm with me. On Fridays, I do something called Fine Art Fridays, where I'll release a new piece of work or celebrate something I've posted before. On Saturdays, I might put up something interesting and engaging, perhaps a second fine art piece, and then I'll take a break to let people breathe a little. Then, maybe mid-week, I'll put up a conservation piece of some kind.

> " My social media platforms have become extremely important to me because they are how I make a living."

So, I post a range of things. When I posted about a film that Cristina and I made for Sony, the post received 400,000 likes and 131,000 comments. That's a small city of people who stopped what they were doing and took time to comment, to engage. When I see well-known people outside of our immediate network engage with something, I know we're reaching further afield.

It's all about pacing; putting out the right content in the right way at the right time. You have to be true to who you are – people can spot inauthenticity a mile off. It's also about buckling in for the long haul. You're building and engaging with a real base, an audience that cares, and that is a very powerful tool.

I'm always humbled when people come up to me and say they follow me on Instagram, and that they love such and such a post. These people have real passions and real concerns for our planet and are on this journey with me.

Ultimately, when it comes to social media, the advice I would give is, don't spend all your time on it, getting caught in a vortex of scrolling and watching reels all day, because it'll suck you in and get you down.

Far better to clear your mind, clear your schedule, get outside and make your art. Do a post when you feel that you have something meaningful to say or show. But don't obsess over every last word or listen to the critical voices in your head, or the people who are trying to bring you down. Go on your journey, shoot what you want to shoot, make the strongest images you can, tell the best stories possible. Learn to write or how to use your words well if you are already a competent writer. Put your stories out there, that's all you can do. From there, the growth will happen naturally.

" You have to be true to who you are – people can spot inauthenticity a mile off."

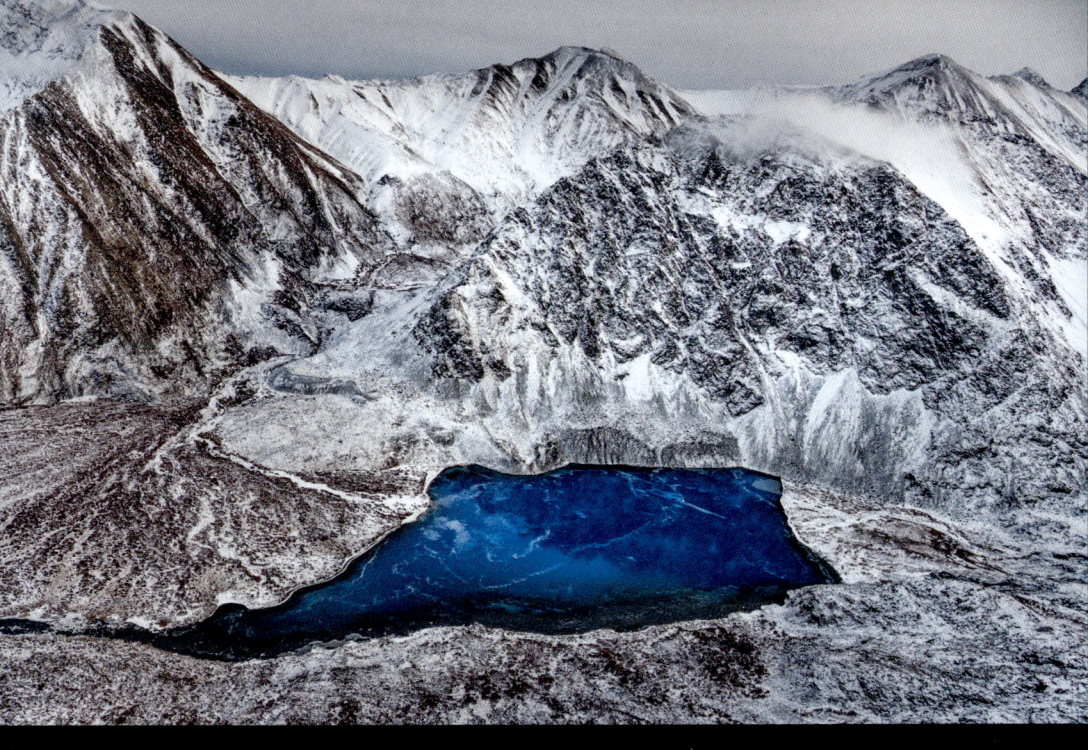

Above: *Deceiving Beauty*, Yukon, Canada, 2010.
Overleaf: *Echoes of the Andes*, Patagonia, Chile, 2024.

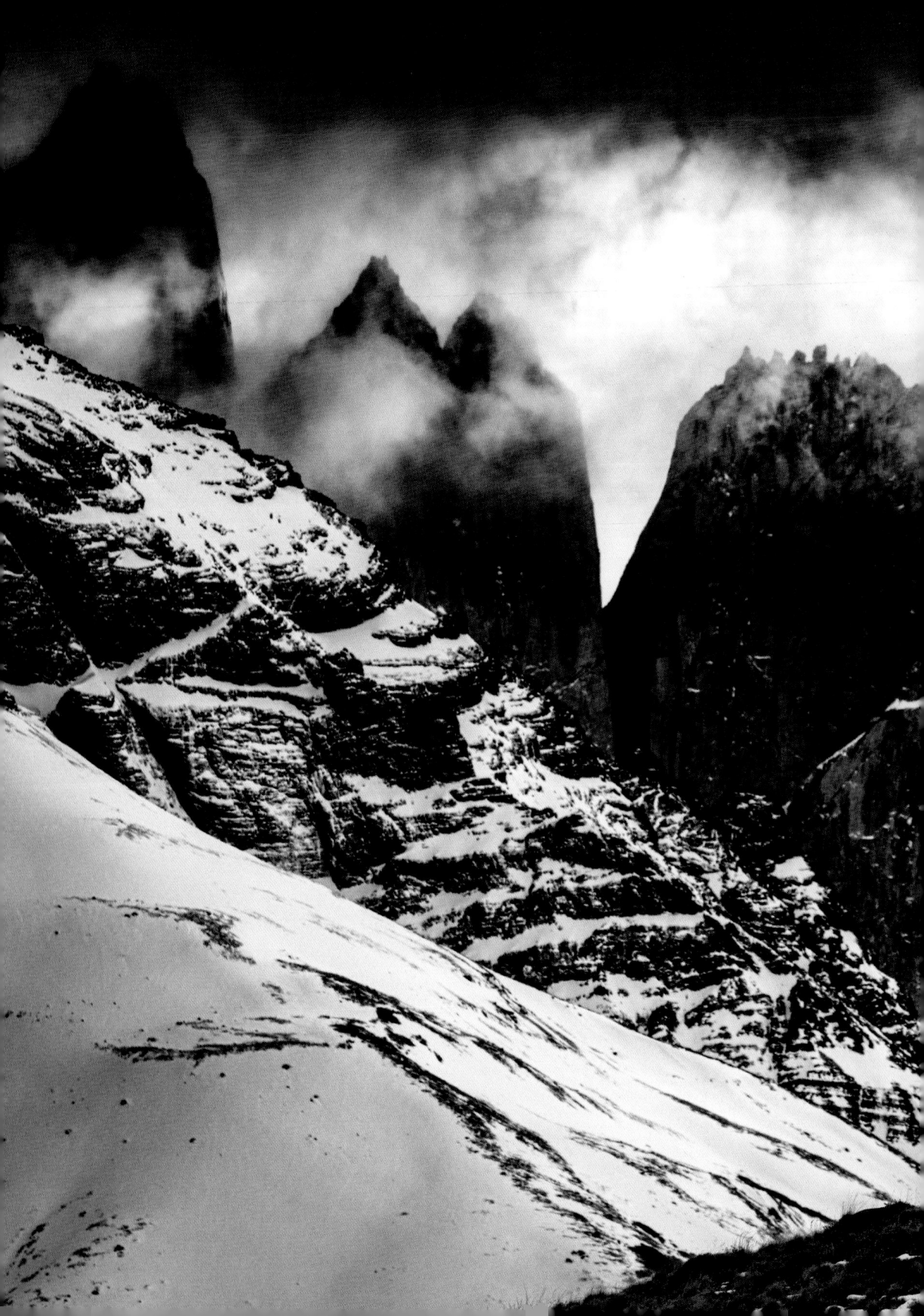

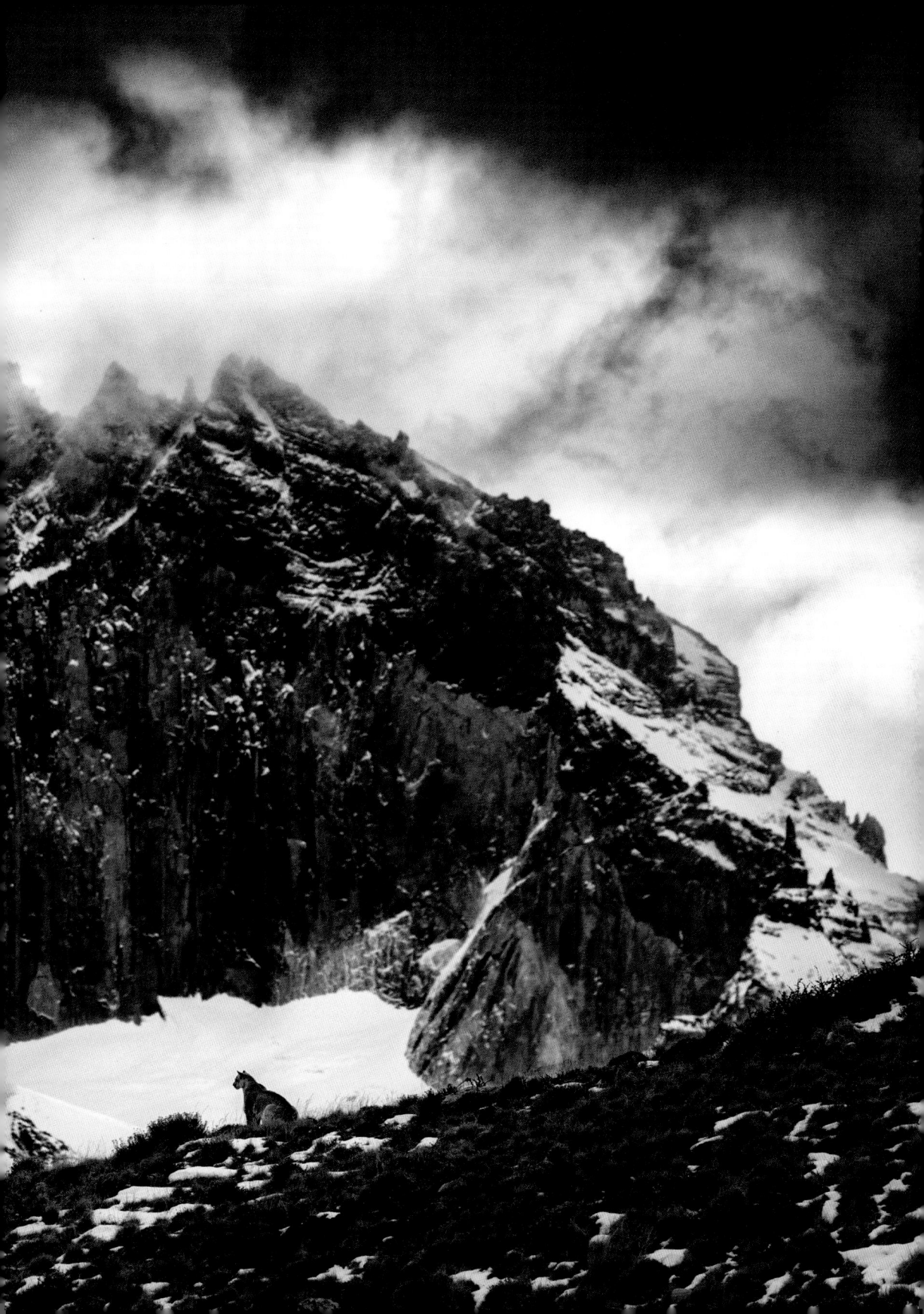

Postscript

After sharing everything I've learned and every failure I've made on my journey as a photographer, I want to thank you for picking up and reading this book.

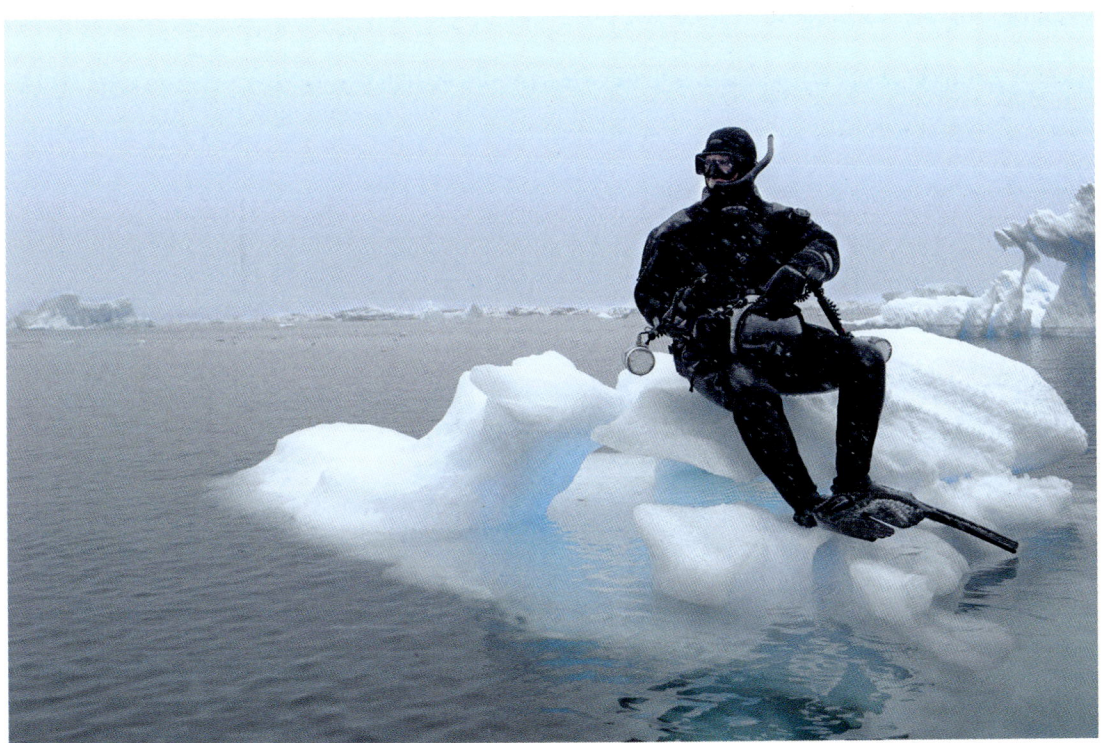

Above: Paul waiting for the return of a leopard seal (taken by Göran Ehlmé), Antarctic Peninsula, Antarctica, 2006.

I may never get the chance to meet you, but I know you are out there, on my team, on the frontlines of conservation, tackling some of the most important issues of our time.

Through photography and communication, we really can change the world. Together, we can help to fuel a movement, we can help drive change. This is our last stand for our planet.

It's a journey of ups and downs, there are great challenges and inevitable failures ahead, but those are the things that make the victories – the wins with your camera – taste even sweeter.

I'll see you out there.

Index

Page numbers in *italics* refer to image captions.

Acknowledgements

My Masters of Photography course – and now this book – are born from decades spent in the wild, learning from nature and from the people who dedicate their lives to protecting it. I'm endlessly grateful to the animals who've let me into their world, and to the colleagues, guides and storytellers who've inspired and supported this journey.

To Cristina Mittermeier – my partner in life, adventure and conservation – your passion is the foundation of this work. To the SeaLegacy team and our broader creative family: thank you for your talent, commitment and belief in storytelling as a tool for change.

To the team at Masters of Photography – especially Chris Ryan, Gilles Storme, Stuart Ashton and, by extension for this production, Oren Lawson – thank you for believing in this vision and helping bring it to life with such care and clarity; and to Kait Burgan for shepherding this project, along with Ryan Tidman.

To the many field partners, editors and mentors who've shaped this work – and to the Indigenous communities who've generously shared their wisdom – this journey is richer because of you.

And to my fellow Photography Masters – it's an honour to be considered among you. Your work continues to push and inspire me.

Finally, to everyone picking up a camera with purpose: thank you. The more we teach each other to see, the more we can protect what matters.

– *Paul*

Creating Paul Nicklen's Masterclass was a truly unforgettable experience. We witnessed his deep connection to the wild, his passion for conservation, and his incredible talent behind the lens, which has made his photography journey so extraordinary.

We were honoured to work so closely with him, capturing not just his technical skill but his vision and ethos. Paul's generosity, wisdom and storytelling made this project something truly special.

We are deeply grateful to all those who helped to make this possible and immensely proud to share this with the world. Thank you, Paul, my friend. It was so inspiring, great fun, and an absolute privilege to step into your world and create this masterclass together.

– *Chris at Masters of Photography*

Quarto

First published in 2026 by Frances Lincoln
an imprint of The Quarto Group.
One Triptych Place, London, SE1 9SH
United Kingdom
T (0)20 7700 9000
www.Quarto.com

EEA Representation, WTS Tax d.o.o.,
Žanova ulica 3, 4000 Kranj, Slovenia
www.wts-tax.si

A catalogue record for this book is available from the British Library.

ISBN 978-1-83600-981-8
Ebook ISBN 978-1-83600-982-5

10 9 8 7 6 5 4 3 2 1

Text by: Gemma Padley
Editorial Director: John Parton
Editor: Róisín Duffy
Photographer: Paul Nicklen
Book Design: Claire Warner Studio
Senior Designer: Isabel Eeles
Senior Production Controller: Rohana Yusof

Printed in Guangdong, China TT122025

MIX
Paper | Supporting
responsible forestry
FSC® C016973
FSC
www.fsc.org